LIBRARY OF HEBREW BIBLE/
OLD TESTAMENT STUDIES

450

Formerly Journal for the Study of the Old Testament Supplement Series

DEATH AND SURVIVAL
IN THE BOOK OF JOB

Desymbolization and Traumatic Experience

Dan Mathewson

t&t clark

NEW YORK • LONDON

T & T Clark International, 80 Maiden Lane, New York, NY 10038

T & T Clark International, The Tower Building, 11 York Road, London SE1 7NX

T & T Clark International is a Continuum imprint.

Library of Congress Cataloging-in-Publication Data
Mathewson, Dan, 1973-
    Death and survival in the book of Job : desymbolization and traumatic experience / Dan Mathewson.
        p. cm. -- (Library of Hebrew Bible/Old Testament studies ; 450)
    Includes bibliographical references (p.) and index.
    ISBN 0-567-02692-2 (hardcover)
    1. Bible. O.T. Job--Criticism, interpretation, etc. 2. Death--Biblical teaching. I. Title. II. Series.
    BS1415.6.D34M38 2006
    223'.106--dc22
                            2006007653

Printed in the United States of America

06 07 08 09 10   10 9 8 7 6 5 4 3 2 1

CONTENTS

ACKNOWLEDGMENTS

The following work originated as my dissertation, and as everyone who has been granted the Ph.D. knows, it takes a small tribe to keep a dissertation-writer motivated, productive, and above all happy. My thanks go out to my tribe. First and foremost among whom is Carol Newsom, my dissertation director, who dazzled me throughout my graduate education with her seemingly limitless list of talents. I thank her for enabling me to think in new directions, and for her gentle and not-so-gentle corralling when I wandered too far off track. As I tell anyone who will listen, Carol is the scholar that all of us want to grow up to be one day. Deep gratitude also extends to Cathy Caruth whose quick mind and challenging ideas shaped the direction of much of my work. Unfortunately Cathy had the incredibly bad judgment to allow a Religion punk into her circle of respectable Comparative Literature students. She created more work for herself in the long run, and for that I thank her. Thanks, also, to Martin Buss for patiently reading my manuscript and offering his many insights and suggestions.

I wrote the bulk of my dissertation while a fellow at Emory University's Center for Humanistic Inquiry. My thanks go to CHI's director, Tina Brownley, and her CHI staff for creating a vibrant intellectual environment. I also thank the other nine fellows who taught me lots about poetry, philosophy, music, foreign cultures, ancient texts, and the concerns and insights that all of us share across our respective areas of learning.

Special thanks goes to my "lunchpail" crew, Ted Smith, Susan Hylen, and Rob von Thaden, all fellow dissertators with the blue-collar approach to writing: punch your ticket in the morning, work all day, punch out in the evening. Your company day-in and day-out—if just at lunchtime and then for tea in the afternoon—provided the energy to sustain what could have been a very lonely several months.

Last of all, my thanks go to my wife, Naho Kobayashi. Just what you were thinking marrying a graduate student, I'll never know. But your presence in my life provided and continues to provide me with indescribable happiness. I thank you for your love, support, and tolerance of my hockey-playing habits. One day I will stop injuring myself. One day...

ABBREVIATIONS

ANEP   *The Ancient Near East in Pictures.* Edited by J. B. Pritchard. Princeton, N.J.: Princeton University Press, 1954

ANET   *Ancient Near Eastern Texts Relating to the Old Testament.* Edited by J. B. Pritchard. 3d ed. Princeton, N.J.: Princeton University Press, 1969

ASV   American Standard Version

AV   Authorized Version

BDB   F. Brown, S. R. Driver, and C. A. Briggs. *A Hebrew and English Lexicon of the Old Testament.* Oxford: Clarendon, 1907

IDBSup   *Interpreter's Dictionary of the Bible: Supplementary Volume.* Edited by K. Crim. Nashville, 1976

JB   Jerusalem Bible

KJV   King James Version

KTU   *Die keilalphabetischen Texte aus Ugarit.* Edited by M. Dietrich, O. Loretz, and J. Sanmartín. Neukirchen–Vluyn, 1976

LXX   Septuagint

MT   Masoretic text

NAB   New American Bible

NEB   New English Bible

NIV   New International Version

NJPS   New Jewish Publication Society

RSV   Revised Standard Version

RV   Revised Version

Chapter 1

INTRODUCTION: DEATH AND DIVINE JUSTICE

Few biblical books resonate with people in the contemporary world as power-fully as the book of Job.[1] Not that the setting of the book is familiar, nor the language in which it was written; rather, *Job*'s seeming contemporaneity stems from the topics with which it deals: suffering and death, and the attempt to find meaning in light of them. Of course, the present age has no special claim on suffering and death. Disaster and suffering have punctuated the course of human history, and death is the biological necessity of *all* humans. *Job*'s themes are exemplary human themes that have ensured the book's relevance—and popular-ity—throughout the centuries.

It is also true, however, that special interest in the book of Job has risen in the late twentieth century in light of the particular circumstances of this age. Specifi-cally, the enormity of the Holocaust spurred a new encounter with *Job* as interpreters turned to the ancient sufferer for insight into contemporary evils. *Job* offered the truth of the "depth, breadth and honesty of expression of human suffering"[2] to those grappling with the realities of the suffering of genocide. Elie Wiesel went so far as to call Job "our contemporary,"[3] despite the millennia that separate the composition of the book of Job from the disaster that Wiesel lived through. According to the latter, "Whenever we attempt to tell our own story, we transmit [Job's]. The opposite is true also: those of his legends we presumed invented, we live through; those of his words we thought illusory, proved to be true; we owe them our experience of evil and death."[4] In Maurice Friedman's words, modern humans, like the character Job, "have in common…the experi-ence of the most terrible exile: that sense of abandonment that undermines the very meaning of existence and makes life insupportable."[5] Friedman aptly gives

1. In order to avoid confusion between *the book of* Job and Job *the character*, I will italicise the word "Job" whenever the use of this term would be ambiguous (i.e. when it is without chapter/verse reference, and without overt reference to "the book."

2. Steven Kepnes, "Job and Post-Holocaust Theodicy," in *Strange Fire: Reading the Bible after the Holocaust* (ed. Tod Linafelt; New York: New York University Press, 2000), 252–66 (253).

3. Elie Wiesel, *Messengers of God: Biblical Portraits and Legends* (trans. Marion Wiesel; New York: Summit Books, 1976), 211.

4. Ibid, 211–12. Or, as André Neher argues, "[T]he story of Job is not a legend, for Satan appears in real life: he is Nebuchadnezzar, he is Hitler" (*The Exile of the Word: From the Silence of the Bible to the Silence of Auschwitz* [trans. David Maisel; Philadelphia: Jewish Publication Society of America, 1981], 195).

5. Maurice Friedman, *Problematic Rebel: Melville, Dostoievsky, Kafka, Camus* (rev. ed.; Chicago: University of Chicago Press, 1970), 463.

the name "Modern Job" to the contemporary quest to understand the experience of radical evil as the reality of one's existence and then to confront it head-on:[6] "[Modern Job] helps us to take unto ourselves the problematic of modern man and shape from it an image of meaningful human existence, an image that neither leaves out the problematic, nor simply reflects it, but wrestles with it until it has found a new way forward."[7]

The Modern Job that Friedman describes shares many features with what the psychohistorian, Robert Jay Lifton, would call the survivor of trauma, "one who has come into contact with death in some bodily or psychic fashion and has remained alive."[8] The traumatic survivor, like the Modern Job, experiences the undermining of the meaning of existence through the paralysis of the psychic forms that normally provide order and rationality to the world of experience. The traumatic encounter with death causes a rift in the world that can only be mended by the evolution of new "[psychic] forms that include the traumatic event, which in turn requires that one find meaning or significance in it so that the rest of one's life need not be devoid of meaning and significance."[9] As with Friedman's Modern Job, the new way forward entails a radical confrontation with that which caused the rupture in the world: death and disaster.

In very broad terms the following pages will explore the particular resonance that the book of Job has with the contemporary age. Specifically, I will examine the representation of death in *Job* and the discourse surrounding the meaning of death that is woven throughout the book. The character, Job, I will argue, is a survivor figure (in Lifton's sense), whose own encounter with death triggers the collapse of a moral and theological world—a collapse that Job articulates, wrestles with, and eventually attempts to move beyond. The function of death in the book, therefore, is of primary importance. How does Job's encounter with death and disaster alter his world? In the context of tragic death, how does Job understand death's meaning? What is the relation between life and death in light of disaster? What must Job do in order to go on living in a world rent apart by traumatic death? What lessons does *Job* offer the contemporary age about death and life? These are the types of questions I will attempt to answer.

---

6. See ibid., 461–93; Maurice Friedman, *To Deny Our Nothingness: Contemporary Images of Man* (Chicago: University of Chicago Press, 1978; repr., Chicago: Midway, 1984), 309–54. Others, however, are not so quick to parallel the Holocaust with the book of Job. Richard L. Rubenstein ("Job and Auschwitz," in Linafelt, ed., *Strange Fire*, 233–51), for example, though noting that *Job* does deal with the problem of innocent suffering, argues for a fundamental incongruence between what *Job* articulates and experience of the Holocaust in terms of the fundamental breakdown of the self in the death camp. For other examinations of *Job* in light of the Holocaust, see Emil L. Fackenheim, *The Jewish Bible after the Holocaust: A Re-reading* (Bloomington: Indiana University Press, 1990), 71–99; Neher, *Exile of the Word*, 27–33, 192–98.

7. Friedman, *To Deny Our Nothingness*, 347. Friedman identifies Elie Wiesel as "the most moving embodiment of the Modern Job" (p. 348).

8. Robert Jay Lifton, *The Broken Connection: On Death and the Continuity of Life* (New York: Simon & Schuster, 1979), 169.

9. Ibid, 176. Later I will examine Lifton's works much more closely.

1.1. *Death in* Job

The Hebrew Bible (HB), as many note, is fairly reticent about discussing death. In contrast to other literature of the ancient Near East (ANE), it rarely shows much interest in post-mortem existence, or the nature of the underworld, or funerary practices, or general discussions of what death means and how one ought to interpret it.[10] According to Segal, in contrast to other ANE literature, the HB deliberately avoids discussing death because "This life with its inevitable death is what the Bible wants to emphasize."[11]

Whether or not Segal is correct about why the HB is reticent about death, there are some HB books that seem to run counter to the general trend and display more of a proclivity to discussing various aspects of death. This is the case most obviously in Qoheleth where death is a topic of overt, almost philosophical, discussion. In fact, death is absolutely central to one of Qoheleth's main theses, that all of life is הבל: "[T]he fate of the sons of men and the fate of beasts is identical: as one dies, so dies the other; they all have the same breath. Man has no advantage over the beasts, everything is vanity. All go to one place: all are from the dust, and all turn to dust again" (3:19–20). Later he suggests that "This is an evil in all that is done under the sun, that one fate comes to all" (9:3). Qoheleth links death to hopelessness and then ironically suggests that life does maintain a modicum of hope:

> But he who is joined with all the living has hope—a living dog is better than a dead lion. For the living know that they will die, but the dead know nothing, and they have no more reward. Even the memory of them is lost. Their love and their hate and their jealousy have already perished, and they have no more forever any share in all that is done under the sun. (9:4–6)[12]

---

10. In contrast, the cognate literature of the ANE displays a much greater interest in these matters. For discussions of this literature, see Lloyd R. Bailey, *Biblical Perspectives on Death* (OBT; Philadelphia: Fortress, 1979), 5–21; Philip S. Johnston, *Shades of Sheol: Death and Afterlife in the Old Testament* (Downers Grove, Ill.: Apollos, 2002), 230–39; Brian B. Schmidt, *Israel's Beneficent Dead: Ancestor Cult and Necromancy in Ancient Israelite Religion and Tradition* (FAT 11; Tübingen: Mohr, 1994), 14–130; Klaas Spronk, *Beatific Afterlife in Ancient Israel and in the Ancient Near East* (AOAT 219; Kevelaer: Butzon & Bercker, 1986), 86–236.

11. Alan F. Segal, "Some Observations about Mysticism and the Spread of Notions of Life After Death in Hebrew Thought," *SBL Seminar Papers, 1996* (SBLSP 35; Atlanta: Scholars Press, 1996), 385–99. For more on the biblical silence concerning death, see Richard Elliott Friedman and Shawna Dolansky Overton, "Death and Afterlife: The Biblical Silence," in *Judaism in Late Antiquity*. Vol. 4, *Death, Life-after-Death, Resurrection and the World-to-Come in the Judaisms of Antiquity* (ed. Alan J. Avery-Peck and Jacob Neusner; Leiden: Brill, 2000), 35–59.

12. Qoheleth's conclusion that in light of certain, hopeless death one must "Enjoy life with the wife whom you love, all the days of your vain life, which he has given you under the sun, because that is your portion in life and in your toil at which you toil under the sun" (9:9), resonates with the contemporary philosopher Simon Critchley (*Very Little—Almost Nothing: Death, Philosophy, Literature* [Warwick Studies in European Philosophy; New York: Routledge, 1997], 1–28) who concludes that death is meaningless and that all we can do is seek to find our meaning in the ordinariness of life. Critchley, in a Qoheleth-esque vain, expressing the disappointment of such a conclusion, suggests that it is "very little…almost nothing," but at it is at least an "almost." Similar

Qoheleth's treatment of death is unique among biblical texts: here death is pondered in an almost philosophical vein and is found to be problematic—or at least to cause problems to prevailing beliefs about happiness and justice. Also unique among biblical books for its emphasis on death is *Job*. In fact, *Job* may be the most death-oriented book in the entire Bible, though its emphasis is different than Qoheleth's. *Job* displays its death-orientation in two ways: by the sheer variety and quantity of words used for "death" throughout the book; and by the apparent strategic narrative placement of depictions of death and conversations about death in the prose and poetic sections.

Altogether, there are 47 words in *Job* that mean "death" in one way or another, occurring over 140 times.[13] This impressive array of words for death includes words that literally mean "death," or "kill," or the like; words that pertain to the grave and the realm of the dead; euphemisms for death; and words that have "death" or "kill" or the like as one of several meanings, but which clearly connote death in the context in which they appear. Every chapter of the book, except possibly 23 and 25 (and from Elihu's Speeches, 32, 35, and 37), contains words for death, whether they be few (chs. 2, 11, 12, 13, 15, 19, 22, 25, 29, 40, 41 and 42) or abundant (chs. 3, 4, 7, 10, 14, 16–17, 18, 21, 27 and 30) or somewhere in between. What makes death in *Job* unique, however, is not so much the variety and frequency of "death" words, but the strategic usage to which the "death theme" is put in the book.

Death, first of all, is a narrative vehicle that both brackets the prose tale and sustains its plot. After a brief description of setting (both Job's and the heavenly setting in 1:1–5, 6–12), the implementation of *haśśatan*'s plan to test Job supplies the crisis that moves the plot forward—and it is a crisis of death (1:13–19): of who dies (those who take care of Job's possessions and cattle, those whom Job most desperately tried to protect from death [his children]), and who dies when (a succession of servants' deaths culminating in the death of Job's children). Death now dominates the tale: Job's response to these deaths is to perform rites of mourning (1:20) and to speak of life and death in the context of God's actions (1:21); *haśśatan*'s next plan is to strike Job but not cause his death (2:6); Job's wife encourages Job to curse God and die (2:9); then Job and his friends perform various mortuary rites (2:11–13). Finally, the prose tale supplies the ending to the whole book with the narration of Job's own death (42:17). The narrative arc of the action of the prose tale is therefore from death to death.

Although the final ending of the book terminates with a description of death in 42:17, scholars have long noted that the end of the prose tale, which doubles as the end of the entire book, is not the *only* ending in the book. *Job*, rather, is made up of several loosely related, but likely originally separate parts, all of which begin and end in turn: the prose tale ends early (2:13), only to give way to the poetic dialogues, which end much later (27:23), giving way to the Wisdom

---

attitudes toward death are found in other literature of the ANE. See, e.g., "A Dispute over Suicide," translated by John A. Wilson (*ANET*, 405–7); and "The Dialogue of Pessimism between Master and Servant," translated by Robert H. Pfeiffer (*ANET*, 437–38).

13. For more on these words, see below, section 1.5.1.

poem (ch. 28) and Job's final speech (chs. 29–31). The Divine Speeches pick up after the end of Job's last speech and themselves end with Job's last words (42:6). With this the prose tale is born again (42:7) and then ends again (42:17).[14] Coinciding with each of these endings, like the final ending of the book, is a death of one sort or another.

First of all, the ending of the first part of the prose tale portrays a death scene, although not the narrated death of a character as in 42:17. Instead, mortuary and mourning rites are depicted (wailing, rent garments, dust thrown on the head)[15] coupled with perfect and full silence (seven days) evoking the ultimate silence and silencing of death.[16]

The dialogues between Job and his friends, for their part, end with Job's discussion of the death of the wicked (27:13–23). Prior to this ending, though, there are numerous references to death, most notably toward the end of certain of Job's key speeches (3:11–23; 7:1–21; 10:18–22; 17:13–16; 21:23–34). The friends also reserve death for special consideration in their speeches (4:7–11, 17–21; 5:17–27; 15:17–35; 18:5–21; 20:4–29). For Job, death signifies multiply: at once a sought-after respite from God's terrors (ch. 3); a subjectively felt attack from God (16:13–16); grounds for a plea for mercy from God (7:20–21; 10:18–22; 14:5–6); grounds for a call for compassion from his friends (ch. 19); and proof of injustice (9:22–24; ch. 21). The friends discuss death differently: death to them proves divine justice to be operative. It is reserved for the wicked, and would not be for Job if only he would repent (4:3–9; chs. 18; 20).

Job's final speech in chs. 29–31 ends neither with a depicted death scene nor a discussion of death, but with a distant allusion to a death now effaced: the statement that "the words of Job are ended (תמּו)" (31:40). The root תמם has no singular connotation: it suggests the completion, finishing, or exhaustion of a variety of things, such as money (Gen 47:15), years (Gen 47:18; Lev 25:29; Ps 102:28; Jer 1:3), strength (Lev 26:20), song (Deut 31:30), and, by extension, the completion or finishing of human life, namely, death.[17] On occasion תמם occurs in parallel to מות, making the "death" connotation more explicit.[18] In the context in Job 31:40, however, תמם is used of the end of words, namely to express that Job's spoken words are finished. But in a book so rife with talk of human death, the echoes of End-of-Life תמם with End-of-Words תמם still can be heard. So the phrase might be translated, "The words of Job are terminated."

---

14. For good discussions of how historical critics typically understand the composition and composite nature of *Job*, see John E. Hartley, *The Book of Job* (NICOT; Grand Rapids: Eerdmans, 1988), 20–33; Carol Newsom, "Job," *NIB* 4:320–25; Marvin H. Pope, *Job* (3d ed.; AB 15; Garden City, N.Y.: Doubleday, 1973), xxi–xxviii; Harold Henry Rowley, *From Moses to Qumran: Studies in the Old Testament* (New York: Association Press, 1963), 146–70.

15. See below, section 1.5.1, for more discussion of these rites.

16. Curiously, no one has died at this point in the tale. The deaths of Job's servants and children occurred as part of Job's first "test" (1:13–19), but in this second "test" Job only is afflicted physically.

17. See Num 14:35; 17:28; Deut 2:14, 15, 16; Josh 5:6; 2 Kgs 7:3; Pss 9:7; 104:35; Jer 14:15; 24:10; 27:8; 44:12 (twice), 18, 27. See also, Josh 10:20; 1 Kgs 14:10; Ps 73:19; Isa 16:4.

18. תמם would fall under the group one, sub-category four "death" words according to the linguistic analysis below (section 1.5.1).

The Divine Speeches also end with death—this time with a double reference to death, both of which evoke death from previous parts of the book. First, the Leviathan speech closes with a flourish on the impossibility of killing the beast with human weapons (41:18–21; sword, spear, missile, lance, arrow, club, javelin)—weapons, which, as instruments of death, Job used previously to describe his own murder at God's hands.[19] For Leviathan, however, these weapons of death are powerless and cannot cause the death of this great monster, a startling image given the traditional mythological associations with Leviathan as the chaos monster that the deity slays.[20]

Second, Job's response to God's soliloquy on the Leviathan that cannot be killed itself ends with an obscure reference to dust and ashes (42:6). The phrase "dust and ashes" is used in only two other places in the HB, Gen 18:27 and Job 30:19. In the former context the phrase clearly refers to a human as a finite, created creature in contrast to God. While it is difficult to determine the exact reference in the latter case, the phrase seems to suggest the dishonor and dissolution that accompany humiliation. Taken separately, "dust" in *Job* frequently is connected euphemistically to the mortality of humans and their deaths,[21] while "ashes," although used infrequently in *Job* (2:11; 13:12; 30:19; 42:6) is associated with ritual acts of mourning elsewhere in the HB,[22] at times referring to the remains of a corpse consumed in fire.[23] Finally, the "dust and ashes" of Job 42:6 recall the dust and ashes in the first half of the prose tale: Job sitting on the ash heap and the friends throwing dust upon their heads as part of the mourning/ mortuary ritual. Although it is rather unclear exactly what Job intends with these dust and ashes in 42:6,[24] that these are items connected with human mortality, death, and death rites seems sure. Fittingly, they are the last of Job's words in the book.

In sum, death in *Job* seems to have strategic importance. All the characters make death the topic of parts of their speeches, many of which terminate with a consideration about the meaning or importance of death. Likewise, discussions or descriptions of death tend to coincide with the endings of the various components of the book of Job (prose tale, dialogues, etc.). Death appears all throughout the book, in all different contexts and in the various discourses of all the different characters.

Zuckerman, therefore, surely is correct when he claims that "verse-for-verse," no book in the Bible is more death-oriented than *Job*."[25] However, unlike

19. Job 6:4; 16:12–14. Frequently various weapons are connected to death by synecdoche. See 20:24; 34:6, and below, section 1.5.1, for further elaboration.

20. See Isa 27:1; 51:9 and section 6.2.1.2 below for more elaboration.

21. See Job 7:21; 10:9; 17:16; 20:11; 21:26; 34:15, and possibly 4:19 and 40:13. This connection of dust to death is made early in the HB in Gen 3:19.

22. Esth 4:1, 3; Isa 61:3; Jer 6:26; Ezek 27:30; Jonah 3:6.

23. See Num 19:9, 10; Ezek 28:18. Mal 4:3 might also have this connotation.

24. See Newsom's discussion of the interpretations of this troubling verse in Carol A. Newsom, "Considering Job," *CR:BS* 1 (1993): 111–12. She traces six distinct attempts to understand this verse. See also my discussion of this verse in Chapter 6, below.

25. Bruce Zuckerman, *Job the Silent: A Study in Historical Counterpoint* (New York: Oxford University Press, 1991), 118.

Qoheleth where death is a topic of special consideration as it buttresses one of the book's central theses, *Job* explicitly is *not* a book whose central topic is death, nor does death have so clear and unproblematic a relation to *Job*'s theses. For, as Pope suggests, scholars have "generally assumed that the purpose of the book is to give an answer to the issue with which it deals, the problem of divine justice or theodicy."[26] *Haśśatan* initially raises this "problem"—inadvertently, it seems—in the prose introduction, when he questions not divine justice, but the existence of unmotivated piety: "Is it for nothing that Job fears God?" (1:9–11). If God rewards piety, does this corrupt the divine–human relationship? Do humans serve God only because they know they will be rewarded? The only way to answer these questions is for God to sanction the infliction of loss and suffering on the pious Job, thus raising the issue of theodicy to prominence.

Such is the topic of the dialogues. The friends maintain a belief in a completely just and good God, and therefore hold suffering to be the occasion for "moral and religious self-examination and reflection":[27] suffering is judgment for the wicked (15:20–35), a warning for those with questionable ethics (5:17–19), discipline for the ethically immature (33:14–30), or cause to return to God in trust and prayer (11:13–19; 22:21–30). Job, however, views his suffering as completely unwarranted, and his response is to confront God and call God to account for this affliction. He accuses God of violating justice (27:2), acting maliciously (7:12–20), and striking out in rage (16:9–14). "The friends argue for the goodness of God, the moral order of the world, the purposiveness of suffering, and the importance of humble submission to God. Job questions the justice of God, describes the world as a moral chaos, depicts suffering in terms of victimization, and stakes his life on the possibility of legal confrontation with God."[28]

Taken together, the prose tale and the poetic dialogues explore two potentially problematic flaws of the Israelite ideology of divine justice: if God truly upholds divine justice, do humans serve God only because God rewards them? And, more fundamentally, does God truly uphold divine justice? Yet the question remains, if divine justice really is at issue in the book of Job, why is there so much death everywhere and why does it seem to be placed strategically? What sort of relation exists between divine justice and the ubiquitous death-talk in the book? What is it about the problematic aspects of the system of divine justice that draws representations of death, discussions of death, and images of death into its orbit? Is the meaning of death influenced by the collapse of divine justice?

This project will be an attempt to answer these questions. I will examine the meaning(s) of death in the book of Job, and the relation of "death" to the theological/moral systems in *Job*. I will argue that death emerges as a main "figure" in *Job* precisely because the book contests the operation of divine justice in the world and does not take it for granted as the operative theological system

26. Pope, *Job*, lxviii.
27. Newsom, "Job," 334
28. Ibid., 336.

by which God directs the universe. In other words, the book of Job wrests the "meaning" of death—who dies and for what reasons—from its traditional moral/ theological context in the system of divine justice and allows death to emerge as a question alongside other moral/theological questions such as the nature of God, the operation of the world, the fate of the wicked, and the value of piety. Before I proceed to explain my own approach to death in *Job* in more detail, I would first like to examine typical ways scholars have approached the study of death in the HB, in general, and in *Job*, in particular.

1.2. *A Select History of the Interpretation of Death in the Hebrew Bible*

Studies of death in the HB are legion, having been produced at a steady pace throughout the centuries. Brichto suggests that "Nothing short of a full monograph woud [*sic*] do justice to the history of interpretation of this [topic]."[29] Although no monographs on this topic have been produced, there are at least two good summaries of the history of interpretation of death in the HB: one covering works until the mid- to late nineteenth century by Spiess;[30] and one covering the early Jewish and Christian periods and the late nineteenth century until about 1980 by Spronk.[31] Before the nineteenth century, when modern research on the topic emerged, it was generally argued that there was no difference between what the HB taught about death and the afterlife and what the Church said about these issues, although this was contested by the Socinians in the sixteenth century and a couple of centuries later by the Deists.[32]

Since the rise of historical criticism, however, there has been an increasing movement to examine death in the context of ancient Israel, apart from Church teaching. The overriding question that has driven the vast majority of these studies is, "What did the ancient Israelites believe about death and about what happens to the individual after death?"[33] Most of the earlier historical-critical

---

29. H. C. Brichto, "Kin, Cult, Land and Afterlife: A Biblical Complex," *HUCA* 44 (1973): 1–54 (1).

30. Edmund Spiess, *Entwicklungsgeschichte der Vorstellungen vom Zustande nach dem Tode: Auf Grund vergleichender Religionsforschung* (Jena: Hermann Costenoble, 1877), 409–16.

31. Spronk, *Beatific Afterlife*; see pp. 4–24 for the early Jewish and Christian eras, including information about how death was interpreted by those who revised certain texts in the Targumim, LXX, and MT, and pp. 25–83 for the Modern period, especially, the late nineteenth century until the publication of his book. For a quick look at the diversity of scholarly opinion about the ancient Israelite conception of death, see Bailey, *Biblical Perspectives*, 25–28.

32. Spiess, *Entwicklungsgeschichte*, 411–13; Spronk, *Beatific Afterlife*, 25–26.

33. Spronk argues that the beginning of modern research on the ancient Israelite understanding of death came with Spiess' 1877 study, which suggested that Israel's conception of death needs to be clarified through comparisons with Israel's neighbors (Spiess, *Entwicklungsgeschichte*, 417–18; Spronk, *Beatific Afterlife*, 28–29). Anthropological theories about the worship of the dead in "primitive" cultures were next to impact studies of ancient Israelite beliefs about death. According to Spronk, one of the first biblical scholars to utilize anthropology in this manner was Lippert who examined the HB with the assumption that ancestor worship is at the root of all religions (Julius Lippert, *Der Seelencult in seinen Beziehungen zur althebräischen Religion: eine ethnologische Studie* [Berlin: Theodor Hofmann, 1881]).

studies accepted the argument for the existence of ancestor worship in ancient Israel and tended to focus on a cluster of issues pertaining to death: the idea of the "soul";[34] mourning customs;[35] funerary rites;[36] worship of the dead in the

34. See, e.g., Carl Grüneisen, *Der Ahnenkultus und die Urreligion Israels* (Halle: Max Niemeyer, 1900), 20–60; Adolphe Lods, *La croyance à la vie future et le culte des morts dans l'antiquité israélite* (2 vols.; Paris: Fischbacher, 1906), 1:43–75. Pedersen articulated the view that came to dominate the field: Israel did not separate the body from the soul and therefore in death "the dead is still a soul, but a soul that has lost its substance and strength: it is a misty vapour or a shadow" (Johannes Pedersen, *Israel: Its Life and Culture* [trans. A. Møller and A. I. Fausbell; 2 vols.; London: Oxford University Press, 1926], 1:180). For examples of those who generally adopt this point of view, see Bailey, *Biblical Perspectives*, 42–47; Walther Eichrodt, *Theology of the Old Testament* (trans. J. A. Baker; 2 vols.; OTL; Philadelphia: Westminster, 1961), 2:214; Robert Martin-Achard, *From Death to Life: A Study of the Development of the Doctrine of the Resurrection in the Old Testament* (trans. John Penney Smith; Edinburgh: Oliver & Boyd, 1960), 18–20, 31–33; Lou H. Silberman, "Death in the Hebrew Bible and Apocalyptic Literature," in *Perspectives on Death* (ed. Liston O. Mills; Nashville: Abingdon, 1969), 13–32 (19–21). For more on the conception of the soul in the research of the early historical critics, see Spronk, *Beatific Afterlife*, 29–33.

35. Johannes Frey, *Tod, Seelenglaube und Seelenkult im alten Israel: eine religionsgeschicht-liche Untersuchung* (Leipzig: Deichert, 1898), 33–52; Lods, *Croyance à la Vie future*, 1:116–23; Friedrich Schwally, *Das Leben nach dem Tode: nach den Vorstellungen des alten Israel und des Judentums einschliesslich des Volksglaubens im Zeitalter Christi, eine biblisch-theologische Untersuchung* (Giessen: Ricker, 1892), 9–20; Roland de Vaux, *Ancient Israel*. Vol. 1, *Social Institutions* (New York: McGraw–Hill, 1965), 59. For more on mourning rites in the research of the early historical critics, see Spronk, *Beatific Afterlife*, 33–35. More contemporary analyses of mourning rites may be found in Gary A. Anderson, *A Time to Mourn, a Time to Dance: The Expression of Grief and Joy in Israelite Religion* (University Park: Pennsylvania State University Press, 1991); Xuan Huong Thi Pham, *Mourning in the Ancient Near East and the Hebrew Bible* (JSOTSup 302; Sheffield: Sheffield Academic Press, 1999); and Johnston, *Shades of Sheol*, 47–65.

36. During the early decades of modern research when funerary rites tended to be examined in connection with a cult of the dead (see, e.g., Schwally, *Das Leben nach dem Tode*, 27–53) it was hard to arrive at sound conclusions regarding the cult of the dead based on the material remains of the ancient Israelites because of the paucity of materials unearthed. In the last couple decades, scholars have returned to this issue, and based, in part or in whole, on new archaeological evidence of tomb sites, have argued for the existence of a cult of the dead. See, e.g., Elizabeth Bloch-Smith, "The Cult of the Dead in Judah: Interpreting the Material Remains," *JBL* 111 (1992): 213–24; idem, *Judahite Burial Practices and Beliefs about the Dead* (JSOTSup 123; Sheffield: JSOT Press, 1992), 109–54; Rachel S. Hallote, *Death, Burial, and Afterlife in the Biblical World: How the Israelites and their Neighbors Treated the Dead* (Chicago: Dee, 2001), 54–68; Theodore J. Lewis, *Cults of the Dead in Ancient Israel and Ugarit* (HSM 39; Atlanta: Scholars Press, 1989) (though Lewis' study is mostly based on textual, rather than artifactual, evidence). For other studies that have examined ancient Israelite beliefs about death, the afterlife, a cult of the dead, ancestor worship, and the like based on archaeological evidence, see John R. Abercrombie, "Palestinian Burial Practices from 1200 to 600 B.C.E" (Ph.D. diss., University of Pennsylvania, 1979), 14–196; Robert E. Cooley, "The Contribution of Literary Sources to the Study of the Canaanite Burial Pattern" (Ph.D. diss., New York University, 1968), 34–38, 80–188; Rivka Gonen, *Burial Patterns and Cultural Diversity in Late Bronze Age Canaan* (ASOR Dissertation Series 7; Winona Lake, Ind.: Eisenbrauns, 1992); George C. Heider, *The Cult of Molek: A Reassessment* (JSOTSup 43; Sheffield: JSOT Press, 1985); Philip S. Johnston, "The Underworld and the Dead in the Old Testament" (Ph.D. diss., Cambridge University, 1993); Herbert Niehr, "Aspekte des Totengedenkens im Juda der Königszeit," *TQ* 178 (1998): 1–13; John Whalen Ribar, "Death Cult Practices in Ancient Palestine" (Ph.D. diss., University of Michigan, 1973), 13–71; David Volgger, "Auch in Israel haben die Toten eine Botschaft," *Anton* 74 (1999): 227–52; Robert Wenning, "Bestattungen im königszeitlichen Juda," *TQ* 177 (1997): 82–93.

context of the family;[37] ritual laws and practices;[38] and, perhaps most relevant to *Job*, an examination of the transition in the HB from the belief in Sheol to that of resurrection. I will elaborate on this last point more fully.

Since the rise of historical criticism, scholarly consensus has been that the bulk of the HB speaks of the afterlife as a shadowy, gloomy existence, completely separate from Yahweh.[39] The most an Israelite could hope for is a good, long life with a son.[40] Although generally supporting this theory, the early historical critics were troubled by references in the HB both to Sheol and the grave

37. Many early historical critics found evidence in the HB itself for the worship of the dead in the family context. See, e.g., Robert Henry Charles, *Eschatology, the Doctrine of a Future Life in Israel, Judaism, and Christianity: A Critical History* (Schocken Paperbacks 49; New York: Schocken, 1963), 23–27; Lods, *Croyance à la vie future*, 2:43–87; Julian Morgenstern, *The Rites of Birth, Marriage, Death, and Kindred Occasions among the Semites* (Cincinnati: Hebrew Union College Press, 1966), 166–79; Schwally, *Das Leben nach dem Tode*, 21–25; and more recently, Joseph Blenkinsopp, "Deuteronomy and the Politics of Post-Mortem Existence," *VT* 45 (1995): 1–16; Bloch-Smith, *Judahite Burial Practices*, 122–26; Brichto, "Kin, Cult, Land," 1–54; Hallote, *Death, Burial, and Afterlife*, 54–68; Karel van der Toorn, "Ein verborgenes Erbe: Totenkult im frühen Israel," *TQ* 177 (1997): 105–20. This position has come under attack by Schmidt (*Israel's Beneficent Dead*, 274–93). For a history of interpretation of the cult of the dead from the early historical critics, see Ribar, "Death Cult Practices," 4–10. For more on the worship of the dead in the family context in HB texts, see Spronk, *Beatific Afterlife*, 37–39; Johnston, *Shades of Sheol*, 150–95.

38. The consensus among early historical critics was that Yahwism gained a monopoly over religion and banned ancestor worship, but was unable to get rid of it altogether. The old animistic views continued to survive on a popular level and eventually they were able to influence Yahwism in its development of the belief in retribution for the individual after death (see, e.g., Lods, *Croyance à la Vie future*, 2:128; Schwally, *Leben nach dem Tode*, 75–76). Among more contemporary scholars the "consensus" view is that that a cult of the dead did exist, although it was likely opposed by official Yahwism (see, e.g., Blenkinsopp, "Deuteronomy," 1–16; Bloch-Smith, "Cult of the Dead," 220–24; idem, *Judahite Burial Practices*, 130–32; Brichto, "Kin, Cult, Land," 1–54; Hallote, *Death, Burial, and Afterlife*, 54–68; Heider, *Cult of Molek*, 383–408; Lewis, *Cults of the Dead in Ancient Israel and Ugarit*, 1–4; Martin-Achard, *From Death to Life*, 24–31; Thomas Podella, "Nekromantie," *TQ* 177 [1997]: 121–33; Gerhard von Rad, *Old Testament Theology* [trans. D. M. G. Stalker; 2 vols.; OTL; Louisville, Ky.: Westminster John Knox, 2001], 1:275–77; Ribar, "Death Cult Practices," 78–84; Toorn, "Ein verborgenes Erbe," 105–20. But see, for opposing views, Bailey, *Biblical Perspectives*, 32–36; Cooley, "Contribution of Literary Sources," 198–201; Eichrodt, *Theology*, 2:221–22; Johnston, *Shades of Sheol*, 167–95; Gisela Kittel, *Befreit aus dem Rachen des Todes: Tod und Todesüberwindung im Alten und Neuen Testament* [Biblisch-theologische Schwerpunkte 17; Göttingen: Vandenhoeck & Ruprecht, 1999], 91–92; Horst Dietrich Preuss, *Old Testament Theology* [2 vols.; trans. Leo G. Perdue; OTL; Louisville, Ky.: Westminster John Knox, 1991], 2:262–63; Helmer Ringgren, *Israelite Religion* [trans. David E. Green; Philadelphia: Fortress, 1966], 241; Schmidt, *Israel's Beneficent Dead*, 274–93; Wenning, "Bestattungen," 82–93).

39. See, e.g., Bailey, *Biblical Perspectives*, 45–47; Christoph Barth, *Die Errettung vom Tode in den individuellen Klage- und Dankliedern des Alten Testamentes* (Zollikon: Evangelischer Verlag, 1947), 76–122; Eichrodt, *Theology*, 2:210–28; Hallote, *Death, Burial, and Afterlife*, 52–53; Martin-Achard, *From Death to Life*, 36–40; Susan Niditch, *Ancient Israelite Religion* (New York: Oxford University Press, 1997), 63–64; Preuss, *Theology*, 2:261–62; Ringgren, *Israelite Religion*, 244–45; Silberman, "Death," 20–21; Nicholas J. Tromp, *Primitive Conceptions of Death and the Nether World in the Old Testament* (BibOr 21; Rome: Pontifical Biblical Institute, 1969), 176–99.

40. For a full statement of this argument, see Bailey, *Biblical Perspectives*, 47–61. According to Bailey, the hope for living on in the family name took the place of the hope for an afterlife. See Bailey, *Biblical Perspectives*, 58.

as abodes of the dead. These early historical critics assumed the existence of a cult of the dead based on anthropological theories about "primitive" religious beliefs, and according to these theories, the cult should be connected with a single grave, not a realm of the dead in general. Pedersen, however, argued that the grave and Sheol cannot be separated, the individual grave forming a whole with the graves of one's kin, which is now the majority opinion among contemporary scholars. Pedersen went on to argue that Sheol is not only a place one goes to after death, but the living can confront it in life through illness, suffering, or the like. He argued that the Israelites had a great sense of totality, so that if Israelites sensed any part of Sheol within them, they experienced all of Sheol.[41] Barth worked out this position with the help of extra-biblical material and argued that death in ancient Israel was not necessarily physical death, since in the Psalms illness, poverty, persecution, and the like are regarded as a way of being in Sheol. These texts suggest that one might be rescued from this Sheol-in-life, and so they do not point to a hope for eternal life.[42] Some scholars have regarded Sheol to be an active force in life, threatening the living with all manner of evils,[43] while others have viewed it as a part of the natural order of things, established by God.[44]

For the many scholars, *the* question when considering the ancient Israelite conception of death is how Israel moved from a belief in the gloomy, shadowy existence in Sheol to a belief in the resurrection and eternal life as exhibited by some of the latest texts of the HB (Isa 25.8; 26.19; Dan 12.2).[45] Most scholars

41. Pedersen, *Israel*, 466–67.

42. Barth, *Errettung vom Tode*, 152–66. Others have expressed similar views about death and also about the Israelite conception of life. See Aubrey R. Johnson, *The Vitality of the Individual in the Thought of Ancient Israel* (Cardiff: University of Wales Press, 1949), 88–107; Martin-Achard, *From Death to Life*, 3–51.

43. Tromp is probably the most ebullient: "Sir death is the enemy par excellence, death is the summary of all evil" (Tromp, *Primitive Conceptions*, 213). So, for Tromp, persecution, sickness, and the like are felt as types of partial (but real) death, and they are manifestations of the archenemy. See also Martin-Achard, *From Death to Life*, 44–45; Preuss, *Theology*, 2:261. Bailey recognizes that death is understood in places in the HB as a power in opposition to the created order. He argues, however, that this conception of death is somewhat tempered because Yahweh was considered to be the sole power by the Israelites. See Bailey, *Biblical Perspectives*, 39–40. For others who argue that the Israelites viewed death with horror, see, e.g., Hallote, *Death, Burial, and Afterlife*, 52–53; Kittel, *Befreit*, 12–19; Bruce Vawter, "Post-Exilic Prayer and Hope," *CBQ* 37 (1975): 460–70 (470); Hans Walter Wolff, *Anthropology of the Old Testament* (trans. Margaret Kohl; Philadelphia: Fortress, 1974), 102.

44. Bailey, *Biblical Perspectives*, 57–61; Eichrodt, *Theology*, 2:501–2; von Rad, *Theology*, 1:390; Ringgren, *Israelite Religion*, 239; Silberman, "Death," 23–25. For more on all these issues, see Spronk, *Beatific Afterlife*, 66–71. For others who argue that the Israelites had little anxiety about death, see, e.g., Lloyd R. Bailey, "Death as a Theological Problem in the Old Testament," *Pastoral Psychology* 22 (1971): 20–32 (21); Walter Brueggemann, "Death, Theology of," *IDBSup*, 219–22 (220); von Rad, *Theology*, 1:390; Ringgren, *Israelite Religion*, 239.

45. Bailey is unique among those who examine Israelite conceptions of death and the afterlife (vs. those who examine burial practices, for example) in that he states that he will not trace the historical factors that led to a belief in life after death (Bailey, *Biblical Perspectives*, 23–24). See also Nico von Uchelen, "Death and the Afterlife in the Hebrew Bible of Ancient Israel," in *Hidden Futures: Death and Immortality in Ancient Egypt, Anatolia, the Classical, Biblical and Arabic-*

today argue that the rise in the belief in resurrection was a late development that occurred, at least partially, as a result of the influence of beliefs of foreign peoples, including Egyptians, Persians, Mesopotamians, Greeks, and various Canaanites.[46] Ringgren, for example, argues that a belief in resurrection arose late, under the influences of old Canaanite beliefs about dying and rising gods, and of Persian beliefs about resurrection, in conjunction with the old Yahwistic conviction that Yahweh is stronger than death and Sheol.[47] Spronk, similarly, argues that Israel was introduced to the idea of resurrection at least twice, early on from the Canaanite belief in resurrection connected with the Baal agricultural myth (which Israel rejected) and later from contact with Egyptian, Greek, and Persian beliefs (which were adapted in various ways only after an Israelite version of resurrection grew out of specifically Israelite theological considerations).[48] Silberman argues that the shift in Israelite belief came as a result of Iranian influence, although internal Israelite developments paved the way.[49]

Virtually every study of the rise of the belief in resurrection in Israel points to native Israelite developments in addition to, or exclusive of, foreign influence. Spronk suggests that the three most commonly cited factors within official Yahwism that contributed to the development of the belief in resurrection are: a growing sense of individuality, which would lead to an increasing curiosity in

Islamic World (ed. Jan Maarten Bremer, P. J. van den Hout, and Rudolph Peters; Amsterdam: Amsterdam University Press, 1994), 77–90.

46. For history of interpretations of foreign influences, see Franz König, *Zarathustras Jenseitsvorstellungen und das Alte Testament* (Wien: Herder, 1964), 8–39; Spronk, *Beatific Afterlife*, 55–65; Günther Wied, "Der Auferstehungsglaube des späten Israel in seiner Bedeutung für das Verhältnis von Apokalyptik und Weisheit" (Ph.D. diss., Universität Bonn, 1967), 7–18 (Wied also gives a history of interpretation of arguments for inner-Israelite changes that resulted in a belief in resurrection). Some scholars reject altogether any sort of foreign influence on Israel's beliefs. See, e.g., Eichrodt, *Theology*, 2:509–25; Martin-Achard, *From Death to Life*, 186–205. Tromp rejects the influence of Canaanite, but not Egyptian, Greek, or Persian beliefs on official Yahwism (Spronk, *Beatific Afterlife*, 344–346).

Albright and Dahood are among a minority of scholars who argue that a belief in resurrection comes from an early period in Israel's history. Albright connects the Israelite במה to hero cults comparable to the Greek hero cults, and then argues that the latter influenced Yahwism's development of a conception of resurrection early on. See William Foxwell Albright, "The High Place in Ancient Palestine," in *Volume du Congrès: Strasbourg, 1956* (ed. G. W. Anderson; VTSup 4; Leiden: Brill, 1957), 242–58. Dahood, on the other hand, adduces from a comparison of certain Proverbs and Psalms with the literature of Ugarit, an early conception of resurrection in Israel. See Mitchell J. Dahood, "Immortality in Proverb 12,28," *Bib* 41 (1960): 176–81. See also John F. Healey, "Death, Underworld and Afterlife in the Ugaritic Texts" (Ph.D. diss., University of London, 1977), 297–300, 309; idem, "The Immortality of the King: Ugarit and the Psalms," *Or* 53 (1984): 245–54; Spronk, *Beatific Afterlife*, 77–81. Most scholars have criticized both Albright's and Dahood's theories, a fact noted by Dahood, himself (*Psalms III* [AB 17a; Garden City, N.Y.: Doubleday, 1970], xli–xlv).

47. Ringgren, *Israelite Religion*, 323.

48. Spronk, *Beatific Afterlife*, 237–346.

49. Silberman, "Death," 26–29. Martin-Achard (*From Death to Life*, 193–95) has argued that Persian influence is hard to trace for several reasons: first, resurrection seems to be a very late development in Persian religion; second, it is extremely difficult to date the Persian texts; and third, the conception of resurrection in Persian texts seems to differ from that in the HB. Comparative Persian evidence seems to be handled with a great deal of caution in recent scholarly discussions.

the fate of the individual in the afterlife; a belief in Yahweh's power (which would be increasingly thought to extend even to Sheol) and justice (which would have increasingly have been thought to be meted out to individuals after death); and increasing hope for a lasting communion with God.[50] Spronk discusses briefly the most cited texts.[51] First, many cite texts such as Deut 32:39; 1 Sam 2:6; Amos 9:2; and Ps 139:18 as indicative of the belief that Yahweh's power was thought to extend to Sheol (in contrast to earlier texts, which envision Sheol as a place marked by God's absence). These texts would have led to the belief that one day death itself would be overcome by Yahweh.[52] Second, 1 Kgs 17:17–24; 2 Kgs 4:18–37; 13:20–21 speak about the revivification of dead people, although most scholars argue these stories are fundamentally different from the later texts that speak of resurrection.[53] Third, Gen 5:24 and 2 Kgs 2:1–8 speak about the assumptions of Enoch and Elijah, respectively; but these, too, are generally regarded as fundamentally different from the later texts that will speak of resurrection.[54] Fourth, texts such as Jer 31:29–30 and Ezek 18:1–4 argue that the sins of parents do not get passed on to future generations. Some scholars suggest that this would have caused theological problems for those who assumed a retributive ethical framework—a problem leading to the creation of a belief in an afterlife where justice would be meted out.[55] Fifth, texts such as Ps 16:10–11; 49:16; 73:23–24; and Job 19:25–27 speak of a continuing relationship with Yahweh after death. Many scholars argue these contributed to a hope in a beatific afterlife.[56]

Other suggestions for native Israelite developments that would have led to a belief in resurrection include: the waning importance of avoiding Canaanite beliefs about resurrection in the context of the exilic and post-exilic Diaspora;[57]

---

50. In contemporary studies, the latter two seem much more prevalent than the first.

51. For what follows, see Spronk, *Beatific Afterlife*, 72–81.

52. See, e.g., Kittel, *Befreit*, 26–33; Martin-Achard, *From Death to Life*, 86–102; idem, "'Il engloutit la mort à jamais'. Remarques sur Esaïe 25,8aα," in *Mélanges bibliques et orientaux en l'honneur de M. Mathias Delcor* (ed. A. Caquot, S. Légasse and M. Tardieu; AOAT 215; Kevelaer: Butzon & Berker, 1985), 283–96; Ringgren, *Israelite Religion*, 323.

53. Spronk argues that these were folk traditions influenced by Canaanite agricultural myths, but not sanctioned by official Yahwism (Spronk, *Beatific Afterlife*, 345–46). Silberman argues that these exceptional miraculous revivals would have had a positive influence in the rise in belief in resurrection (see Silberman, "Death," 26–29).

54. See, e.g., Martin-Achard, *From Death to Life*, 65–72.

55. See, for a comprehensive working out of this theory, Dermot Cox, "'As Water Spilt on the Ground' (Death in the Old Testament)," *Studia Missionalia* 31 (1982): 1–17.

56. See, e.g., Eichrodt, *Theology*, 2:517–25; Kittel, *Befreit*, 27–44; Martin-Achard, *From Death to Life*, 147–81; Niditch, *Israelite Religion*, 66–67; Spronk, *Beatific Afterlife*, 344–45. According to Spronk, Sellin argued that such texts led to two separate developments: one leading to the belief in individual resurrection, and the other to a more mystical conception of the afterlife (see Spronk, *Beatific Afterlife*, 75, and E. Sellin, "Die alttestamentliche Hoffnung auf Auferstehung und ewiges Leben," *NKZ* 30 [1919]: 232–89 [266–67]). See also Michael S. Moore, "Resurrection and Immortality: Two Motifs Navigating Confluent Theological Streams in the Old Testament (Dan 12,1–4)," *TZ* 39 (1983): 17–34; Harold Henry Rowley, "The Future Life in the Thought of the Old Testament," *Congregational Quarterly* 33 (1955): 785–99.

57. Hallote, *Death, Burial, and Afterlife*, 136–42.

the elaboration of prophetic conquest of death motifs, which themselves were responses to the perceived contradiction in beliefs about death, namely, that it is ordained by God who calls humans into fellowship *and* determines that they will be cut off from God in death;[58] the extension beyond the boundaries of life into the realm of death of the fellowship with Yahweh assumed in the covenant;[59] extensions and applications of the images of national resurrection in Ezek 37:1– 14 and the vindication of the servant in Isa 53 to righteous individuals;[60] and shifting conceptions of God and God's relation to the community of Israel in light of the collapse of national structures following the Babylonian invasion and subsequent exile.[61]

1.3. *A Brief History of the Interpretation of Death in* Job

Studies of death in the book of Job tend to belong to one of three categories: the first includes those, mentioned above, that examine death in *Job* only insofar as it pertains to a larger study of death in the HB; the second includes studies that tend to focus on one small section of *Job*, typically Job's speech in ch. 3; and the third category includes "literary" examinations of death in *Job*.

Studies in the first category rarely examine *Job* at great length because the object of study is the Israelite conception of death evidenced throughout the HB, not just in *Job*. References to death in *Job* are utilized, along with references to death in other places, to support a particular argument about the nature of Sheol or about the rise in the belief in resurrection. Tromp, for example, refers to *Job* more than any other biblical book except for the Psalms, but does not have a chapter or section that examines death in *Job* exclusively.[62] Instead he cites verses in *Job* that describe the nature of Sheol as evidence of the Israelite conception of death. Martin-Achard, on the other hand, examines the rise in the belief in resurrection and turns to a passage in *Job* that might suggest a sense of life after death.[63] According to Martin-Achard, in 19:25–27 Job confesses his utter and absolute need for God as his only resource in the face of sorrow. In fact, Job's sense of the importance of the Divine Presence is such that it transforms traditional beliefs about life and death:

> Without reaching the positive assertion of the immortality or resurrection of the believer, being primarily concerned with tasting or seeking the fullness of the presence of their Lord, they are preparing the way for future generations to proclaim that death is impotent against those who are living in communion with the Living God.[64]

58. Eichrodt, *Theology*, 2:496–529.
59. David Leonard Miller, "The Development of the Concept of Immortality in the Old Testament" (Ph.D. diss., New York University, 1977), 298–12.
60. Martin-Achard, *From Death to Life*, 93–123.
61. Shannon Burkes, *God, Self, and Death: The Shape of Religious Transformation in the Second Temple Period* (Boston: Brill, 2003).
62. See Tromp, *Primitive Conceptions*.
63. Martin-Achard, *From Life to Death*, 166–81.
64. Ibid., 181. See also Eichrodt, *Theology*, 2:517–25; Kittel, *Befreit*, 27–44; Niditch, *Israelite Religion*, 66–67; Spronk, *Beatific Afterlife*, 344–45.

Very few of these types of analyses of death in the HB spend a great deal of time on *Job*. A notable exception is the recent study by Kittel, which includes an entire section on death in *Job*.[65] Kittel's general approach is at home with the overwhelming majority of studies of death in the HB—at least those whose primary data are the texts of the HB, rather than comparative material and archaeological evidence. Her main objective is to trace the development of the conception of resurrection and beatific afterlife in Israel from a prior belief in Sheol as a shadowy existence outside of God's presence. Kittel argues for four native theological developments in this progression. First is what she calls "das Grundbekenntnis der Psalmisten" ("the basic confession of the Psalmist"), that is, that Yahweh is the God who saves from death-in-life experiences (sickness, persecution, and so on). Second is the notion, developed in the post-exilic literature of *Job*, certain Psalms, and Isa 53, that the communion between God and the individual will not be broken even after death. Third is the development of the belief in Ezek 37 and Isa 26:19 that God can recreate and revive dead humans. Last is the development of the notion of the death of death altogether in Isa 25:8.[66]

Specifically, Kittel examines *Job* for those places where it displays an advance over earlier conceptions. She is able to locate three such advances. First, Kittel understands Job's wish in ch. 14 to be taken to Sheol while God's anger abates as the wish for death not to sever his relationship with God. As soon as he wishes it, though, he abandons this hope as impossible.[67] Second, she interprets Job's appeal to his witness in heaven in ch. 16 as an appeal to a God who saves and liberates, as opposed to the presentation of God in the prose tale who maintains a system of retributive justice (an "early" conception of God in ancient Israel). Job desires an unbroken relationship with this "new" God.[68] Third is Job's statement in ch. 19 that he knows that his redeemer lives and that he will see him. Kittel, like Martin-Achard, understands this as a statement of the continuing relationship with God after death.[69]

Studies such as Kittel's, which trace the development of the conception of death and the afterlife in ancient Israel, focus on those places in the HB where a portrayal of death seems to contradict its portrayal elsewhere. These contradictions are explained as diachronic changes in the conception of death in Israel. Such studies are valuable insofar as they proffer hypotheses regarding how and why these diachronic changes occurred. However, such studies are vulnerable to the tendency to miss an extremely important, and frequently overlooked, aspect of death: the rhetorical function of death in a text. By treating occurrences of death and death-talk in the HB as opportunities to delve "beneath" the text, as it were, to the conceptual world that these texts reference, one risks missing a crucial feature of these "death" texts, namely, that "death" necessarily is imbedded textually, in a linguistic and rhetorical context. First and foremost,

---

65. Kittel, *Befreit*, 45–56.
66. Ibid., 90–102.
67. Ibid., 42–50.
68. Ibid., 50–51.
69. Ibid., 51–56.

"death" needs to be read and interpreted in its immediate literary context before, or at least, alongside its conceptual understanding.

This critique also applies to the second category of Joban death studies, namely, the specialized study of a smaller passage in *Job*. Job's death wish in ch. 3, in particular, has received a fair bit of analysis by scholars wishing to locate the sentiments of this speech in the greater ANE context. Strauss, for example, argues that the attitudes expressed in ch. 3 are unique to the HB and compares them to Egyptian beliefs about death.[70] Blumenthal compares the sentiments of ch. 3 with the Egyptian "Songs of the Harper."[71] Jacobsen and Nielsen examine Job 3 in light of several Akkadian texts (Damu Lament, Lament over Ur, Gilgamesh, Atrahasis) and Jer 20:14.[72] And Burns compares Job's death wish with the *Iliad*, the Erra Epic, and Jer 20:14–18.[73]

Like the previous category of studies of death, this category is also interested in the "history of ideas," seeking to trace the origins of and/or parallels to Job's conception of the desirability of death in other, cognate literatures. And like the previous category of studies, this one also has a tendency to miss the textuality of death, its rhetorical value in its literary context.[74]

The third category comprises those studies that do examine the rhetorical value of death in *Job*. Such studies are very few and I will limit my discussion only to the noteworthy ones by Zuckerman and Crouch. In Zuckerman's chapter, entitled "The Art of Parody: The Death Theme," in his book, *Job the Silent*,[75] he treats death as a motif or literary strategy in *Job*, employed for the accomplishment of certain rhetorical goals. According to Zuckerman, the author of the poetic dialogues uses the death motif in order to parody certain well-established theological traditions in ancient Israel. In particular, he focuses on two uses of death in Job's speeches: the death wish and the particular emphasis on the finality of death. According to Zuckerman, the death wish (prominently displayed in ch. 3) alludes to the righteous sufferer motif seen in many Psalms. But contrary to traditional usage, Job does not employ this motif to direct God's attention to his miserable plight with the goal of having God rescue him from his affliction. Rather, Job depicts himself as a righteous sufferer whose only wish is to die. So, instead of groveling before God with a cry for mercy and restoration (the traditional righteous sufferer motif), Job announces his affliction as his opening battle cry against God, desiring to be separated from God in Sheol

---

70. Hans Strauss, "Tod (Todeswunsch; »Jenseits«?) im Buch Hiob," in *Gottes Recht als Lebensraum: Festschrift für Hans Jochen Boecker* (ed. Werner H. Schmidt Peter Mommer, Hans Strauss; Neukirchen–Vluyn: Neukirchener Verlag, 1993), 239–49.

71. Elke Blumenthal, "Hiob und die Harfnerlieder" *TLZ* 115 (1990): 721–30 (722–29), though Blumenthal also examines other places where Job suggests that Sheol is a positive place.

72. Thorklid Jacobsen and Kirsten Nielsen, "Cursing the Day," *SJOT* 6 (1992): 187–204.

73. John Barclay Burns, "Cursing the Day of Birth," *Proceedings* 13 (1993): 11–22.

74. Another study that might be cited in this context is Roland E. Murphy, "Death and Afterlife in the Wisdom Literature," in Avery-Peck and Neusner, eds., *Judaism in Late Antiquity*, 4:101–16. Murphy compares the presentation of death in *Job* to its presentation in Wisdom Literature in general (pp. 105–7). He, also, is mainly concerned with conceptual, rather than literary, matters.

75. Zuckerman, *Job the Silent*, 118–35.

rather than be restored into fellowship with God. According to Zuckerman, Job's battle cry, with his implicit refusal to kowtow before God, functions to emphasize the key issue of the dialogues: Is God a moral deity?[76]

The other key theme of the death motif in *Job* is that of death as permanent non-existence. Here Zuckerman examines two key passages (chs. 14 and 19) and argues that they explicitly reject a possibility of resurrection from the dead. This, according to Zuckerman, is a conscious usage of Israelite tradition (finality of death) by the author of the dialogues to counter conflicting tradition (resurrection from the dead). What makes this strategy by the author of the dialogues particularly forceful is that, according to Zuckerman's reconstruction, the original folktale included the resurrection of Job's children from the dead as part of Job's restoration. So the treatment of death in the poetic dialogues is a direct challenge to the hopeful message in the tale: the pious cannot hope that their dead will live again.

Although many will be reluctant to affirm Zuckerman's hypothetical reconstruction of the supposed original folktale, along with his subsequent usage of this hypothesis in his analysis of the death motif in the dialogues, at least in his general approach Zuckerman has opened new avenues for the study of death in the HB. Whereas the majority of studies, including Kittel's, implicitly posit that behind every appearance of death in the HB there lies a particular mind-set, conception, or worldview among ancient Israelites—and these necessarily must be somewhere in the background of every occurrence of the death motif in *Job*—Zuckerman shows that death also has rhetorical value that contributes to the goals and messages of the text.[77] "Death" as a theme can be manipulated and amplified in innumerable ways.

Death in *Job*, though, is far more subtle and complex than Zuckerman's brief analysis allows. First of all, death has an *excessive* quality in *Job*, appearing seemingly at every turn in the book. As such, some part of death shares in nearly every discourse, every argument, every illustration, every lament, every narration, and every verbal attack in the book. But in order to be so ubiquitous, death, as a figure, must be a supple figure—here conforming to this discourse, here conforming to this argument, here conforming to this narration. As an excessive figure, death has to have excessive meaning. It cannot only be "death as parody" (Zuckerman), but also has to be "death as test" (1:13–19), "death as relief" (3:11–19), "death as justice" (4:6–9), "death as guarantor of the created order" (5:17–21), "death as grounds for forgiveness" (7:21), and so on. Death as motif must be protean, it must contain an excess of meanings; it must be overdetermined.[78]

This excessive quality of death, however, is not particular to *Job*. In fact it is inscribed in the very word, "death." For death stands for that which is beyond

76. Ibid., 118–27.

77. See von Uchelen, "Death and the Afterlife," 81–84, for a similar, but more general, analysis of what he calls "literary-metaphorical" death in the HB (especially the Psalms).

78. See also von Uchelen (ibid., 79–86), who seems to be attuned to the quality of "literary" death in the HB.

the realm of human knowledge and it can only be discussed as the negation of
what is known: it is not-life, not-being. The referent of "death" is therefore a
void or an absence, ensuring, paradoxically, that the word "death" foregrounds
as a presence what is finally and ultimately absent and "beyond." As Stewart
argues, "it is the intransigent abstraction death that persists across literary history as a semantically unoccupied zone of utterance, at once a linguistic horizon
and void."[79] And so death's place in literature marks an absence whose referent
is filled in by death's linkage to other signifiers in its semiological context.[80]
According to Stewart,

> Once established as sheer term—whether as noun, adjective, or verb—the amorphous
> shape of death can manifest and ramify itself only by rhetorical ingenuity. More inven-
> tion than evocation, death necessitates a mastery of "the Impossible" by style. When
> the linguistic forms *death*, *dead*, and *die* are extrapolated from their own referential
> vacuum into anything like a subjective episode of narrated dying, language unfolds a
> definitive instance of pure story…[81]

That is, literary "death" necessarily has no meaning except as it unfolds in the
literary context. And "death" is defenseless against context: it is always the
malleable trope for its own rhetorical and semantic space.

One study of death in *Job* is sensitive to this unique function of death in
literature: Crouch's *Death and Closure*.[82] He does not, however, begin his study
with this consideration, but first links death and life with the question of existential meaning and then relates these to the interpretation of narrative. Crouch
argues that while one is living, one's life is in flux and one does not have the
ability to understand and thus master one's life and "sum it up" in a manner that
allows one to control it. Only after death can one's life be viewed from beginning to end and then summed up and ordered (by someone else in a biography).
Novels, on the other hand, since they are written with the ending already known
(by the author) have an order and coherence built in. Humans read novels in
order that, by reaching the end and understanding the whole story from the
perspective of the end, they can master their own lives. "Thus we experience a
'whole' by reading a story, or by watching a movie. The repetition of this
experience, the completion of many wholes, gives us a sense of mastery over the
experience itself and a sense of mastery over our own lives,"[83] albeit an illusory
sense of mastery.

Crouch goes onto suggest that the desire to read the end of a story (an impossible end to know in one's life) and thus the desire to understand coherence and
wholeness (which cannot be understood in one's life), may be related to an

---

79. Garrett Stewart, *Death Sentences: Styles of Dying in British Fiction* (Cambridge, Mass.:
Harvard University Press, 1984), 4–5.

80. According to von Uchelon, when interpreting death in the HB "Within the specific literary
context the turns of metaphor have to be followed" (von Uchelen, "Death and the Afterlife," 86).

81. Stewart, *Death Sentences*, 5.

82. Walter B. Crouch, *Death and Closure in Biblical Narrative* (Studies in Biblical Literature 7;
New York: Peter Lang, 2000).

83. Ibid., 8.

unstated desire for death, namely, the Freudian death drive. For, similar to Freud's conception of life and death, one begins a story in nothingness, from which a start comes. This is followed by tension and disequilibrium, which creates a desire for the end. When the end arrives, answers are forthcoming and there is release from tension as the story returns again to nothingness. Desire is satisfied.[84] "Death, not our possession, is the only resolution to the narratability of life, the only state in which a satisfactory equilibrium can be reached, that of nothingness."[85]

Having linked death with narrative, Crouch now considers the unique status of death, mentioned above. He argues that the figure "death" in narrative acts as a "negative materiality"; that is, "death" stands for something absolutely unknowable and beyond the realm of human experience. As such, "death" is a symbolic content whose meaning is only supplied by its treatment in particular texts. Crouch's goal will be to examine how certain biblical texts (John, *Job*, and Jonah) treat death as symbolic content, and at the same time how a narrative's ending brings about a sense of closure. The manner in which a narrative speaks about death and how it ends are important to the readers' sense of desire and satisfaction (desire for their own end and completion). An examination of these will help explain how certain biblical texts give a sense of hope whereas others do not. He calls this type of analysis "narrative mortality."

In his specific examination of *Job*, Crouch argues that the chief interpretive problem of *Job* is the relationship of the prose frame to the poetic sections. In his understanding, the tradent (poetic section author) attempts to counter the view of the prose frame, but fails: the frame's theological view of life and death prevails due to the effects of narrative sequence, ending, and closure. The tradent's attempt to question the fundamental notions of Israel's faith as expressed in the prose frame (belief in the sovereignty and integrity of God; belief in piety and faithfulness in the face of mistreatment; belief in retributive justice) unintentionally reinforces them in that despite the questions raised in poetic sections, the expected closure and coherence of the prose frame return and dominate. The ultimate message is that God will indeed make things right in this life. Crouch calls this a closed view of death (death is final, and since there is no resurrection, God will repay humans in this life). Finally, since the prose frame trumps the poetic section, and since the prose frame ends with a high degree of closure in that all the narrative details are wrapped up, *Job* has a "congruent narrative mortality": the way death is discussed (as the absolute end of life) is congruent with the narrative ending (the finalized closure of the book), which explains why *Job* leaves readers with a sense of hope.[86]

Crouch's understanding of death as a negative materiality is unique among biblical critics, as is his attempt to juxtapose death and The End. Crouch's study, however, fails to account for the diverse complementary and contradictory

84. Ibid., 8–12.
85. Ibid., 12.
86. Ibid., 151–59. My own sense is that *Job* leaves at least as many readers troubled as it leaves readers with a sense of hope.

functions "death" has in *Job*, and the multitude of rhetorical zones "death" is made to occupy. Like Zuckerman, Crouch does not notice the *excessive* quality of death in *Job*. Nevertheless, Crouch's observations about death as a negative materiality, when pushed a little farther, as I will do in the following paragraphs, can bring into focus the basic issues presently under consideration: the theoretical link between death's multiple meanings in *Job* and the collapse of divine justice, the main "topic" of the book.

1.4. *Death and Theory*

What is it that makes death unique? Death, after all, is not uncommon; it is the biological necessity of all living creatures. Yet despite its universal character, death certainly is an unknown quantity: if all living creatures necessarily must die, all living creatures also necessarily cannot have knowledge of their own deaths as lived experience. This is a different statement than Becker's influential thesis that in order for humans to cope with the anxiety of their own deaths, they must establish elaborate systems that meticulously enable them to evade and deny their own deaths and convince them that their existence has some sort of significance.[87] This thesis implies that death is a known quantity that must be denied, and it is similar to Kittel's (and the type of analysis of death in the HB that she represents), Zuckerman's, and even Crouch's understandings of death in *Job*. For these biblical scholars, death is a known idea or belief that can be discerned in the biblical text (Kittel), a consciously shaped literary motif that functions consistently in *Job* (Zuckerman), or a deep-seated value that operates in concert with the rhetorical shape of the book (Crouch). Like Becker's, all of these analyses assume death to be a known quantity (by ancient Israelites, by the author) that can be discerned in analysis.[88]

The aspect of death that I wish to study is, rather, its capacity as an unknowable experience and as an elusive figure. Kenneth Burke writes about this aspect of death: "So far as this world of our positive experience is concerned, death can only be an *idea*, not something known by us as we know our bodily sensations."[89] And again later: "whatever the evidence of Death, we have no direct experience of it. To experience Death is, by the same token, to be beyond the terms of our existence here and now."[90] But to claim that death is pure idea without any possible basis in the world of lived human experience is to claim that death is a pure signifier whose connection to a referent can never be established. Instead one can only know "death" in reference to other signifiers in some sort of semiological complex.[91] As Derrida writes, "It is well known that if there is

87. See Ernest Becker, *The Denial of Death* (New York: Free Press, 1973). His thesis is stated in the clearest terms in the opening paragraph (p. ix).

88. Despite Crouch's claim that death is a negative materiality.

89. Kenneth Burke, "Thanatopsis for Critics: A Brief Thesaurus of Deaths and Dying," *Essays in Criticism* 2 (1952): 369–75 (369).

90. Ibid., 373.

91. For example, a biological definition of death would be in reference to the negation of the signifier "life."

one word that remains absolutely unassignable or unassigning with respect to its concept and to its thingness, it is the word 'death.'"[92]

And yet the word "death" always has meaning, though this meaning is never a given. It is constructed, maintained, and modified by cultures, for to "understand" the "meaning" of death, one does not grasp "death's" referent (or thingness, according to Derrida), but rather in "understanding" death one "produce[s] a reading that depends upon the physical and subjective context."[93] According to Bronfen and Goodwin, "Death is thus necessarily constructed by a culture; it grounds the many ways a culture stabilizes and represents itself, and yet it always does so as a signifier with an incessantly receding, ungraspable signified, always pointing to other signifiers, other means of representing what finally is just absent."[94]

Because the meaning of "death" is never given and is always a culturally constructed reality, and because "death" signifies only in relation to other signifiers in a signifying complex, the meaning of "death" in any given society can be analyzed and understood by examining the various rites of death (funerals and other mortuary rites), artifacts of death (tombs, tomb decorations, and so forth), artwork depicting death and dead bodies, and literature that represents death and death rituals.[95]

In fact, "death" might be a privileged signifier, not in Derrida's sense of a(n) (illusory) transcendental concept that arrests and grounds the flow signification in the semiotic process,[96] but in the sense of a signifier that is linked to some of the most basic and dear values of a culture. Many sociologists have noted this connection between "death" and cultural values. According to Huntington and Metcalf, "In all societies...the issue of death throws into relief the most

---

92.   Jacques Derrida, *Aporias: Dying—Awaiting (One Another at) the "Limits of Truth"* (trans. Thomas Dutoit; Stanford: Stanford University Press, 1993), 22. Bronfen and Goodwin similarly argue that "In any representation of death, it is strikingly an absence that is at stake, so that the presentation is itself at a remove from what is figured" (Elisabeth Bronfen and Sarah Webster Goodwin, "Introduction," in *Death and Representation* [ed. Elisabeth Bronfen and Sarah Webster Goodwin; Baltimore: The Johns Hopkins University Press, 1993], 3–25 [7]).

93.   Margaret Higonnet, "Speaking Silences: Women's Suicide," in *The Female Body in Western Culture: Contemporary Perspectives* (ed. Susan Rubin Suleiman; Cambridge, Mass.: Harvard University Press, 1986), 68. She goes on to say, "when we categorize a death we do not record a pure fact."

94.   Bronfen and Goodwin, "Introduction," 4. I am making a special case for death as an empty signifier that can be known only in reference to other signifiers, but as Derrida and others have demonstrated, this is the nature of all signification. See Jacques Derrida, *Of Grammatology* (trans. Gayatri Chakravorty Spivak; Baltimore: The Johns Hopkins University Press, 1998), for an extended analysis of the implications of this insight. Bronfen and Goodwin therefore suggest that "Representations of death...often serve as metatropes for the process of representation itself: its necessity, its excess, its failure, and its uses for the polis" (Bronfen and Goodwin, "Introduction," 4).

95.   Ariès has pioneered such work. See Philippe Ariès, *The Hour of Our Death* (trans. Helen Weaver; New York: Oxford University Press, 1991); idem, *Images of Man and Death* (trans. Janet Lloyd; Cambridge, Mass.: Harvard University Press, 1985); idem, *Western Attitudes toward Death: From the Middle Ages to the Present* (Johns Hopkins Symposia in Comparative History; Baltimore: The Johns Hopkins University Press, 1974).

96.   The notion of a transcendental signified comes up repeatedly in Derrida, *Of Grammatology*.

important cultural values by which people live their lives and evaluate their experiences. Life becomes transparent against the background of death, and fundamental social and cultural issues are revealed."[97] Bronfen and Goodwin argue that "much of what we call culture comes together around the collective response to death"[98] and that "death" as a cipher for cultural values can become a political weapon used to confirm moral and cultural values that seem to be crumbling.[99] Berger argues that cultures are constructed in order to stave off the debilitating effects of the perception of chaos and disorder, whose chief representative is death: "every nomos is an edifice erected in the face of the potent and alien forces of chaos. This chaos must be kept at bay at all costs."[100] Bradbury argues that the descriptions in societies of particular deaths as "good" or "bad" function to delineate the social order and provide a general pattern of death that seemingly masters its arbitrariness.[101]

The particular aspect of death's connection to cultural values that I wish to explore pertains to the representation of death in literature. Friedman has probed along these lines and has argued that "More than any other manifestation, narratives of death and dying reflect a culture's symbolic and mythic truths."[102] While it may be true that representations of death in literature function to uphold a culture's "symbolic and mythic truths" (as is likely the case with the examples Friedman cites), I am not convinced that such representations *always* function this way. It seems equally possible to me that representations of death might attempt to subvert or disrupt such cultural truths—as might be the case in the book of Job. Kenneth Burke's analysis of the function of "death" in poetry is more along the lines I wish to pursue. He argues, as stated above, that death necessarily is beyond the realm of human experience and therefore death can only be an idea, and not something known by experience. Because "death," according to Burke, is pure idea or pure symbol, poets, who deal in symbols, talk a lot about death. But since poets cannot know death from experience, they imagine it necessarily with images not belonging to it.

Burke then goes on to give a list of "'deflections' that the idea of death reveals as a literary topic. The assumption is that if death is not an immediate experience, then the ubiquitous talk of death can very readily be talk of something else."[103] The list of such "deflections" includes "logical fulfillment" where expressions of hunger, disease, misfortune, hardship, sorrow, and the like find

97. Richard Huntington and Peter Metcalf, *Celebrations of Death: The Anthropology of Mortuary Ritual* (Cambridge: Cambridge University Press, 1979), 2.

98. Bronfen and Goodwin, "Introduction," 3.

99. Ibid., 8–9.

100. Peter L. Berger, *The Sacred Canopy: Elements of a Sociological Theory of Religion* (Garden City, N.Y.: Doubleday, 1967), 24.

101. Mary Bradbury, *Representations of Death: A Social Psychological Perspective* (London: Routledge, 1999), 142–46. See also Maurice Bloch and Jonathan P. Parry, "Introduction: Death and the Regeneration of Life," in *Death and the Regeneration of Life* (ed. Maurice Bloch and Jonathan P. Parry; New York: Cambridge University Press, 1982), 1–44 (15–18).

102. Friedman, *Fictional Death*, 5.

103. Burke, "Thanatopsis for Critics," 369.

their logical fulfillment in death and "hence as imagery they may share its essence";[104] "cloacal" connotations of death as the analogue of corruption, or the morally or physically repugnant; death as "dignification" wherein since praise and honor go to the dead, by associating a poem with death, the poem "has a good chance of gaining solemnity";[105] death as a the "dialectical opposite" of life as a way of celebrating life by contrast; death as the "entelechial" motive wherein "death" as "end" can be the image of fulfillment or purpose and thus it can name the "'logic of a life'...by whatever way of dying is felt to be the fitting culmination of such a life";[106] death as a surrogate for sexual union; death and dying as an image of rebirth and change; death as mental unbalance; death as mystery, secrecy, that which lies beyond; and many more.

I will explore the ramifications of Burke's thesis for the presentation of death in the book of Job. More precisely, I will examine the particular "'deflections' that the idea of death reveals as a literary topic" in *Job*. But an analysis of these "deflections" must take into account the main topic of *Job*, which is not death, but divine justice. If, as I have argued, death has multiple meanings in *Job* and displays a variety of "deflections," then somehow these relate to the depicted collapse of divine justice and the ramifications of this collapse, which are worked out throughout the book. To help elucidate the implications of the connection between the representation(s) of death and the collapse of the religious system of divine justice I turn to the work of the psychohistorian, Robert Jay Lifton, who is very much interested in the link between death and cultural systems.

1.4.1. *Robert Jay Lifton and the Link between Symbol Systems and Death*

On a broad level Lifton's work can be characterized as a probing of the connections that exist between culture, the self, and individual and cultural understandings of death and life in light of situations of cultural upheaval and disaster. The specific disasters Lifton has studied have ranged from the effect of the A-Bomb on Hiroshima survivors, Nazi doctors and their "patients," subjects who underwent Chinese thought reform, Vietnam war veterans, survivors of local disasters, and others. Through extensive interviews Lifton has heard survivors articulate their sense of the collapse of traditional symbol systems and their struggles to go on living. Inevitably discussions turn to the meaning of life and death and to the effort of the individual to reassert life's vitality in the face of devastation and death.[107]

Based on his extensive work among survivors of disasters, Lifton has argued that there exists a link between cultural symbol systems (which are shared in various degrees by individuals within a culture) and cultural and individual beliefs about life and death. Individuals, claims Lifton, "require [a] symbolization of continuity—imaginative forms of transcending death—in order to confront

104. Ibid., 369.
105. Ibid., 370.
106. Ibid., 370.
107. For a brief look at Lifton's publishing history and research on disaster, see Charles B. Strozier, "Introduction," *The Psychohistory Review* 20 (1992): 103–5.

genuinely the fact that [they] die."[108] A sense of immortality is not a denial of the reality of death (Freud), "Rather it is a corollary of the knowledge of death itself, and reflects a compelling and universal inner quest for continuous symbolic relationship to what has gone before and what will continue after our finite individual lives."[109] Culture furnishes individuals with sets of symbols that enable them to assert a sense of life and vitality in light of the knowledge of death, a sense of life that Lifton names "symbolic immortality."

According to Lifton, five modes of symbolic immortality have been utilized by various cultures in a variety of ways throughout history. First is the "biological mode," which is epitomized by emphasis on family continuity and living on and through one's progeny. Second is the "theological" or "religious mode," which might include the belief in an afterlife, and which always includes the basic idea of death as rebirth into the immortality of the deity, however the deity is conceived. Third is the "creative mode," which is exemplified in great works of art, literature, and science, in which the artistic creation is seen somehow to escape death. ("[E]ach…investigator becomes part of an enterprise larger than himself, limitless in its past and future continuity."[110]) Fourth is the "natural mode," in which there is a perception that the natural environment is limitless in space and time, and will therefore remain eternally, despite one's own individual death. Last is the "experiential transcendent mode," which is classically the mode of the mystic: the ecstatic feeling of extraordinary psychic unity whereby all of life, as well as death, is absorbed into the oneness of the deity.[111] What the various modes of symbolic immortality accomplish is to provide the self with a sense of vitality or inner harmony, what Lifton calls "the state of near-perfect centering,"[112] virtually eliminating the destructive aspects of the death symbol: imagery of separation, stasis, and disintegration; meaninglessness; and impaired image-making ability.

In his observations of situations of mass trauma and disaster, however, Lifton has witnessed the collapse of traditional cultural symbol systems, the "breakdown of social and institutional arrangements that ordinarily anchor human lives,"[113] or what he calls, "desymbolization." According to Lifton,

> During these upheavals, symbols of longstanding authority are undermined, confronted, or shattered in ways that can produce powerful and painful collective experiences of death and rebirth. There is an outpouring of death imagery, publicly and privately, as well as feelings of separation, disintegration, and stasis (what I call "death equivalents") and a questioning of larger human connectedness or symbolic immortality.

108. Lifton, *The Broken Connection*, 17.

109. Ibid. The quote is copied, almost verbatim, in Robert Jay Lifton, *The Life of the Self: Toward a New Psychology* (New York: Simon & Schuster, 1976), 31.

110. Lifton, *The Broken Connection*, 21.

111. For more on these modes, see Lifton, *The Broken Connection*, 13–35; idem, *Life of the Self*, 29–34; and idem, *Boundaries: Psychological Man in Revolution* (New York: Random House, 1970), 21–26.

112. Lifton, *The Broken Connection*, 34.

113. Robert Jay Lifton, *The Protean Self: Human Resilience in an Age of Fragmentation* (New York: Basic Books, 1993), 14.

At such times, our psychological viability as the cultural animal…is under duress—until new combinations can reanimate our perceived place in the great chain of being.[114]

Lifton's writings about disaster and its effect on the human psyche provide a useful vantage point from which to understand the dynamic between death's multiple "deflections" and the collapse of divine justice in the book of Job. In part, the process that Lifton observes among survivors of mass disaster, stated in the terms employed earlier, is the process of the severing of the meaning of death from its cultural symbol systems, which function to provide the semiological context for the negative materiality, "death." When people witness mass and/or problematic death, frequently they sense that the cultural symbol system that normally would provide death its meaning now no longer applies. In these cases death ceases to have its normal signification and its meaning is unknown. Death, then, represents an absence or void, a blank space that means nothing, but can also mean anything. As Lifton suggests, only when a new symbol system is found does death again attain a stable meaning, as it re-gains an operative semiological context. I will examine death's multiple meanings in *Job* as a consequence of the collapse of divine justice. Whereas divine justice acts as a symbol system that grounds the meaning of death for Job's friends, when Job experiences disaster and senses that this symbol system collapses, death for Job loses its anchor. Job's struggle throughout the book will be to articulate a new symbol system in order that his experiences of suffering can be understood in a new and newly meaningful context. This new context will also supply Job a stable place from which to understand death.[115]

My argument that the book of Job narrates the struggle of a character to articulate a new symbolic system following a disaster supports Lifton's claim that fictional literature is a place where the creative processes of articulating new types of symbol systems transpires. According to Lifton, the artist is a person who can arrange the fragments of collapsed symbol systems into new combinations. More specifically, Lifton points to the literature of survival as the place for these new combinations (a survivor being one who has encountered death in a bodily or psychic fashion and has remained alive).[116] All survivors struggle toward inner form and formulation, which is the quest to find significance in

114. Ibid., 15. Although Lifton adduces examples of such symbolic breakdown from the Renaissance until the present in the West, and also from various periods in non-Western history, he argues that the late twentieth century exhibits this type of disintegration best (see ibid., 15–17).

115. For further introduction to Lifton's theories, see Eric Markusen, "Comprehending the Cambodian Genocide: An Application of Robert Jay Lifton's Model of Genocidal Killing," *The Psychohistory Review* 20 (1992): 145–54; Charles B. Strozier and Michael Flynn, "Lifton's Method," *The Psychohistory Review* 20 (1992): 131–44; Gregory J. Walters, "Religious Totalism in the Preconciliar and Postconciliar Church: An Application and Critique of Robert Jay Lifton's Psycohistorical Paradigm," *The Psychohistory Review* 20 (1992): 171–80. For a history of the origins of psychoanalytic movement that Lifton helped pioneer, see Petteri Pietikainen and Juhani Ihanus, "On the Origins of Psychoanalytic Psychohistory," *History of Psychology* 6 (2003): 171–94.

116. Robert Jay Lifton, *Death in Life: Survivors of Hiroshima* (New York: Random House, 1968), 479–541; idem, *Life of the Self,* 113–14.

one's death encounter and remaining life experiences. Survivors have potential for new wisdom in encountering death, which can be deadening and immobilizing, by grasping death and rendering it significant through the reordering of their own experience.[117] Artists are particularly deft at this reordering, for "The artist is a prophet of forms... [T]he artist suggests patterns of reordering, even if, in the process, seeming to contribute further to the disarray. For it is the artist's task...to reveal to us the exquisite details of the experience of desymbolization."[118] Lifton, therefore, examines several novelists in terms of their symbolization of death: Albert Camus, Kurt Vonnegut, Günter Grass, Yoko Ota, Michihiko Hachiya, Toshiyuki Kajiyama, Hiroyuki Agawa, and Kin Kokubo.[119]

Does the book of Job qualify as literature of survival? There is no way of answering this question for the simple reason that there is no foolproof way of knowing the circumstances of the composition of *Job*. Although some scholars do argue that the perspective of the book of Job demonstrates a delayed response to exile,[120] throughout history scholars and religious authorities have achieved nothing remotely resembling a consensus on the date of the book. It has been dated anywhere from the tenth to the fourth century based on supposed historical allusions,[121] linguistic evidence,[122] literary dependency,[123] theology,[124] and other reasons.[125]

117. Lifton, *Life of the Self*, 114–115.

118. Ibid., 113.

119. See ibid., 115–30; idem, *Death in Life*, 397–439. Lifton's works contain numerous other shorter references to a host of novelists, for example, Martin Amis, Isaac Asimov, John Barth, Donald Barthelme, Samuel Beckett, William Burroughs, Don DeLillo, Ralph Ellison, William Faulkner, F. Scott Fitzgerald, James Joyce, Franz Kafka, Herman Melville, Thomas Pynchon, Salman Rushdie, and many others.

120. This argument dates back to the Talmud (*b. Bat. 15b*). Among contemporary critics, see Martin Buber, *The Prophetic Faith* (trans. Carlyle Witton-Davies; New York: Macmillan, 1949; repr., New York: Harper & Row, 1960), 188; Alfred Guillaume, *Studies in the Book of Job* (ed. John Macdonald; Annual of Leeds University Oriental Society Supplement 2; Leiden: Brill, 1968), 7–14. See also Charles L. Feinberg, "Job and the Nation of Israel," *BSac* 96 (1939): 405–11, who reads Job's story against Israel's experience of suffering in the exile, though he argues that *Job* was written much earlier than the exile.

121. J. J. M. Roberts, "Job and the Israelite Religious Tradition," *ZAW* 89 (1977): 107–14, examines in detail the scholarly attempt to locate historical details in *Job*.

122. Avi Hurvitz, "Date of the Prose-Tale of Job Linguistically Reconsidered," *HTR* 67 (1974): 17–34; David A. Robertson, *Linguistic Evidence in Dating Early Hebrew poetry* (SBLDS 3; Missoula, Mont.: Society of Biblical Literature, 1972), 135–56; Harold Henry Rowley, *The Book of Job* (NCB; Grand Rapids: Eerdmans, 1980), 23–25; Norman Henry Snaith, *The Book of Job: Its Origin and Purpose* (SBT 2/11; London: SCM Press, 1968), 104–12.

123. Robert Gordis, *The Book of God and Man: A Study of Job* (Chicago: University of Chicago Press, 1965); Hartley, *Job*, 19–20; Samuel L. Terrien, "Job," *IB* 3: 875–1198 (888–90); Robert H. Pfeiffer, "The Dual Origin of Hebrew Monotheism," *JBL* 46 (1927): 193–206 (202–6).

124. Rowley, *Job*, 21–23.

125. Among the historical-critical works, Hugh Anderson ("The Book of Job," in *Wisdom Literature and Poetry: A Commentary on Job, Psalms, Proverbs, Ecclesiastes, the Song of Solomon* [ed. Charles M. Laymon; Interpreter's Concise Commentary 3; Nashville: Abingdon, 1983], 1–41 [5–6]) dates the composition of *Job* some time after the destruction of Jerusalem (586 BCE), but before 250 BCE; Edouard Dhorme (*A Commentary on the Book of Job* [trans. Harold Knight;

Although it is uncertain whether *Job* qualifies as literature of survival, *Job* certainly does merit consideration in terms of Lifton's categories if qualification for analysis is the *content* of the literature.[126] For *Job* does depict the collapse of a symbol system, whose ramifications form the main content of the book as the main character, Job, gropes toward the articulation of a new symbol system from the fragments of the old one. Specific facts of the historical origin of *Job*, therefore, have little or no bearing on the main issues of the book—on the moral and theological problems that emerge in the encounter with death and suffering.

1.5. *The Selection of Death Passages in* Job

One of the difficulties of analyzing death in the book of Job is deciding upon which passages to include in one's analysis, and which ones to exclude, for nearly every chapter of the book, as mentioned above, seems to contain either representations of, or discussions about, death. Presumably, one ought to select for examination those passages that have an abundance of death imagery in them. This, however, raises another, related problem: How does one decide what does and does not count as "imagery" of death? It seems that "death" needs some sort of definition in order to locate the imagery in *Job* that participates in death's "realm." Yet, this runs counter to the fundamental orientation of this project: as I argued earlier, "death" is an empty signifier whose meaning emerges only within a specific semiological context. Part of the task of my project is to discover what meaning(s) of "death" emerge(s) in the particular context(s) of the book of Job. Defining "death" beforehand would therefore run counter my goals.

Instead of giving "death" and "death imagery" some sort of *a priori* definition, I propose to undertake an analysis of the distribution of words for death in *Job*. I will attempt to see what kinds of words are used to refer to death and in which passages in *Job* they occur so that I might locate passages with clusters of "death" words. This will also enable me to examine the other words and images that occur in parallel to, or in the context of, these death words. If certain types of words or images recur frequently with these death words, I will be able to

Nashville: Nelson, 1984], clxix–clxxi) and Gordis (*Book of God and Man*, 147–52) date it to the second temple era in the fourth–third centuries. Samuel Rolles Driver and George Buchanan Gray (*A Critical and Exegetical Commentary on the Book of Job: Together with a New Translation* [2 vols.; ICC 14; Edinburgh: T. & T. Clark, 1921], 1:lxv–lxxi) date it somewhere between the first and the fifth centuries. Guillaume (*Studies in the Book of Job*, 7–14) and Terrien ("Job," 890) date it after the fall of Jerusalem in the sixth century. Zuckerman probably has the most complex analysis of the composition of *Job*. He uses the metaphor of the fugue to discuss how the book was composed: first the traditional tale of Job the sufferer circulated (1:1–2:13; 42:7–17 + a middle section now lost); the poem was composed in order to parody and refute the theological and moral views of the tale (3:1–31:40; 38:1–42:6); the Wisdom poem (ch. 28) and the Elihu Speeches (32:1–37:24) were added later still in order to counter the perspective of the poem. See Zuckerman, *Job the Silent*, 13–84. For an examination of the range of scholarly arguments about the dating of the book, see Rowley, *From Moses*, 173–74 n. 2.

126. Roberts ("Job," 107–14) similarly argues that a period of acute national crisis is irrelevant to the content of *Job*.

make a case that they are death images whose meanings overlap with that of death in various ways. The passages with the densest clusters of death words will be those that will be selected for my analysis of death in *Job*.

I have to admit, though, that this method of locating death passages is not completely "pure" or infallible. As will be indicated below, some of the words that can be identified as death words in *Job* can only be so identified due to their usage in the particular passages in *Job*. So, in some instances, it is not so much, "this is a word that means death, and here is where it is used in *Job*" but rather, "here is a word that in this context seems to mean death." But when the situation is phrased this way, we are back to the problem of giving death an *a priori* meaning that can then be located in *Job*. I see no way of getting around this problem entirely, but when I identify such words, I will use a minimal definition of death as "cessation of life."

1.5.1. *Words for Death in* Job

Zuckerman's claim that *Job* is the most death-oriented book in the Bible is borne out by the sheer number of words in *Job* that mean death. When attempting to analyze them one is struck not only by the quantity of such words, but by the varieties of categories of words that are employed, from words whose meaning pertains to death or killing or the like, to euphemisms for death, to words that pertain to the grave or realm of the dead, to words that have various meanings (including death), but in their context in *Job* likely pertain to death. Furthermore, there are categories of words that seem to connote death metaphorically or by synecdoche. A variety of words for "darkness" function this way, as do various words for war weapons. Lastly, there are several words that pertain to mourning rituals, whose connection to death is indirect. I have divided these words up into four main groups, the first of which has several sub-categories.

The first main group contains words that by themselves seem to connote some aspect of death, in some cases because of their context. I have divided this group into four sub-categories, which are listed below in descending order of importance and/or certainty (although each sub-category contains words whose connection to death is stronger than others).

Words that simply mean "death" or "kill" or "murder" or the like comprise the first sub-category. *Job* employs seven in total (רצח, קטל, הרג, גוע, מות), including one word that means "miscarriage" (נפל) and one that means "strangulation" (מחנק). Every usage of these words, except three, clearly refer to the death of a human (or human embryo).[127]

The second sub-category of death words in *Job* are those that pertain to the grave or the realm of the dead. Included here are well-known words like קבר ("grave, to bury"), גדיש ("tomb"), שאול ("Sheol"), שחת ("Pit"), אבדון ("Abaddon"), and רפאים ("Rephaim, shades, ghosts"), as well as two whose

---

127. In 14:8; 18:13; and 38:17, מות refers to the death of a tree stump, the firstborn of death, and the gates of death, respectively.

reference to the Underworld, while no means certain, is at least a distinct, if not likely, possibility: רעב ("Hungry One", namely Mot) in 18:12; and מלך ("King [of the Underworld]") in 18:14.

The third sub-category of death words in *Job* are those words and phrases that seem to be euphemisms for killing or death: נכה חרב ("put to sword"), שלה נשק ("extract a life"), נסע יתר ("pull up the tent cord"[128]), שלח ("dispatch, send away"), מפח נפש ("expiring of life, exhaling of life"), קצר ימים ("short of days"), לא קיץ ("not wake up"), שנה ("sleep"), שכב ("lie down"), אין ("not be"), בית מועד ("meeting house"), רעה ("evil"), כלה ("end, fail, finish, be complete"), and less obviously שקט ("at rest, tranquil, at peace"), נוח ("rest"), and שלה ("be at ease"). Of these, some seem to be rather obvious euphemisms for death (נכה חרב, קצר ימים) while others seem to function euphemistically due to their context (אין,[129] רעה,[130] שלח[131]). Some of the words pertaining to sleeping and resting seem certainly to be death euphemisms in certain contexts (לא קיץ, שנה, שכב),[132] but are less obviously so in other contexts (שקט, נוח, and שלה).[133] The verb כלה is most frequently used not in connection with the "ending" of human life, but with the "ending" of something related to human life by synecdoche (eyes, days, flesh).[134] Lastly, the exact translation and meaning of מפח נפש is disputed, but very well might be a euphemism for death.

The last sub-category of death words in *Job* are those that, by themselves, have several meanings—some of which do not necessarily pertain to death—but in their particular contexts in *Job* likely refer to death. Included here are בלע ("swallow, destroy"; 2:3; 8:18; 10:8), אבד ("perish, vanish, go astray, be destroyed"),[135] טמן ("hide, conceal, bury"; 3:16; 40:13), כחד (Niphal: "be hidden, be effaced, be destroyed"; 4:7; 22:20 [in reference to cities in 15:28]), דכא ("crush, be crushed, be contrite, be broken"; 4:19; 6:9; 34:25), כתת ("beat, crush to pieces"; 4:20), בצע ("cut off, sever, finish, complete"; 6:9; 27:8), חלל ("slay, pierce"; 24:12; 39:30 [in reference to a serpent in 26:13]), מחץ ("smite through, shatter"; 26:12, used in reference to Rahab), נכב ("be smitten, be stricken"; 30:8). Several other words might have this same force, although whether they do is less certain: שוף ("bruise, crush"; 9:17), שמם ("destroy, devastate, ravage, show horror, be desolate"; 16:7), לאה (Hiphil: "weary, make

---

128. Parallel to the verb מות in 4:21.

129. See 7:8, 21; 8:22; and 24:24. It does not function this way in numerous other places.

130. Used in reference to death and disaster in 2:11 and 42:11. In 20:12; 22:5; and 24:21 it does not seem to operate euphemistically.

131. See 8:4 and possibly 14:20.

132. See 7:21; 14:12; 20:11; 21:26.

133. See 3:13, 26, where these are used in Job's description of the experience of Sheol. The term שכב is also used in this connection in 3:13.

134. See 7:6; 11:20; 21:13; 33:21; and 36:11 (perhaps also 17:5 and 31:16). In 7:9 the "ending" of a cloud is parallel to vanishing in Sheol. The root is also used in connection with the "ending" of human life in 4:9 and 9:22, bringing these occurrences more in line with the next category of death words in *Job*.

135. See 4:7, 9, 20; 20:7; 29:13; 31:19 in reference to the perishing of human life. Other occurrences refer to the perishing of things non-human: 3:3 (day); 4:11 (lion); 6:18 (caravan); 8:13 (hope); 11:20 (way of escape); 12:23 (nations); 14:19 (hope); 18:17 (memory); and 30:2 (strength).

weary, exhaust"; 16:7), פרר (Pilpel: "break to pieces, shatter, split, divide"; 16:12), פצץ (Pilpel: "shatter, dash to pieces"; 16:12), and נפח ("cause to breathe out, snuff out"; 31:39).

Of all the sub-categories, the line of distinction between the third and the fourth is most blurred. It is difficult, and perhaps unnecessary, to establish exact criteria for distinguishing euphemisms from words that connote death since this connotation often operates euphemistically.

The second main group comprises an array of words pertaining to darkness that do not, by themselves, seem to have anything in particular to do with death, but by their specific usage in *Job*, and by their tendency to appear in contexts where death is under discussion, seem to connote a certain gloominess or darkness of death. That is, these words seem to hover near and around death in *Job*, and therefore, seem strong candidates to be identified as "death imagery."

All of this is true for all of the darkness words, except for one, צלמות. This lone word seems to make the connection between darkness and death explicit by itself seemingly being an amalgamation of צל and מות.[136] The former has several connotations: shadow as protection from the sun; shadow as threat of the loss of light; shadow as the transitory nature of life. The first and last senses of צל are found in *Job*[137] and throughout the HB (especially Qoheleth for the latter and the Psalms for the former).[138] Moreover, all three senses of צל seem to be wrapped up in צלמות: death as the ephemeral nature of life; death as fear-inducing threat; death as protection or relief from life's burdens. This latter sense is found in several places in Job's speeches, where death is viewed as relief from his misery. This is somewhat ironic, given that צל frequently is used in reference to the shelter and protection of God (especially in the Psalms).[139] In *Job*, though, God is the one from whom shelter is needed, which is the shelter of death.

The other "darkness" words do not make explicit this connection between darkness and death, but when they appear in *Job* they do tend to hover around "death" contexts. They do so in two ways. First, they frequently appear in lines and phrases wherein they parallel צלמות.[140] And secondly, and more importantly,

---

136. Against those that revocalize the word to צלמות from the root צלם ("to be dark"; see, e.g., *HALOT*), Clines and others argue it is doubtful that this root is attested in West Semitic. See David J. A. Clines, *Job 1–20* (WBC 17; Dallas: Word, 1989), 69; idem, "The Etymology of Hebrew Ṣelem," *JNSL* 3 (1974): 19–25. For discussions of this word, see Walter L. Michel, *Job in the Light of Northwest Semitic*. Vol. 1, *Prologue and First Cycle of Speeches, Job 1:1–14:22* (BibOr 42; Rome: Biblical Institute Press, 1987), 42–46; idem, "ṢLMWT, 'Deep Darkness' or 'Shadow of Death,'" *BR* 29 (1984): 5–20; D. Winton Thomas, "צלמות in the Old Testament," *JSS* 7 (1962): 191–200.

137. 40.22 and 7:2 for first; 8:9 and 17:7 for second.

138. D. Winton Thomas argues that מות is used here as a superlative and has absolutely no reference to death or the underworld. The term צלמות, he argues, translates to "very deep shadow" (Thomas, "צלמות" 197–98). However, as Clines argues, "if using מות is a way of expressing the superlative…it does more than simply express a superlative: it does so by using "death" as the intensifier" (Clines, *Job 1–20*, 223). The translation of the word ought also to retain this deathly connection, hence, "shadow of death."

139. See Pss 17:81; 36:8; 57:2; 63:8; 91:1; 121:5.

140. See 3:4–6; 10:21–22; 12:22; 28:3; 34:22; and perhaps 38:17–19. This is true for כמריר, עיפה, and אפל (although it stands alone in 30:26, and parallel to חשך only in 23:17). The most common word for darkness, חשך, appears in clusters of darkness words along with צלמות (see 3:4–6

they tend to appear in contexts alongside numerous group-one death words where death is the "topic" of discussion, indicating clearly that the darkness words comprise some of the imagery of death.[141] Key passages for consideration will be those wherein large clusters of darkness words accompany large clusters of group-one death words.

The next group of words are those related to battle and warfare, including, and especially, various names of weapons. Of themselves, they do not necessarily suggest an immediate connection with death,[142] but frequently, in their usage in *Job*, they seem to be used metaphorically to stand for "instrument of killing/death." This is most obvious for חרב in the euphemism נכה חרב,[143] but is also true of nearly all of the other occurrences of this word in *Job*.[144] Other words for weapons (נשק, קשת, חץ, להב, כידון, אשפה, חנית, שריה, רב[145]), which occur considerably less frequently in *Job*, seem to hover somewhere between a synecdochic relationship to "instrument of killing/death" and a synecdochic relationship to "warfare."[146] And like the darkness words, words for weapons tend to cluster around contexts wherein death is under discussion or is evoked.[147]

The last group of words and phrases that evoke death are the words for mourning rituals on behalf of the dead. These occur almost exclusively in the introductory prose tale in two places. The first is 1:20 where Job receives news of the death of his children and his reaction is to tear his robe (קרע מעיל) and shave his head (גזז ראש).[148] The second occurs in 2:12–13 where the friends, upon seeing Job, treat him "as a person already dead."[149] They weep (בכה),[150] tear their robes (קרע מעיל), sprinkle dust upon their heads (זרק עקר),[151] and sit

and maybe 3:9; 10:21–22; 12:22, 25; 28:3; 34:22; perhaps also 38:17–19) but more frequently it stands by itself.

141. See 10:18–22; 15:22–23; 17:12–16; and 38:17; possibly also 18:12–18; 20:4–29; and 24:12–24. Job 3:3–10 certainly also belongs to this list, although the "death" that is being envisioned here is Job's day of birth, which is a way of discussion one's non-existence by circumlocution.

142. Although the leap from warfare to death is relatively small.

143. 1:15; 1:17, discussed above.

144. See 5:20; 15:22; 19:29; 27:14; 41:18. It is unclear how חרב functions in 5:15 and 40:19. In 39:22 it seems to be a synecdoche for warfare.

145. The term רב, of course, means "archer" and is not a weapon.

146. See 6:4; 16:13; 20:24; 34:6; 39:21, 23; 41:13, 18, 20, 21. Words for warfare or battle (קרב, מלחמה) and words that describe warfare (גדור, "troop"; חנה, "encamp, lay siege against") although rather infrequent, also might be included here. Their connection to death is mainly through mental association with what happens in warfare.

147. See 5:20; 16:12–13; 20:23–26; 27:13–15; and likely, 41:18–21, although no other death words are used in connection with the weapon words here. Also, 15:22–23 might be included though, again, no death words are found here (darkness words are employed, however).

148. Gordis considers Job falling to the ground and worshipping (1:21) also to be mourning rituals (Robert Gordis, *The Book of Job: Commentary, New Translation, and Special Studies* [Moreshet Series 2; New York: Jewish Theological Seminary of America, 1978], 17), as does Pham (*Mourning in the Ancient Near East*, 25), who cites Josh 7:6–7; Ezra 9:5–6; and 1 Macc 4:36–40 as supporting evidence.

149. Clines, *Job 1–20*, 61.

150. בכה seems also to have the sense of a mourning rite in 27:15 and perhaps 30:31.

151. Although it is a bit unclear how the השמימה functions in this phrase.

on the ground (לאֶרֶץ) in silence[152] for seven days.[153] While there is disagreement concerning what precisely these rituals signify,[154] it is clear that they were performed throughout the ANE as mourning rites in connection with death.[155]

1.5.2. Selection of Passages

When examining the distribution of the above words for death in *Job* it becomes apparent that dense clusters of the words appear in several passages. In the prose tale, words for death are clustered toward the latter portions of the two "scenes" of the tale. So, the story of Job's first test (1:6–22) has one word from the literal "death" words (group one, sub-category one), two euphemisms (group one, sub-category three) and three words/phrases for mourning—all of which appear from 1:15 onward. The story of Job's second test (2:1–13) has one literal "death" word, one euphemism, and five mourning words/phrases—all of which appear from 2:9 onward. And finally, the prose epilogue ends with the narration of Job's actual death (42:11).

The poetic dialogues also display several clusters of death words, the most obvious of which are chs. 3,[156] 7,[157] and 10:18–22.[158] Death words in chs. 3 and

152.   Norbert Lohfink ("Enthielten die im Alten Testament bezeugten Klageriten eine Phase des Schweigens," *VT* 12 [1962]: 260–77) has argued that silence is part of the mourning ritual. See also, Edward Lipiński, *La liturgie pénitentielle dans la Bible* (LD 52; Paris: Cerf, 1969), 31–35; Eileen F. de Ward, "Mourning Customs in 1, 2 Samuel," *JJS* 23 (1972): 1–27 (17–20). Isa 23:1–3a and Ezek 26:16–17a seem to depict speechlessness as part of the mourning ritual (see Pham, *Mourning*, 29–31).

153.   A seven-day ritual mourning period seems to be common in many texts of the ANE. See, e.g., "The Curse of Agade," 4:195–209 (Jerrold S. Cooper, *The Curse of Agade* [JHNES; Baltimore: The Johns Hopkins University Press, 1983], 59, 61); "Gilgamesh," Meissner Fragment, 2.1–13 (Anderson, *Time to Mourn*, 78); "Harran Inscription of Nabonidus" (C. J. Gadd, "Harran Inscription of Nabonidus," *Anatolian Studies* 8 [1958]: 35–92); and probably "Aqhat" (*KTU* 1.17.1.1–19; translated by H. L. Ginsberg, *ANET*, 150) although here no one has died; Danil simply acts like a mourner (see also Anderson, *Time to Mourn*, 77, for a discussion of this passage). For more on the significance of a seven-day period of ritual mourning, see Anderson, *Time to Mourn*, 77–84. See also, Gen 50:10; 1 Sam 31:13; 2 Sam 12:15–24; Sir 22:12. Also significant is the fact that the friends come to comfort (נחם) Job. Anderson argues this is a ritualistically important attitude of mourners, who assume a state of mourning alongside a mourner in order to bring about the cessation of mourning (Anderson, *Time to Mourn*, 84–87; see, also, Gen 24:67; 37:34–35; 2 Sam 12:24; 1 Chr 7:22–23; Isa 61:2, 10; Jer 31:13).

154.   Spronk (*Beatific Afterlife*, 33–35) lists several theories of earlier generations of historical critics: the rituals are attempts to ward the souls of the dead away from the living; they are attempts of the living to show their submission to the dead; they are attempts by the living to communicate with the dead; they are attempts by the living to cope with death; they are expressions of humility before God.

155.   See Anderson, *Time to Mourn*, 49–97; Pham, *Mourning*, 16–35. For biblical examples of the above mourning rites, see Gen 37:34, 35; Josh 7:6; 1 Sam 4:12; 2 Sam 1:2, 11; 13:19; Jer 7:29; Mic 1:16; Jdt 4:11–12.

156.   In the 26 verses of ch. 3, of the group-one death words, ch. 3 has four occurrences of sub-category one words (words that mean "death"), one sub-category two word (words that pertain to the realm of the dead), two sub-category four words (words that in this context mean death), six possible occurrences of sub-category three words (euphemisms), and six occurrences of "darkness" words.

157.   Of ch. 7's 21 verses, it has eight group-one death words (two sub-category one, six sub-category two, and one sub-category three).

10:18–22 coincide with the topic of these passages, which is Job's fantasy about Sheol. In ch. 7, similarly, the death words are used by Job in the context of his description of his soon-to-be death and his stated desire for death rather than God's terrors.

Several other passages also contain clusters of death words, although, perhaps, not quite as densely as the above three. These other passages include 4:7–11;[159] 4:17–21;[160] 5:17–26;[161] ch. 14;[162] 17:11–16;[163] 18:5–21;[164] 21:7–34;[165] 26:5–14;[166] and 27:2–23.[167] Death words appear quite frequently throughout the three cycles of speeches, but tend to recede slightly in Job's final impassioned statement of his innocence in ch. 31.

In the Elihu Speeches, death words generally are infrequent, except for 33:12–30[168] and in a smattering of other places in other speeches (e.g. 34:20–25 and 36:11–14).

In the Divine Speeches, the familiar mixture of the groups of death words is no longer apparent. Only three group-one words are present in the entire four chapters (one sub-category one word in 38:17, two sub-category four words in 40:13), along with only three darkness words (38:2, 17, 19[169]). On the other hand, there are a plethora of weapon/war words in these speeches, most of which are concentrated around the description of the horse (39:19–25) and Leviathan (41:18–21).

In the following chapters I propose to analyze the passages in the book of Job that are most rife with death words, but I also desire to examine death in all the various sections of *Job*—prose, dialogues, and Divine Speeches. So, although both Job's last speech in chs. 29–31 and the Divine Speeches in chs. 38–41 have

---

158. Of these five verses, two are group-one death words (one sub-category one, one sub-category two) and five are "darkness" words.

159. These five verses contain five group-one death words (one sub-category three word, four sub-category four words).

160. These five verses contain five group-one death words (one sub-category one word, one sub-category three word, three sub-category four words).

161. These eleven verses contain two group-one death words (one sub-category one word, two sub-category two words), one darkness word, and three weapon/war words.

162. These 22 verses contain eleven group-one death words (four sub-category one words, one sub-category two word, five sub-category three words, and one sub-category four word).

163. These six verses contain three group-one death words (three sub-category two words) and two darkness words.

164. These 17 verses contain four group-one death words (one sub-category one word, two sub-category two words, one sub-category four word) and two darkness words.

165. These 28 verses contain seven group-one death words (two sub-category one words, three sub-category two words, and two sub-category three words).

166. These ten verses contain five group-one death words (three sub-category two words and two sub-category four words) and one darkness word.

167. These 22 verses contain five group-one death words (two sub-category one words, one sub-category two word, one sub-category three word, two sub-category four words), one weapon/war word, and one mourning word.

168. These 19 verses have seven group-one death words (one sub-category one word, five sub-category two words, and one sub-category three word).

169. Although חשׁך in 38:2 seems to have little to do with death.

significantly fewer death words in comparison to various portions of the dialogues, I think it is important to see what happens to "death" in these new contexts, and especially to examine the dominant metaphors and tropes that appear
instead of death.

Chapter 2 will be an examination of death in the introductory section of the
prose tale (chs. 1–2). I will probe the rhetorical function death plays in the plot
of the tale as I trace the movement of the tale from a picture of life and vibrancy
(1:1–5) to death and mourning (2:11–13).

Chapters 3 through 5 will examine death in the poetic dialogues, and the three
chapters together function as a unit as they describe Job's sense of the breakdown of his symbolic system (Chapters 3 and 4) and then Job's attempt to
articulate a new symbolic system from the fragments of the old one (Chapter 5).
Chapter 3 will focus mainly on ch. 3; 7:1–6; and 10:18–22 from Job's speeches,
and then on Eliphaz's response to Job in chs. 4–5. Emphasis will be placed on
the ways Job conceptualizes and fantasizes about death, and how he expresses
death's intrusion or impingement on his life. Contrast will be drawn between
Job's experience and understanding of life and death with those of Eliphaz. This
will be the only place that I examine one of the friends' conceptions of death.
Although they lace some of their later speeches with discussions of death, the
friends doggedly maintain one conception of death throughout their speeches, a
conception that I will discuss in my examination of chs. 4–5.

Chapter 4 will examine a shift that occurs in Job's discussions of death in the
latter portions of the first cycle and throughout the second. Now Job will
understand his death as divine murder and he will associate it with absolute
hopelessness. My focus will be on several passages that display these themes:
7:20–21; 9:21–24; 14:7–22; 16:7–22; 17:11–16; 19:6–20.

Chapter 5 will analyze the clusters of death imagery in chs. 21 and 27 and
then chs. 29–31, in general, and focus will be on Job's reconceptualization of
the function of death in light of his articulation of a new symbolic system.

Chapter 6 will examine chs. 38–41 as the divine response to the new symbolic system Job has just articulated in chs. 29–31. Specifically, I will argue that
the Divine Speeches function as a rival to Job's new symbolic system and that
the differences between the two are obvious by the way death signifies in each.

I will end with a short concluding chapter where I interpret Job's own death
in light of all of my previous analysis.[170]

In sum, I propose to analyze death imagery in most of the major sections of
Job. Absent from my analysis is the large block of material that comprises the

---

170.   I realize that one potential objection to the organization of my chapters is that, in contrast
to the poetic dialogues and the Divine Speeches, I do not account for the prose tale as a whole.
Instead, I account for its two pieces separately. Although many scholars accept that the two pieces of
the prose tale once circulated as a unit independent of the dialogues, for the purposes of this project I
am not interested in the textual pre-history of the book of Job. No doubt the figure "death" takes on a
different guise when one reads the entire prose tale as a unit. However, when one reads the sequence
of the book as a whole, "death" now signifies in this bifurcated tale, which has been combined with a
particular sequential arrangement of poetic units.

Elihu Speeches (chs. 32–37). These speeches have received their fair share of negative criticism in the history of interpretation, being accused of being later additions (with the implication drawn that they are not worth serious consideration) due to their inferior Hebrew style and their content, which seems to be an orthodox defense against Job's accusations.[171] All of this may or may not be true, but my decision to exclude them is based more on the considerations of the larger project. First, as I have already mentioned, these speeches demonstrate a relative lack of death words; and second, when the Elihu Speeches do employ death imagery, it tends to conform to how death imagery was used previously in the speeches of the friends. In contrast to the Divine Speeches, where death imagery also seems to occur less frequently, in the Elihu Speeches the death imagery that is present simply echoes what has already been seen before.

The driving question that will animate my analysis of the book of Job will be the relationship of the presentation of death to divine justice and its depicted collapse. I will intersperse my analysis of *Job* with discussions of Lifton's theories about psychohistorical dislocation. My hope is that by juxtaposing the two each source will function as a critical edge to provide astute and important insights into the other, including plausible answers to some of the vexing critical problems that interpreters of both sources encounter. In *Job*'s case, Lifton's theories enable the apparent disunity of *Job*—its multiple genres and voices—to be read as a strategy of the narration of psychohistorical disruption, while *Job* supplies for Lifton a satisfying resolution to a nagging tension in the presentation of his conception of the self.

---

171. According to Gordis (*Book of God and Man*, 106, 332) this argument was made early in the rise of historical criticism by Eichhorn and de Wette (Johann Gottfried Eichhorn, *Einleitung in das Alte Testament* [3d ed.; 3 vols.; Leipzig: Weidmann, 1803], 3:597–98; Wilhelm Martin Leberecht de Wette, *A Critical and Historical Introduction to the Canonical Scriptures of the Old Testament* [trans. Theodore Parker; 3d ed.; 2 vols.; Boston: Rufus Leighton, 1859], 2:558–60). It was then repeated in S. R. Driver's influential *An Introduction to the Literature of the Old Testament* (Meridian Library 3; New York: Meridian Books, 1960), 428–30. Recent scholarly analysis has looked upon the Elihu Speeches more favorably. See, e.g., David Noel Freedman, "Elihu Speeches in the Book of Job," *HTR* 61 (1968): 51–59; Gordis, *Job*, xxxi–xxxii; Norman C. Habel, *The Book of Job: A Commentary* (OTL; Philadelphia: Westminster, 1985), 35–39; J. Gerald Janzen, *Job* (Int; Atlanta: John Knox, 1985), 22–25, 218; Roland E. Murphy, *The Book of Job: A Short Reading* (New York: Paulist, 1999), 87. Good chooses not to treat Elihu's Speeches as fully as the other material, not because he believes they were interpolated, but because he "find[s] Elihu a pompous, insensitive bore" (Edwin M. Good, *In Turns of Tempest: A Reading of Job, With a Translation* [Stanford: Stanford University Press, 1990], 321). Gordis provides one of the fullest discussions of the critical issues involved, together with his own conclusion that the author of the Elihu Speeches was the same person who composed the poetic dialogues, only he did so at a later date (Gordis, *Book of God and Man*, 104–16). For contemporary scholars who regard the Elihu speeches as secondary additions, see A. de Wilde, *Das Buch Hiob* (OtSt 22; Leiden: Brill, 1981), 2–5; J. C. L. Gibson, *Job* (The Daily Study Bible Series; Philadelphia: Westminster, 1985), 219–20, 268–70; Newsom, "Job," 320–25.

Chapter 2

SYMBOLIC WHOLENESS AND LIFE, DESYMBOLIZATION AND DEATH (CHAPTERS 1–2)

Haśśatan voices the fundamental issue of the prose tale when he inquires of God, "Is it for nothing that Job fears God?" (1:9). This question is not merely about the greatness of Job's piety or nature of his sincerity, but is a profound and troubling inquiry into the coherence of a powerful Israelite moral system. Are humans pious only because God showers them with blessings? If blessings were withheld, would humans still be pious? What really *is* the source of human piety? As the prologue unfolds, God and *haśśatan* test Job's virtue by removing all of his blessings, and then seeing how Job responds: Will he maintain his integrity, or will he curse God?

Although the question of unmotivated piety is the fundamental issue of the prologue, in the telling of the tale—in the recounting of the test of Job's virtue—what might be called (for lack of a better term) "the death theme" rises to prominence. *Haśśatan*'s first plan against Job consists of the loss and death of Job's livestock, the deaths of his servants, and culminates in the deaths of his children (1:13–19). Job's response to these deaths is to speak of his own mortality (1:21). *Haśśatan*'s second plan against Job stops just short of the latter's death, and when Job's wife implores Job to take action, she urges him to "curse God and die" (2:9). Mortuary rites punctuate the prologue: Job performs them upon hearing of his children's deaths (1:20); and the final scene of the prologue shows a mortuary ritual involving Job's friends and Job himself (2:12–13).

In this chapter I will examine more closely what is at stake in the depiction of death in the prologue. I will try to show what death does as a narrative vehicle and why death is of supreme importance to the basic issues of the prologue. As an *entré* into this discussion I will contrast the deathly ending of the prologue with its lively beginning.

2.1. *Endings vs. Beginnings*

Aristotle has argued that the plot of the tragedy has three parts—beginning, middle, and end—all joined by necessary and probable causes.[1] A tripartite division of plot has also influenced the way biblical scholars conceptualize the plot of Hebrew prose. Gunn and Fewell, for example, in their *Narrative in the*

---

1. See Aristotle, *Poetics* 1450b.26–34.

Hebrew Bible, argue that the plot structure of Hebrew prose consists of an exposition, which sets the scene; conflict, which introduces the fundamental question or problem of the story; and a resolution, where the question is answered or the problem is solved.[2] While many stories do demonstrate this type of flow, it is also true that many do not: whether intentionally or not, some do not achieve a level of resolution, while others barely have enough conflict to sustain a plot.[3] In any case, the introduction and conclusion (or resolution) are key in any story. To borrow liturgical terms, the former operates as the processional, wherein the reader is acclimatized to the story world of the tale; while the latter functions as the recessional, wherein the reader exits the story world and transitions back into the "real" world, having been altered by the story told. Furthermore, the ending of a story provides the vantage point from which the story as a whole can be perceived, analyzed, and in many cases, understood.[4]

The book of Job, as argued previously, is a book of multiple beginnings and endings. As such, it does not lend itself easily to an Aristotelian analysis. But the introductions and conclusions *are* of fundamental importance to the story told in *Job*, nowhere more so than in the prose tale (chs. 1–2; 42:7–17), for it raises to prominence the important issue of what bearing the ending of a story has on the story itself. If, as numerous scholars suggest, both parts of the prose tale originally circulated as a unit, then the tale seems to tell a fairly straightforward story that can be traced using Aristotle's or Gunn and Fewell's terms (exposition—1:1–5; conflict—1:6–2:10; resolution—42:7–17). *Haśśatan*'s fundamental question, concerning the existence unmotivated "piety," is answered: after experiencing calamity, Job refuses to curse God. Unmotivated piety is proven to exist, and God restores Job's fortunes.

But this is not how the tale appears presently in the book. Instead, the prose tale is split in two, with voluminous poetic sections separating the two parts, forming a vast, extended pause in the action of the tale, before it reaches its resolution. This pause has two drastic effects on the tale. First, whatever resolution 42:7–17 provided to the unified prose tale is now altered by the themes and issues raised in poetry of 3:1–42:6. The interruption in the prose tale does not allow the point of the tale simply and exclusively to be an affirmation of the existence of unmotivated piety. Second, 1:1–2:13 now functions as a prologue to the book as a whole, meaning that it not only raises the question of the existence of unmotivated piety (*haśśatan*'s question), but also, because of where the tale is interrupted (before the resolution), shifts the focus from *haśśatan*'s question to the implications of the question—the problematics of innocent suffering. This now becomes the question with which the poetic sections will struggle.

---

2. David M. Gunn and Danna Nolan Fewell, *Narrative in the Hebrew Bible* (Oxford Bible Series; New York: Oxford University Press, 1993), 102.

3. As recognized by Gunn and Fewell, who argue that their analysis of plot structure is for heuristic purposes and that many stories in the HB do not conform to it (ibid., 102–12).

4. See Peter Brooks, *Reading for the Plot: Design and Intention in Narrative* (New York: Knopf, 1984), 19; Paul Ricoeur, "The Narrative Function," *Semeia* 13 (1978): 177–202 (182). For a critique of this position, see Gunn and Fewell, *Narrative*, 105–6, who argue that some endings fail to bring resolution and/or to clarify what has come before.

Moreover, 1:1–2:13 is a unique type of prologue. It does not share generic connections to the main body it introduces. Its genre, in fact, clearly distinguishes it from the main poetic body of the work, and marks it as a different, separable entity with its own beginning (1:1–5), middle (1:6–2:10), and ending (2:11–13). Chapter 1:1–5 now acts as the processional to the prologue, orienting the reader to its world, while 2:11–13 acts as the recessional, wherein the reader exits the world of the prologue. A comparison between the two will demonstrate them to contrast sharply and will raise the question about what sort of story is capable of sustaining the movement from the one to the other. A comparison will also allow the "death theme" to come into focus more clearly, revealing its fundamental importance in the book of Job, in general, and in the prologue, in particular.

2.1.1. *Conclusion of the Prologue and Death*

The book of Job, as mentioned previously, is a book of multiple endings coinciding with multiply layered deaths. The first such death-ending occurs in the prologue where the cessation of the prose narrative occurs simultaneously with an explosion of death imagery in the depiction of various mortuary rites (weeping, tearing of robes, sprinkling of dust upon heads, sitting on the ground in silence for seven days).[5] Various passages in the HB confirm the mortuary nature of these rituals. When Jacob received news of his son Joseph's death he tore his garments and mourned with weeping (Gen 37:34–35). Likewise did David and his men upon receiving the news of Saul's and Jonathan's deaths (1 Sam 1:11–12). After the men of Ai killed some Israelites in battle, Joshua tore his clothes, and he and the elders put dust on their heads and lay with their faces to the ground (Josh 7:6). In 1 Sam 4:12 and 2 Sam 1:2, messengers with torn clothes and dust on their heads brought news of defeat and death. In Ezek 26:15–17, the mourning over the fall of, and slaughter in, Tyre includes stripping of garments, trembling, sitting on the ground, and being appalled (שׁמם).[6] Joseph observed a seven-day mourning period in Gen 50:10, and the men of Jabesh-gilead fasted for seven days over the deaths of Saul and his sons (1 Sam 31:13).[7]

Common as these mourning rites may have been, what sets off the rites at the end of the prologue in *Job* from the others is that whereas the other passages all include the death of someone or some group of people as what prompts the

---

5.   See section 1.5.1 for more on the mourning ritual.

6.   Pham (*Mourning in the Ancient Near East*, 30) argues that שׁמם "connotes the idea of being speechless and motionless out of fear" in the mourning rite to which she compares the silence in Job 2:13. See also Isa 23:1–3a for speechlessness as part of the mourning ritual.

7.   Other mourning rites included fasting, shaving the beard, gashing the body, beating the breast, striking the thigh, and walking around bowed down (ibid., 27). For more on mourning in the HB, see Anderson, *Time to Mourn*, 82–91; E. Kutsche, "'Trauerbräuche' und 'Selbstminderungsriten' im AT," *ThSt* 78 (1965): 25–42; Pham, *Mourning in the Ancient Near East*, 24–35; Ward, "Mourning Customs," 1–27; Arent Jan Wensinck, *Some Semitic Rites of Mourning and Religion: Studies on their Origin and Mutual Relation* (Verhandelingen der Koninklijke akademie van wetenschappen te Amsterdam. Afdeeling Letterkunde. Nieuwe reeks 18; Amsterdam: J. Müller, 1917), 1–101.

mourning rites, in *Job*, there is no death that can be shown to prompt the mourning ritual.[8] Granted, the prologue does narrate the deaths of Job's servants and children (1:13–19), but the mourning ritual at the end of the prologue likely is not a response to these deaths for two reasons. First, Job already does perform mourning rites on behalf of these in 1:20–21; and second, all of the events of 1:13–19 are quite distinct from the events in 2:11–13 from a narrative point of view. Structurally, 1:6–22 and 2:1–10 comprise two parallel, but distinct and self-contained narrative units of the prologue. Each begins with a heavenly scene wherein God and *haśśatan* agree to test Job's virtue (1:6–12; 2:1–6); each narrates a calamitous event (1:13–19; 2:7–8); each relates Job's response to his calamity (1:20–21; 2:9–10a); and each ends with the narrator's evaluation of Job (1:22; 2:10b). The scenes in 1:13–22; 2:1–10; and 2:11–13 form self-contained, separate story units whose actions and events are to be related to actions and events of that particular scene, including the friends' mourning rituals in the second scene, which are a response to seeing Job, as if something about Job's appearance prompted this reaction. In fact, not only is 2:11–13 distinct from 1:13–22, it even seems to be distinct from the entire prologue altogether. For whereas every other scene in the prologue is arranged in alternation between earthly scenes (1:1–5, 13–22; 2:7–10) and heavenly scenes (1:6–12; 2:1–7),[9] 2:11–13 breaks the pattern and stands by itself. Its sole purpose seems to be to introduce the friends and therefore to act as a narrative link between the prose prologue and the poetic dialogues that follow.

In any case, in the symbolism of the friends' actions in 2:11–13, Job is "treat[ed] as one already dead."[10] And yet Job is not dead, nor has there been a death to which the friends' mortuary rites point, as in the other biblical examples. Rather, this death scene is symbolically ambiguous: mortuary rites connected not to death, but to not-death. What then does this death scene mean? What is symbolized in this death scene without death? Relatedly, how did we get here? What route did the prologue take to end with this narrated death/non-death?

2.1.2. Introduction to the Prologue and Life

These questions are all the more relevant given the beginning of the prologue and its dual emphasis on Job's piety and, contra the conclusion, on life, fecundity, and liveliness. First, the former. The beginning of the prologue to *Job* establishes a story world of wonderful simplicity with a focus on a single man of the deepest moral character. It is a fairytale type of beginning, vaguely and cursorily introducing Job's historical and geographic setting, but elaborating on

---

8.   The closest parallels to the friends' actions occur in Jonah 2:5–9, where the king of Nineveh performs and orders various mortuary rites in reaction to Jonah's prophecy of destruction, and Ezra 9:3–4, where Ezra likewise performs mortuary rites in reaction to the news that the returned exiles have intermarried with the Canaanites. In both of these cases, however, the mortuary rites can be connected to perceived threats of annihilation—in the former case, God's destruction of Nineveh for its sins; in the latter case the "death of the community" for its sins of intermarriage (see H. G. M. Williamson, *Ezra, Nehemiah* [WBC 16; Waco, Tex.: Word, 1985], 133).

9.   See Clines, *Job 1–20*, 6–8, for more.

10.   Ibid., 64.

the details of his virtue with great relish (1:1). The lack of specificity regarding Job's historical location (היה איש; "There was a man...") and the apparently hazy geographical location of his home, Uz,[11] shifts the significance of this introduction to the specific demarcations of Job's virtue: "blameless and upright, one who fears God and turns from evil." The terms employed to describe Job's virtue (תם; ישר; ירא אלהים; סר מרע) are all loaded terms of high significance in the sapiential circles.[12]

Connected to this emphasis on Job's piety, is the picture of life, fecundity, and liveliness that the introduction foregrounds. There is an exaggerated quality to this life. Not only is Job blessed with children, he had the perfect number of children (ten): seven sons (the number of completion[13]) and three daughters (the "perfect" ratio of sons to daughters[14]). Not only is Job blessed with livestock and servants, like the patriarchs of Genesis, Job possesses an absurdly large number of livestock, again described in terms of symbolically complete numbers. In fact, the silence of the Genesis texts in regards to the quantities of the patriarchs' livestock serves to underscore the exaggeratedly large number of animals owned by Job.[15] Life—human and animal—was bursting at the seams in Job's world.[16]

In the lone example of Job's piety that the narrative offers (1:4–5), themes of life and liveliness predominate. As the tale reveals, Job's children would take turns hosting feasts in their homes to which all the siblings would be invited to

---

11. See Meir Weiss, *The Story of Job's Beginning: Job 1–2; A Literary Analysis* (Jerusalem: Magnes, 1983), 21–33.

12. The word תם appears in scattered places throughout the HB (although not generally in the Prophets), and appears with most frequency outside *Job* in Proverbs (eight times) and the Psalms (nine times). The term ישר is an even more common word, especially in the Deuteronomistic History, Chronicles, the Psalms, and Proverbs, besides *Job*. The two appear as a pair in 1 Kgs 9:4; Pss 25:21; 37:37; Prov 2:7; 29:10 and three times in *Job*, all in the prologue (1:1, 8; 2:3). The "fear of God," though not necessarily a specifically sapiential phrase, does occupy an important role in the theology of Proverbs. As Prov 1:7; 2:5–8; 3:7; and 16:6 make clear it is a "traditional expression of wisdom theology for that total devotion which underlies and motivates those who follow the path of wisdom to salvation and success" (Habel, *Job*, 86). "Turning from evil" is a stereotypical sapiential expression that coincides with the conception that in life one ought to "walk" along the straight "way" of wisdom. To turn from evil is to maintain one's path. See Prov 3:7; 13:19; 14:16; 16:6, 17; Pss 34:15; 37:27, for this metaphor of the wise life. For more on the imagery of the way, see Michael V. Fox, *Proverbs 1–9: A New Translation with Introduction and Commentary* (AB 18a; New York: Doubleday, 2000), 128–31; Norman C. Habel, "Symbolism of Wisdom in Proverbs 1–9," *Int* 26 (1972): 131–57. For more on *Job*'s connections to the Wisdom tradition, see Gordis, *Book of God and Man*, 31–52, and below, section 3.2.2.1.

13. Clines, *Job 1–20*, 13, lists other ancient texts where seven sons is the ideal: Job 42:13; Ruth 4:15; 1 Sam 2:5; Jer 15:9; "Keret" (*KTU* 1.15.2.23; see the translation in J. C. L. Gibson, *Canaanite Myths and Legends* [Edinburgh: T. & T. Clark, 1977], 91); Ovid, *Metamorphoses* 6.182–83.

14. Clines, *Job 1–20*, 13, compares this ratio to 1 Kgs 11:3 where Solomon has 700 wives and 300 concubines.

15. Cf. Gen 12:16; 26:14; 30:43; 46:32. Although not a text dealing with the Patriarchs, 1 Sam 25:2 does number Nabal's sheep (3000) and goats (1000), but even these figures cannot compare to those of the prologue to *Job*.

16. Meier hints at this emphasis on life and fecundity by connecting the description of Job's progeny to the Genesis command to "be fruitful and multiply." See Sam Meier, "Job 1–2: A Reflection of Genesis 1–3," *VT* 39 (1989): 183–93 (186).

join. Movement, merry-making, eating and drinking: life and liveliness to the fullest.

The first word of v. 2 (ויולדו), appearing as a *waw*-consecutive, bridges the dual emphasis on Job's piety (1:1) and life/fecundity/liveliness (1:2–5), establishing a connective link between two. According to Cooper, this *waw*-consecutive does not necessarily imply a causal connection between piety and life (as numerous scholars suggest), only a symmetrical parallel between the two (it may simply mean "and"). Grammatically, Cooper is correct, but he overstates his case when he argues that there is nothing in the text to suggest a *causal* connection in the *waw*-consecutive and that this interpretation is merely a reflection on the interpreter's assumptions.[17] In fact, the connection of piety and life (whether causal or merely symmetrical) is a picture of a moral world order quite common in the HB, especially obvious in Deuteronomy, certain Psalms, and Proverbs.

2.1.2.1. *Piety, Life, and Relationship in Deuteronomy, Psalms, Proverbs.* In Deuteronomy life and death are understood to be wrapped up in the issue of covenant obedience. The rules received by Moses are for the benefit of Israel, that the people might follow them and be blessed by living and occupying their land without interruption. This understanding of the law punctuates Deuteronomy in numerous places throughout the book, functioning as a sort of refrain, and orienting the reader to a correct understanding of the laws established in the book.[18] Most striking about the list of blessings is the emphasis on life and fecundity. The Israelites are told that if they obey, "[God] will multiply [them] and bless the fruit of [their] womb and the fruit of [their] soil, [their] grain, [their] wine and [their] oil, the offspring of [their] cattle and the young of [their] flock" (7:13). Obedience means "life and happiness" (30:15), disobedience means "death and adversity" (30:15).

But this is no impersonal mechanical system of reward (or punishment). In fact, the whole system is personal and relational. God is the one who delivered Israel from Egypt and led them through the wilderness (chs. 1–4). God is the one who will dislodge the inhabitants of the land of Canaan and give it to Israel (6:10; 7:1–2). And most importantly, God is the one who established a covenant with Israel's "fathers," Abraham, Isaac, and Jacob, that if Israel obeys the laws, God will grant Israel life, land, and blessing (7:12–15; 26:16–19).

The key language of this covenant is relational: Israel will obey the laws and therefore show their love (אהב) of God[19] while God will bless Israel with life and therefore show his love (אהב) of Israel.[20] While the use of אהב in covenants implies loyalty and fidelity, it is significant that covenants use the highly

17. Alan Cooper, "Reading and Misreading the Prologue to Job," *JSOT* 46 (1990): 67–79 (69–71).

18. See, e.g., 4:1, 29–31, 39–40; 5:26, 29; 6:1–3, 24; 7:12–15; 8:1; 11:8, 13–14; 12:28; ch. 28; 30:6–10, 15–20; 32:47.

19. 5:10; 6:5; 7:9; 10:12; 11:1, 13, 22; 13:3; 19:9; 30:6, 16, 20.

20. 4:37; 5:10; 7:13; 10:15, 18; 23:5.

personal, emotional, and relational language of "love" to do so.[21] Deuteronomy also emphasizes the "punishment" side of the agreement: abandoning God and following other gods—abandoning one relationship for another—results in death.[22]

One ought not to romanticize this relationship too much, however. Deuteronomy also makes it quite clear that this is a hierarchical relationship, not an egalitarian one. *God* is the one who chose Israel and gave them a covenant. *God* commanded them to obey the laws and serve him. Israel, for its part, has to obey the laws and serve God only. If Israel does so, God will give rewards.

Deuteronomy's connection of obedience, life, and relationship with God also is apparent in many Psalms, although frequently the terms seem to take on a slightly different significance there. Whereas Deuteronomy explores the obedience/life/relationship complex in relation to the law, in the Psalms this complex finds its context in the language of worship. This has the effect of making the complex highly personal, as demonstrated in Ps 145:20a where the general truth that "Yahweh watches over all who love him" leads the Psalmist to the personal declaration, "my mouth shall utter the praise Yahweh" (145:21a).

A movement away from the legal and covenantal context of Deuteronomy also has the effect of shifting the terms of the content of "obedience." Whereas in Deuteronomy obedience consisted of obeying the laws set out as part of the covenant, in the Psalms, obedience is cast more in terms of personal piety. Psalm 37, for example, contrasts the righteous man with the wicked. The former "trusts in Yahweh" (בטח) and "does good" (טוב) (v. 3), abandons "anger" (אף) and "fury" (חמה) (v. 8), "turns from evil" (סור מרא) (v. 27), his mouth "utters wisdom" (חכמה) and "speaks justice" (משפט) (v. 30), and he "waits for Yahweh and keeps to his way" (דרך).[23] This person is called "righteous" (צדיק), "blameless" (תם), "upright" (ישר), and "faithful" (חסיד).

The pious person is the one who will have food to eat in famine (v. 18), will abide forever (v. 27), is preserved forever (v. 28), and will dwell in the land forever (v. 29). As in Deuteronomy, these "life" blessings are not simply results of a mechanical system of piety = reward, but are personal and relational, tied to one's relationship to Yahweh. In acting piously, the righteous are "trusting in Yahweh" (v. 3) and "delighting in Yahweh" (v. 4). Yahweh is the one who "supports" the righteous (v. 17). By his "blessing" do they "inherit the land" (v. 22). As Ps 30:6 says, "when [Yahweh] is pleased there is life."[24]

---

21. For more on this point see Jacqueline E. Lapsley, "Feeling Our Way: Love for God in Deuteronomy," *CBQ* 65 (2003): 350–69.

22. Deut 4:26; 5:22; 6:14; 8:19–20; 9:11–14; 11:17; 13:6, 9–10, 13–19; 17:2–5, 12; 29:17–28; 32:22–31.

23. References to תורה are not entirely absent, for this person has "the תורה of God in his heart." Here, however, תורה does not seem to have the legal sense that it did in Deuteronomy. It refers more generally to "teaching" or "instruction." It likely has this latter sense also in Pss 1, 19, and 119.

24. For more on the life/piety/relationship with God complex in the Psalms, see 1:1–3; 15:1–5; 18:5, 17, 21–25; 19:8; 26:1–12; 30:6; 33:18; 41:2–3; 66:8; 92:13–16; 97:10; 103:3–5; 115:12–18; 118:5, 21–25; 127:3–5; 145:20.

Perhaps one of the most concise statements of the life/piety/relationship complex comes from Ps 15. This short Psalm consists of three parts: a comparatively lengthy middle section, bracketed by two sections that parallel each other structurally. The middle section describes the pious person in similar terms to Ps 37: one who is "blameless" (תם), "does right" (צדק), "speaks truth" (אמת), and so on (vv. 2–5b). The first part of the Psalm describes this person's relationship to the deity using language of co-habitation: this one "dwells" (גור) in Yahweh's "tent" and "abides" (שכן) on Yahweh's "holy mountain" (v. 1). Paralleling this brief initial relational statement is its mirror statement at the end, which describes the fate of the pious person: he "will not be shaken (מוט)" (v. 5c). This short Psalm does not so much establish logical connections between piety, life, and relationship to the deity (such as piety leads to relationship leads to life), but establishes piety as the "middle" term between life and relationship to Yahweh: acting piously is at once to dwell with Yahweh (v. 1) *and* to live securely (v. 5c).

Similar formulations of this complex can be found in Proverbs, a book that is frequently noted for its secularism. But even here piety and life do not comprise an impersonal system of "act–consequence"[25] but form a complex with relationship to God as the third term. Proverbs 11:19–20, for example, establishes this complex with piety as the middle term. The simple chiastic arrangement of the four lines of these two verses contrasts the life of piety with the life of sinfulness:

A: כן צדקה לחיים
   "The pursuer[26] of righteousness finds life" (19a)

B: ומרדף רעה למותו
   "The pursuer of evil finds his death" (19b)

B′:   תועבת יהוה עקשי לב
   "Those of perverse heart are an abomination to Yahweh" (20a)

A′:   ורצונו תמימי דרך
   "Those of blameless ways are his delight" (20b)

While the first and last lines link piety with life and piety with relationship to the deity (A and A′ respectively), the middle lines link impiety with death and impiety with alienation from the deity (B and B′ respectively). So, as in Ps 15, piety, life, and relationship to Yahweh are connected with piety as the middle term. Where there is piety there is life; where there is piety there is relationship to Yahweh (and conversely, where there is sin, there is death; where there is sin there is broken relationship).

Throughout Proverbs this relationship between piety, life, and relationship to God is also evident, although the theme of piety as the middle term is not always apparent. Proverbs 3, for example, intersperses exhortations to pious living ("Let loyalty and faithfulness not leave you" [v. 3]; "do not lean on your

---

25. This phrase is borrowed from David J. A. Clines, "False Naivety in the Prologue to Job," *HAR* 9 (1985): 127–36 (132–33), who uses this term to describe the prologue to *Job*.

26. Inserting the מרדף of Prov 11:19b.

own understanding" [v. 5]; "do not be wise in your own eyes [v. 7], and so on)
with descriptions life and plenty as the benefits of piety ("they will add to you
length of days, years of life and well-being" [v. 2]; "barns will be filled with
plenty and your vats bursting with new wine" [v. 10]) and with statements of
relationship to God ("favor and approval in the eyes of God" [v. 4]; "[God] will
make your paths smooth" [v. 6]). The exhortation to piety is also sometimes
spoken of in terms of relationship to God, further linking the elements of piety,
life, and relationship to God into a complex ("Trust in God" [v. 5]; "acknowl-
edge [God]" [v. 6]; "fear Yahweh" [v. 7]; "honor Yahweh" [v. 9]).[27]

2.1.2.2. *Piety, Life, and Relationship-to-God in* Job. Of particular interest in
Prov 3 is the exhortation to "fear Yahweh" (ירא את יהוה) and "turn from evil"
(סור מרע) in v. 7. This pair, along with the pair "upright" (ישר) and "blameless"
(תם) from Prov 2:7 comprise the four descriptors of Job's character in Job 1:1.
This fact, along with the heavy emphasis on life, liveliness, and fecundity in the
introduction to the prologue in *Job*, suggests to the reader an orientation to the
particular moral–theological world of the piety/life/relationship complex so
prominent in Deuteronomy, Psalms, and Proverbs. The third term of the complex—relationship to the deity—is also present in *Job*, although perhaps not as
prominently as the piety and life themes. It is seen first of all in the description
of Job as being "one who fears God" (ירא אלהים; 1:1), thus linking Job's piety
with a relationship to the deity. The lone example of Job's piety in the introduction further establishes this link—Job's habit of offering sacrifices to God on
behalf of his children. Here Job's concern is that his children might have
affronted God (ברך אלהים; 1:5[28]) and he desires to ensure their proper relationship to God. This relationship, however, is not one-sided as God also reveals his
part by referring to Job in the highly personal and relational term "my servant"
(עבדי; 1:8), a term of intimacy reserved for precious few in the HB.[29]

  In *Job*, therefore, as in Deuteronomy, Psalms, and Proverbs, themes of piety,
life, and relationship to deity coalesce to form a highly coherent complex.
Cooper is quite correct that the introduction to *Job* does not present a picture of
the mechanical operation of "the act–consequence nexus."[30] However, the
introduction does orient the reader to a much more elaborate and comprehensive
moral and theological world.

  27. For further examples of this complex in Proverbs, see 1:33; 2:7–19; 2:21; 3:13–18, 19–26;
4:3–9, 20–27; 5:7–20; 7:1–5; 8:1–36; 9:6, 10–11; 10:2–7, 9, 16a, 17, 27, 30; 11:4, 8, 19–21; 13:3,
14; 14:11, 27; 15:24, 27; 16:17; 19:16, 23; 20:27; 23:12–14.
  28. The term ברך here is functioning euphemistically. See my discussion below, section 2.3.3.
  29. Most frequently it is applied to Moses. It is also applied to Abraham, Isaac, and Jacob, as
well as several prophets in the Deuteronomistic History (see Clines, *Job 1–20*, 24).
  30. Similar to Clines's usage of this phrase to describe the correlation of piety and blessing in
Job, other scholars refer to "retributive justice." See, e.g., Dhorme, *Job*, lxxix–lxxx; Otto Eissfeldt,
*The Old Testament: An Introduction, Including the Apocrypha and Pseudepigrapha, and also the
Works of Similar Type from Qumran: The History of the Formation of the Old Testament* (trans.
Peter R. Ackroyd; New York: Harper & Row, 1965), 467; Rowley, *Job*, 22; Artur Weiser, *The Old
Testament: Its Formation and Development* (trans. Dorothea M. Barton; New York: Association
Press, 1961), 292.

The coherence and comprehensiveness of this world is buttressed in *Job* by the symbolic wholeness of the very language with which the world is described. That is, the form of the introduction to the prologue, as opposed to the content, also establishes the sense of a coherent moral world. Many commentators have noted the symmetry, coherence, and structural unity of these verses. Newsom, for example, comments on the beauty and balance of the language: the short rhythmic phrases arranged in a patterned repetition of three two-word phrases (איש היה, "There was a man"; בארץ עוץ, "in the land of Uz"; איוב שמו, "his name was Job"), one three-word phrase (והיה האיש ההוא, "that man was"), and three two-word phrases (תם וישר, "blameless and upright"; וירא אלהים, "a fearer of God"; וסר מרע, "a shunner of evil"); the parallelism in the description of Job's character (two sets of parallel descriptors); the rhythmic parallelism in the description of Job's children and possessions; significant numbers (round numbers that are grouped to add up to ten and multiples of ten). According to Newsom, "What [these] suggest is a world in which everything adds up, a world of coherency and wholeness. This I would argue, is the most fundamental desire the prose tale elicits and offers to satisfy, the desire for a world that can be experienced as supremely coherent, a world of utterly unbreachable wholeness."[31]

And yet this symbolically coherent, piety/life/relationship complex gives way to a symbolically problematic scene at the end of the prologue, which foregrounds not life, but death, with its puzzling—and even a little incoherent—mortuary rites. The question that will be pursued in the rest of this chapter is how or why does the prologue move from a scene of the coherent world of the piety/life/relationship complex to a scene of incoherent death? What sort of plot will sustain this movement?

2.2. Death, Life, and Symbolization

To answer these questions one ought first to consider what is at stake in the transition from symbolic unity and wholeness, with its related emphasis on life and liveliness, to symbolic incoherence with its connected emphasis on death. These types of questions factor prominently in the works of the psychohistorian, Robert Jay Lifton, whom I introduced in the previous chapter. While Lifton's focus of study—the human psyche and cultural upheaval—may seem to differ radically from what is at stake in the prologue to *Job*, the particular shape of Lifton's theories, and then his own analysis of certain works of literature show him to be thinking through similar problems to those of the book of Job. A brief look at Lifton's work will be a profitable detour before returning to *Job* with a new perspective on the questions of symbolic coherency and incoherence, life and death.

Lifton's fundamental point of reference in his examination of the human psyche stems from the dual facts that humans always interpret and order reality

---

31. Carol A. Newsom, *The Book of Job: A Contest of Moral Imaginations* (Oxford: Oxford University Press, 2003), 53.

mentally, and that all humans must die. Regarding the former, Lifton argues that humans understand only through paradigms and models, furnished initially by culture, but subject to an individual's tweaking and even rejection and replacement.[32] According to Lifton, who relies on the work of the philosophers Ernst Cassirer and Susanne K. Langer, "human mentation consists of continuous creation and re-creation of images and forms. We perceive nothing, so to speak, nakedly; our only means of taking in the world of objects and people around us is through [an] unending process of reconstituting them."[33]

Humans, therefore, are symbolizing animals, constantly re-creating and re-ordering experiences into symbolic clusters of images and forms, or what Lifton seems to refer to by shorthand, a "mental image."[34] This image is both highly personal, comprising many personal symbolizations (of familial relationships, of sexuality, of death, of social and political issues, and so on) and also shared to some extent across one's culture. Insofar as one's mental image connects with those of others, one can speak of shared images and forms.[35]

Each of these symbolic clusters of images is inseparable from all the forms that constitute the sense of the "self," which is an individual's way of symbolizing his/her sense of his/her own organism, for even "self" is a symbolically constituted entity. "The self is the most inclusive of all individual forms, one's symbolization of one's own organism,"[36] and, according to Lifton, "maintaining the life of the self—an overall sense of organismic vitality—becomes the central motivating principle for psychic action, for the creation and recreation of images and constellations."[37] The very core of human life is dependent upon the integrity of the image, for "its absence or breakdown threatens life."[38]

The symbolizing function of humans therefore pertains to matters of life and death. Whereas Freud argued that humans cannot know their own deaths because the organism cannot envision its non-existence without envisioning itself as envisioner,[39] Lifton, in contrast, argues that "Death is indeed essentially a negation—the epitome of all negations—but that does not mean that the mind has no way of 'representing' death, of constructing its versions of death."[40] And again, "[W]hether or not we imagine our own death as a specific event, we do anticipate the end of the self—its annihilation, cessation (stasis) and total

32. Lifton, *Life of the Self*, 22–23.

33. Lifton, *Protean Self*, 28.

34. In other places he calls this image the "structured anticipation of interaction with the environment" (Lifton, *Broken Connection*, 38).

35. But they cannot be reduced to a single form as Freud does with the Oedipus complex, for example (see Lifton, *Life of the Self*, 75).

36. Lifton, *Broken Connection*, 38.

37. Ibid.

38. Ibid., 38–39.

39. "Death is an abstract concept with a negative content for which no unconscious correlative can be found" (Sigmund Freud, *The Ego and the Id* [trans. Joan Riviere; The International Psycho-Analytical Library 12; London: Hogarth, 1950]). Therefore, according to Freud, humans deny their own deaths.

40. Lifton, *Broken Connection*, 48.

separation (from the world)."[41] Lifton agrees with Freud that we deny death to a certain extent, but argues we do not, and cannot, do so absolutely, for we are never fully ignorant of the fact that we will die. We have a "middle knowledge" of death: we know that we will will die, but our actions and expressions belie that awareness. As discussed above, Lifton suggests that humans "require [a] symbolization of continuity—imaginative forms of transcending death—in order to confront genuinely the fact that we die."[42] Humans have a "compelling and universal inner quest for continuous symbolic relationship to what has gone before and what will continue after our finite individual lives."[43] To this continuous symbolic relationship, Lifton gives the name "symbolic immortality" and he outlines five such modes: the biological, religious, creative, natural, and the experience of transcendence (all discussed earlier).

Any individual mode of symbolic immortality is shaped both by cultural influences and by personal death encounters (death of a friend, war, and so on) and by what Lifton calls death equivalents. Death equivalents can be thought of in terms of three dialectics: connection (between a child and parent, between a person and friends, and so on) and separation; movement (sense of empowerment to act) and stasis (feeling of powerlessness, immobility, and the like); and integrity (sense of wholeness) and disintegration (sense of falling apart).[44] The experiences of personal death encounters and death equivalents (separation, stasis, disintegration), and the experiences of life and life equivalents (connection, movement, integrity) become highly symbolized into the ethical and psychological constellations of symbolic immortality, which are constantly shifting and moving.

But they can also collapse. In fact, Lifton is most interested in this collapse and its ramifications, for according to Lifton, the cessation of image building (also called "desymbolization") spells the cessation of the self's very vitality, and is the theme around which mental illness can be described and understood. This collapse is also where Lifton's theories about symbolization and desymbolization, life and death connect with the book of Job and to the structure of the prologue in particular. For, according to Lifton, what in his age (the late twentieth century) has caused the collapse of viable images is the experience of mass death (in epidemics, wars, and various other disasters) and cultural and historical dislocation. This collapse prompts a "breakdown of social and institutional arrangements that ordinarily anchor human lives."[45] As quoted above, according to Lifton,

> During these upheavals, symbols of longstanding authority are undermined, confronted, or shattered in ways that can produce powerful and painful collective experiences of death and rebirth. There is an outpouring of death imagery, publicly and privately, as

---

41. Ibid., 16.
42. Ibid., 17.
43. Ibid. The quote is copied, almost verbatim, in Lifton, *Life of the Self*, 31.
44. For more on death and life equivalents, see Lifton, *Broken Connection*, 53–59, 60–63, 82–88; idem, *Life of the Self*, 35–40.
45. Lifton, *Protean Self*, 14.

well as feelings of separation, disintegration, and stasis (what I call "death equivalents")
and a questioning of larger human connectedness or symbolic immortality. At such
times, our psychological viability as the cultural animal...is under duress—until new
combinations can reanimate our perceived place in the great chain of being.[46]

The premise of the book of Job is the collapse of a long-standing and powerful
theological system, the piety/life/relationship complex. In the pages that follow I
will argue that the piety/life/relationship complex *is* a system of symbolic
immortality and it functions as a theological "constellation" that orders experience into understandable categories. I will flesh out the implications of this
symbolic system and I will argue that the prologue does, indeed, offer a picture
of desymbolization. *Job* is an exemplar of the processes that Lifton describes.

2.3. *Symbolization and Desymbolization, Life and Death in the Prologue*

Lifton provides useful language with which to describe the introduction to the
prologue. The poetically coherent world of the introduction, with its depicted
system of the life/piety/relationship complex can accurately be described in
Liftonian terms as a highly symbolized, moral, and theological image constellation, with an emphasis on symbolic connectedness, movement, and vitality, and
on integrated coherence. Just as in Lifton's theories, where the mental image
functions as that which interprets and orders reality into coherent symbolic
systems and constellations, the world of the prologue is similarly presented as a
highly coherent system. It is the "image" of a world already ordered in terms of
the life/piety/relationship complex.

Stated differently, the life/piety/relationship complex comprises what Lifton
refers to as a "mode of symbolic immortality." This complex provides "a compelling and universal inner quest for continuous symbolic relationship to what
has gone before and what will continue after."[47] Of the five modes of symbolic
immortality that Lifton outlines, it most closely resembles the "biological mode"
whose emphasis is on family continuity and living on and through one's progeny. This connection is most obvious in Deuteronomy where the "life" aspect of
the complex frequently includes the promise of progeny and the guarantee of
their protection.[48] One also finds it in the prologue to *Job* where children seem to
have special importance: they are mentioned first in the list of all of Job's
"possessions" (1:2); Job makes special efforts to ensure their well-being (1:5);
and the description of Job's losses in 1:13–19 climaxes with the deaths of his
children, the final and most wounding blow to Job.

---

46. Ibid., 15. Although Lifton adduces examples of such symbolic breakdown from the Renaissance until the present in the West, and also from various periods in non-Western history, he argues
that the late twentieth-century exhibits this type of disintegration best (see idem, *Protean Self*,
15–17).

47. Lifton, *Broken Connection*, 17.

48. 4:40; 5:26; 6:1–2; 7:12–13; 11:8–9; 12:28; 30:9. It can also be found in scattered places in
the Psalms (18:50; 22:31; 25:13; 89:5, 30, 37; 102:29; 112:2; 127:3–5) and Proverbs (14:26).

However, Lifton's biological mode of symbolic immortality does not fully describe the life/piety/relationship complex. This complex, in fact, seems to form its own category that might be called the "abundant" mode of symbolic immortality. In this mode, life implies an exaggerated sense of fullness, richness, and abundance. To live is not merely to be alive in a biological sense, but it is to experience all the blessings of the deity, including abundant crops, fine wine, fertile cattle, healthy children, security, and health. To live abundant life is also to live piously in relation to the deity. The crowning achievement of abundant life is not immortality or an afterlife; rather, it is contented, even abundant, death—death at an advanced age (see Job 42:17).

The flip-side of "abundant life" is "meager life" or "death-in-life." If abundant life implies piety and relationship to the deity, meager life implies sinfulness or foolishness and alienation from the deity. Meager life means sickness, drought, war, childlessness and death of progeny, and untimely or early death.[49]

Although images of abundant life predominate in the introduction to the prologue, the threat of meager life or death-in-life is also implied. It is most clearly seen in 1:5 as the threat that sin would result in punishment, death, and alienation from the deity. According to 1:5, Job's habit was that after his children had finished their festivities, he would sanctify them: "He would rise in the morning and offer up a burnt offering for each of them, for Job would reason, 'perhaps my sons sinned and cursed[50] God in their hearts in one way or another.'" Job here is not concerned with sin in general, but with the particular sin that would affront God and therefore result in a breach of the life-giving relationship with the deity.[51] The passage does not overtly state that the consequence of this type of sin is early death,[52] but the implication is that Job's prophylactic sacrifice is to avert potential disaster due to this sin. What Job assumes, and what the prologue symbolizes, is that early death, or death-in-life, has a predictable place in a coherent moral world: it is connected to sin and alienation from God and is the flip-side of abundant life. Death-in-life, therefore, is the type of death that abundant life overcomes.

This mode of symbolic immortality has deep theological and moral ramifications. For to live abundantly—to overcome death symbolically—necessitates a particular mode of conduct and a relationship to the deity. Without right living and right relation, abundant life cannot ensue.

---

49. For a treatment of many of these issues in the context of the Psalms, see John Goldingay, "Death and Afterlife in the Psalms," in Avery-Peck and Neusner, eds., *Judaism in Late Antiquity*, 4:61–85.

50. The term בָּרַךְ here is translated euphemistically as "curse," following the lead of the vast majority of commentators. However, Linafelt surely is correct that the translation of the supposed euphemism is not so easily determined in *Job* or in 1 Kgs 21:10, 13, and Ps 10:3 (see Tod Linafelt, "The Undecidability of BRK in the Prologue to Job and Beyond," *BibInt* 4 [1996]: 154–72).

51. Regardless of whether this sacrifice is an example of Job's extreme piety or an example of his hubris as one who thinks he sees from the position of God, knowing good from evil when others do not. See Ellen van Wolde, "A Text-Semantic Study of the Hebrew Bible: Illustrated with Noah and Job," *JBL* 113 (1994): 19–35 (31–32), for this interpretation.

52. But see Job 2:9 and 1 Kgs 21:10. Job 2:9 will be examined in more detail below.

2.3.1. *Symbolization of Death in the Unfolding Story*

If, in the introduction, Job averts death-in-life through proper relationship with the deity (prophylactic sacrifice), in the unfolding plot of the prologue death explodes to the surface. This is evident initially in *haśśatan*'s plan to test the existence of unmotivated piety, a plan that utilizes death—unexpected and problematic death—to meet its goal: the death and loss of cattle, the death of servants, the death of Job's children. How Job deals with this death, his reactions to his loss, and his theological interpretation of highly personal death—these form the climax of this first substantive section of the prologue. They will answer *haśśatan*'s question about unmotivated piety.

However, as in the introduction to the prologue, not only is the content of the story of interest—death and Job's reaction to it—but also the poetic form that the story takes—how the story is told. For the poetic form of the story adds increasing emphasis on these deaths, buttressing the action of the content of the tale. First of all, the very words the messengers use contribute to the sense of an increasing, singular focus on death. Each messenger scene begins and ends identically: they all begin (except the first, for obvious reasons) "While this one was still speaking another entered and said" (עוד זה מדבר וזה בא ויאמר)[53] and all end with, "I alone escaped to report to you" (ואמלטה רק אני לבדי להגיד לך). Structurally this repetition of introductory and concluding phrases calls attention to what lies between: the specific details of death and loss.

Second, the rapid-fire succession of the four announcements of the messengers contributes to the sense of increasing doom and disaster. Each of these reports follows the same basic pattern: the messenger arrives, gives a report of the disaster, states that he is the sole survivor, and is interrupted by the arrival of another messenger.[54] As Gordis suggests, "The impact of the narrative is heightened by its compression"[55] since relatively few descriptive details are provided. We only hear "the impassioned words of each breathless survivor"[56] who layers on news of death with news of death.

Furthermore, the order of the announcements has a sort of cumulative effect whereby the sense of disaster grows with each successive report, climaxing in the news of the death of Job's children. In the first report, the initial description of the oxen and asses going about their normal business ("ploughing" and "grazing") follows on the heels of the narrator's description of Job's children going about their normal festive routine (1:13). Nothing, apparently, is abnormal. This apparent normality is strongly juxtaposed by the very next phrase by the messenger of the destruction by the Sabeans. The point of the messenger's tale is destruction, loss, and death, not the life and liveliness of the introduction. This

---

53. The fourth messenger begins his report with עַד instead of עוד. James Barr and Jeremy Hughes ("Hebrew *'ad*, Especially at Job 1:18 and Neh 7:3," *JSS* 27 [1982]: 177–92) have demonstrated that the former can also mean "while" rather than its more normal meaning "until."

54. As Georg Fohrer notes (*Das Buch Hiob* [KAT 16; Gütersloh: Gütersloher Verlagshaus G. Mohn, 1963], 88–89), the number 4 seems to represent a totality of destruction in the ancient world. He cites as evidence Ezek 14:12–23; Zech 2:3; Gilgamesh 11.177–85.

55. Gordis, *Job*, 16.

56. Ibid.

point is underscored by the reports of the next two messengers who make no concessions to "normal life" but begin their accounts with the agents and actions of destruction and death (אש אלהים in 1:16; כשדים in 1:17).

The order in which Job's livestock are lost and/or killed also contributes to the cumulative effect and heightens anticipation of the deaths of Job's children. First he loses his oxen and asses, followed by his sheep, and last, his camels. This is almost the complete reversal of the order in which the introduction lists his blessings—children, sheep, camels, oxen and asses.[57] As the reports of the deaths and losses of Job's possessions work their way down the list in the first three reports, it becomes apparent that Job has lost everything with which he was blessed by Yahweh, save his most prized blessing, that which Job made extra efforts to protect from alienation from the deity and divine punishment (1:5)—his children. A sense of ominous dread awaits the arrival of the fourth messenger.

Although the report of Job's biggest loss is saved for last, the fourth messenger, unlike the previous two, will not simply jump into the report of the destruction. Instead, his report will parallel the first in that it will begin with a description of normal life. The force of this description is not the same as the first time around. "In the first message, the contrast between the news of peace and the announcement of disaster was the focus; now the expectation is exclusively upon the inevitable disaster that is surely to be reported, and the good news merely increases the tension."[58] That is, the description of "normal life" simply lengthens the report of the final and most devastating loss to Job, the deaths of his children.[59]

As if to drive this point home—to make it more salient, more obvious—whereas the previous messengers announced the deaths of cattle and servants with euphemistic expressions (הכו לפי־חרב in 1:15, 17; תאכלם in 1:16), the final messenger relates the deaths of Job's children non-euphemistically, with the stark announcement simply that "they died" (וימותו). Linguists posit a number of explanations for the usage of death euphemisms in various cultures. Many point to the connection between euphemisms and cultural taboos (sex, bodily fluids, death, and the like) and note that in earlier societies the word not only names something, but is that very thing. Therefore substitutions were found to talk about death in order not to "conjure" death.[60] This supposed superstitious

---

57. Meier ("Job 1–2," 188–89) also comments on this reverse order. He parallels it to a reversal of creation in Gen 1–3, however.

58. Clines, *Job 1–20*, 33.

59. The Hebrew does not explicitly state that the children were killed, only the "lads" (הנערים). Good's description is apt: "Each successive messenger has used [הנערים] to mean Job's slaves who were killed (vv. 15, 16, 17). The fourth messenger has stated the circumstance, that Job's sons and daughters were having their feast, and when he says that the house fell on the [הנערים], perhaps we are at first relieved: 'Oh, only the slaves.' The relief is momentary, for we quickly realize that [הנערים] can include sons, and we must then assume that here…it also includes the daughters. On further reflection, we may be ashamed that we have underplayed the humanity of slaves" (Good, *Turns of Tempest*, 197).

60. See, for various versions of this theory, Brian Cooper, "Euphemism and Taboo of Language (with Particular Reference to Russian)," *Australian Slavonic and East European Studies* 7 (1993):

connection of the word "death" with death itself seems rather weak in the book of Job and in the HB in general, for literal words for death are used with frequency, especially in *Job*.[61] A more likely explanation is offered by Allan and Burridge who theorize other motivations for death taboos in various cultures: fear of the loss of loved ones; fear of the disintegrating body; fear of the end of life and not knowing what comes next; fear of malevolent spirits; fear of an absurd and meaningless death.[62] Further, others suggest that the usage of euphemisms likely pertains to the consideration of one's interlocutor: euphemisms are used "to conceal embarrassing or unpleasant reality," "to minimise painful or disagreeable impressions," or "to develop in the interlocutor a favourable disposition or impression."[63] In this passage in *Job*, the former two seem most probable. If the first three messengers soften the reality of death—or at least its impact—with euphemistic expressions, its cold reality must be confronted in the announcement of the final messenger with the encounter with the literal word, "death."[64] The death taboo has been broken and now Job must face this stark reality.

Of the various explanations for death taboos suggested by Allan and Burridge, the fear of absurd or meaningless death is perhaps the most intriguing in the context of the prologue to *Job*, for *haśśatan*'s plan to test unmotivated piety has been set up as a crisis of death. Previously, in the introduction to the prologue, death found a seemingly natural place in the symbolically coherent moral world. Now, however, *haśśatan*'s plan has, in Lifton's words, desymbolized death: it now marks a place of confusion, an incoherence, an aporia. Death ceases to signify properly in the life/piety/relationship complex, for now Job's piety and his assumed relationship to the deity have resulted in problematic and early death. And in the poetics of the telling of this desymbolization, emphasis steadily marches through the progression of euphemisms that attempt to soften the impact of desymbolized death, climaxing in Job's encounter with literal, stark מות—the bold revelation of the death of Job's children. The question now becomes: How will Job interpret desymbolized death? The taboo now fully transgressed, will death be understood as absurd? Will desymbolized death accomplish its purposes and prove the non-existence of unmotivated piety?

61–84 (62); Kathryn Kirkpatrick, "The Figurative Language of Death," *The Secol Review* 7 (1983): 27–35 (30); Robert Strozier, "The Euphemism," *Language Learning* 16 (1966): 63–70 (63).

61. See my linguistic analysis, section 1.5.1.

62. Keith Allan and Kate Burridge, *Euphemism and Dysphemism: Language Used as Shield and Weapon* (New York: Oxford University Press, 1991), 153–71.

63. Cooper, "Ephemism and Taboo," 62. See also Anna Tambor-Krzyzanowska, "L'euphemisme: Comment parler de la mort en français et en polonais," *Verbum* 16 (1993): 125–30 (125); S. Widlak, "L'interdiction linguistique en français d'aujourd'hui," 43 (1965): 932–45. For the usage of euphemism in the HB, see Marvin H. Pope, "Euphemism and Dysphemism in the Bible," in *Probative Pontificating in Ugaritic and Biblical Literature: Collected Essays* (ed. Mark S. Smith; UBL 10; Münster: Ugarit-Verlag, 1994), 279–91.

64. John Gross, writing about death euphemisms comments that "There are times…when more or less everyone would agree that direct talk of death ought to be carefully avoided… What are needed are words which blur or stave off, if only for an instant, the dreadful finality of the facts" (John Gross, "Intimations of Mortality," in *Fair of Speech: The Uses of Euphemism* [ed. D. J. Enright; Oxford: Oxford University Press, 1985], 203–19).

2.3.2. *Imaging Death*

Job's reaction comes in two varieties, actions and words, which together contain a few puzzling interpretive features. The first is found in Job's actions. That he would perform various mourning rituals—rising and tearing his robe, shaving his head (1:20)—seems a rather reasonable and conventional response to the various disasters. But that he would fall to the ground and worship seems a bit out of place.[65] Newsom is correct to identify the puzzling relation of grief to worship (rather than to a curse, for example) as the "problem" of Job's actions. "Attention turns to Job's words, which bear the weight of rendering persuasive a response that is not self-interpreting."[66]

Job's verbal response, however, is not exactly self-interpreting either. Commentators note with frequency the logical inconsistency in Job's opening phrase "Naked I came out of my mother's womb and naked I shall return there" where mother's womb and womb-of-the earth/Sheol converge metaphorically.[67] The more basic interpretive problem, however, is why Job would utter this statement at all. Why would news of the problematic deaths of his children and servants, and loss and deaths of his livestock prompt Job to utter an existential statement of his *own* mortality? What is the relation of "desymbolized deaths of loved ones" to "my death?"

The contrast to other reactions to news of death in the HB is most instructive. In case after case, the words that accompany the mourning ritual make clear that the focus of mourning is on the loss of a loved one.[68] David's reaction to the news of the death of his son, Absalom, is typical: he weeps and cries out in distress over the fate of his son (2 Sam 18:33). But not Job: for him the loss of those he loved most dearly prompts a highly personal statement of his own movement from the non-existence of the womb to the non-existence of death.

In fact, the very words Job uses to describe this non-existence stand out in contrast to those of the messenger who reported his children's deaths. Having been confronted by this messenger with the stark and bold reality of desymbolized מות, Job now in essence "effaces" this reality with the most genteel of all euphemisms, "I shall return there [to the womb of the mother/earth]" (1:21) —even using a euphemism ("there") for a euphemism ("womb") of death. If

---

65. Good (*Turns of Tempest*, 197) and Gordis (Gordis, *Job*, 17) both argue that worship is part of the conventional mourning rite. Pham (*Mourning in the Ancient Near East*, 25), however, argues that חוה "is not such clearly mourning ceremony vocabulary" as the other words describing Job's actions (although she also lists Josh 7:6–7; Ezra 9:5–6; 1 Macc 4:36–40 as examples of mourning and prayer converging). For other commentators who argue that worship here is distinct from mourning rites, see Clines, *Job 1–20*, 35; Driver and Gray, *Job*, 1:18–19; Hartley, *Job*, 77; Rowley, *Job*, 33. See also Newsom, "Job," 352 who cites as supporting evidence 1 Sam 1:3; Ps 95:6; Ezek 46:9.

66. Newsom, *Contest of Moral Imaginations*, 57.

67. The issue, of course, is the reference of the word שמה. For an elaborate discussion of the issue, including a consideration of how contemporary scholars deal with the issue, see Gregory Vall, "The Enigma of Job 1,21a," *Bib* 76 (1995): 325–42.

68. See, e.g., Gen 37:34–35; Josh 7:6–7; 1 Sam 4:12, 17; 2 Sam 18:32–19:1; cf. 2 Sam 1:2–4 and 11–12 where the narrator makes clear that the focus of mourning is on the deaths of loved ones.

previously מות stood for problematic death—death that failed to signify properly in the abundant mode of symbolic immortality—what is at stake with Job's euphemistic expression wherein he now associates death with the protective, life-giving womb of the mother?

The answer to this question seems to be that for Job the issue is not so much the deaths of ones he loved, but death itself. With one simple phrase, Job has taken all of the cold reality announced by the word מות—problematic, incoherent, desymbolized death—and resymbolized it into a symbolically coherent, simple narrative of the universal human life cycle, for which Job stands as the prime exemplar. "Death" (מות), now, is not that which disrupts the symbolically coherent world of the life/piety/relationship complex; "death" (שׁמה) rather, is the return to the womb of the mother/earth—that protective, safe place. What was desymbolized through *haśśatan*'s plan has now been resymbolized in Job's response. One might say that Job refuses to concede מות. When confronted by it he transforms it into "womb" (בטן).

The second line of Job's verbal response reveals what allows Job's resymbolization of death into this coherent narrative of protective non-existence to protective non-existence: "Yahweh gives and Yahweh takes" (1:21).[69] Job juxtaposes the actions of coming out of the womb and returning to it with Yahweh's actions of giving and taking such that, far from the more typical conception of death as transformation to a shadowy existence in Sheol separate from Yahweh's presence, here non-existence falls under Yahweh's protective care.[70] He is the one who assigns humans to the shelter of the womb. In Job's resymbolization of death, Yahweh is the very guarantor of the coherence of death, the very one who brings about the "return" (שׁוב) to the womb.

But in order to resymbolize death Job has had to reinterpret the terms of the life/piety/relationship complex. First of all, by emphasizing that humans are born and die "naked," that is, with no clothes, no protective shelter, no possessions,[71] life is no longer abundant life—fertile livestock, abundant crops, progeny, and health. It is simply cast as the biological process of birth: coming from the mother's womb. Death, too, is discussed neither positively, as the culmination of an abundant life, nor negatively, as the corollary of sin and alienation from God. Instead it is the structural parallel to birth and simply completes the biological cycle.

Second, in Job's resymbolization piety is completely absent. Humans are not assigned any sort of moral roles in life. They are reduced only to fulfilling the biological necessities of life and death. This fact connects to the third term of the life/piety/relationship, for the transformation of the terms of the relationship to Yahweh is of primary importance. If, in the life/piety/relationship complex the relationship to the deity was understood as hierarchical, now the relationship is

---

69. Newsom ("Job," 352) notes that the Hebrew word order shifts the emphasis from the action of the verbs to the subject of the verbs, Yahweh (יהוה נתן ויהוה לקח).

70. On other aspects of the strangeness of this verse in the context of general conceptions of Sheol in the HB, see Fohrer, *Hiob*, 93.

71. See ibid; Newsom, *Contest of Moral Imaginations*, 57–58.

virtually totalitarian. Traditionally God was considered the dominant partner, choosing Israel, demanding obedience, which he would reward with blessing, while humans contributed to the relationship by choosing to serve God, acting piously, and opting for proper types of behavior. In Job's resymbolization, this reciprocity is lost. Humans have no choices, no duties to fulfill. They are only recipients of what the deity gives and takes, namely, life and death.

Furthermore, God's role in the relationship is also significantly reduced, for God has no part in blessing piety and in protecting and loving humans. God *only* brings humans to life and brings them to death. Adding emphasis to this reduced, minimal conception of the relationship to the deity is that God brings humans into the world naked—implying at once vulnerability (that God does *not* protect and shelter humans) and without possessions (that God does *not* provide the blessings of abundant life).[72] So also do humans come naked to death.

Nowhere is the resymbolization of relationship with the deity more apparent than in Job's usage of "womb" imagery. In Deuteronomy the fertility of the womb (פרי בטנך; "fruit of the womb") forms one of a number of blessings that comprise the abundant life. God provides the fruitful womb as a blessing for the faithful, and it therefore represents both obedience to the law and proper relationship to the deity (see Deut 7:13; 28:4, 11; 30:9). Likewise, in the Psalms the fertile womb is viewed as a reward from God (Ps 127:3), but more than this, the womb also speaks of the deep intimacy between God and the Psalmist. In Ps 139, for example, the Psalmist confesses the tenderness of a God who carefully formed him in his mother's womb. This intimacy then leads the Psalmist to praise God (Ps 139:13–18). Similarly, in Ps 22:10–11 the Psalmist uses the intimacy established from the moment of his birth to plead with God not to abandon their relationship and come to the Psalmist's aid (see also Ps 71:6).

In Job's resymbolization, however, all the rich, intimate "womb" language is gone. Certainly Job still acknowledges that birth is the result of God "giving" life, but this gift no longer establishes the intimate relationship that will sustain life, as it does for the Psalmist. Now, the gift only consists of the biological process of "naked" birth alone, apart from protection, possessions, and other blessings of abundant life. Furthermore, unlike in Deuteronomy where womb imagery ties into the excessive *multiplication* of life (Deut 7:13: "he will *multiply* you and bless the fruit of your womb"), in Job's resymbolization, the womb now represents a narrative of a zero-sum gain: a human is born, a human dies; God gives, God takes. The womb now is no longer a metonymy for abundant life, but for bare, minimal biological existence.

So much has been lost in Job's resymbolization of life and death. Life is no longer abundant life, but stark, nominal existence. Piety is no longer the expression of the human relationship with the deity. Relationship with the deity is minimal and cast in totalitarian terms. But what is lost in this resymbolization is replaced by gain: Job has found an alternative symbolization that renders desymbolized מות intelligible again. Job's resymbolization is both theologically

---

72. For the connection of nakedness with lack of provisions and protection, see Deut 28:48.

crucial and creative: Yahweh's actions of giving and taking now interpret the catastrophic deaths of Job's children and draw these seemingly desymbolized deaths into the coherent world of life and death under God's direction. Job's children did not die (מות) incoherent, desymbolized deaths as the servant claimed; rather, the children were "taken" (לקח) by God into the protective care of the "womb" of the mother. As Lifton theorizes, Job enacts: the facticity of death is not received nakedly, but reconfigured and placed in light of a constellation of imagery with Yahweh at the center.

The expression of loss and gain in Job's resymbolization finds its fitting conclusion in Job's final statement: "ברך be the name of Yahweh" (1:21). Normally ברך is translated "blessed" so that Job's last words in this unit enact the piety of blessing. Such a grateful response to Yahweh no doubt pertains to Job's success in attaining a measure of symbolic immortality for his children, for himself, and for the world.[73] To Job death now is only a piece of a much larger world directed by God, albeit not the same world of the life/piety/relationship complex.

However, in the prologue the meaning of ברך is far from certain. In some cases it fairly obviously a euphemism for "curse" (1:5, 11; 2:5).[74] Here, in 1:21, it is also possible to understand the "curse" sense of the term in Job's words. For just as the positive "blessing" sense of the term as a grateful act of piety corresponds to the positive aspects of what Job gained in his resymbolization (attaining symbolic immortality for his children), so the negative "curse" sense of the term as a protest or rebellion against God would correspond to the negative aspects of what Job has lost in his resymbolization. God *only* provides a minimal life of bare biological existence with no protection, sustenance, or meaningful relationship with the deity. Life is meager at best, and God is wholly responsible. Job, therefore, curses God.

The precise sense of the term ברך depends on how, and with what inflection Job pronounces the line—information impossible to glean from the text. This ambiguity of the sense of ברך, however, indicates that Job's resymbolized world has shifted from what it was previously. To ברך the name of Yahweh is no longer to perform a simple act of piety by the standards of the life/piety/relationship complex. Now, to ברך the name of Yahweh is either to express gratitude for Yahweh's central role in rendering death meaningful again apart from this complex, or it is to express rebellion against the meagerness of life that this resymbolization of Yahweh's role implies.

2.3.3. Desymbolization and Death

Job's resymbolized world, however, is soon to be shaken again when God gives *haśśatan* permission to strike Job (נגע; 2:5–6), a task *haśśatan* sets out to do in the final section of the prologue, 2:7–10. Significantly, this section is the least

---

73. This interpretation is far, indeed, from those that take this phrase as a confession of passive acceptance of whatever the deity doles out (see, e.g., Dhorme, *Job*, 13; Fohrer, *Hiob*, 93–94; Hartley, *Job*, 78; Pope, *Job*, 16). I agree with Weiss (*Story of Job's Beginning*, 61) that Job's statement renders his blessing of Yahweh's name intelligible, but for very different reasons.

74. See below, section 2.3.3, for its meaning in 2:9.

poetically coherent of all sections of the prologue, and it is the most semantically ambiguous.

Unlike Job's response to disaster in 1:20–21, where Job's actions and words were reflections of the coherent moral order that he perceived himself to be living in, here actions and words seem of a different type altogether. The contrast is striking. Previously, Job's response of grief culminated in worship of Yahweh. This time, Job's grief is more muted: he is seated among ashes—symbols of mourning[75]—but he performs no rites.[76] More importantly, previously mourning led to worship of Yahweh; here, mourning leads to nothing—Job only tends his sores. Previously also, mourning and worshipping led to Job's resymbolization such that a confession of Yahweh's direction of life and death could be affirmed; here, Job's wife, not Job, breaks the silence, and her command is terse, caustic, and abrupt: "Curse God and die!" (2:9). And perhaps most tellingly, whereas previously Job's verbal response to his situation provided the interpretive frame in which his actions of grief and worship made sense, here, the verbal response of Job's wife raises more interpretive quandaries than it solves.[77]

Just what does Job's wife mean by ordering her husband to "Curse God and die"? Contemporary commentators see a number of possibilities. Many, following Augustine's lead, suggest that "the narrator has Job's wife serve as the earthly mouthpiece for the hidden Satan"[78] and that her order is another trial that Job must endure.[79] But equally possible, according to other commentators, is that she is being dutiful: she believes in Job's innocence and that he is maintaining his integrity (בתמתך), and she is urging him to die in order that he be released him from his suffering.[80] Newsom suggests that her statement seems to play off of the two meanings of the word "integrity" (תמה)—integrity as conformity to religious norms or integrity as guileless honesty.[81] If taken to be the former, her entire statement seems to mean that if Job blesses God as before (taking ברך literally), she feels he will be committing act of deceit; if the latter, then Job must curse God and therefore violate social integrity that forbids such a

---

75. As a sign of mourning, ashes, functioning quite like dust, were thrown on the head (2 Sam 13:19; possibly Isa 61:3) or on the clothes (Esth 4:1) or were lain on or rolled in (Esth 4:3; Jer 6:26; Ezek 27:30). See further, Morris Jastrow, "Dust, Earth, and Ashes as Symbols of Mourning among the Ancient Hebrews," *JAOS* 20 (1904): 133–50 (133–35); Ward, "Mourning Customs," 6–8.

76. Clines and Newsom argue correctly that the Hebrew syntax implies that Job's sitting on ashes is a continuous action, not a new one. Possibly Job is still mourning for his children (Clines, *Job 1–20*, 5; Gordis, *Job*, 8; Newsom, "Job," 355).

77. See Weiss, *Story of Job's Beginning*, 72–74, for another comparison of Job's reactions in the two scenes.

78. Habel, *Job*, 96.

79. This suggestion comes from at least as early as Thomas Aquinas (see *The Literal Exposition on Job: A Scriptural Commentary Concerning Providence* [trans. Anthony Damico; Classics in Religious Studies 7; Atlanta: Scholars Press, 1989], 94) and is echoed throughout the history of interpretation. For a particularly strong statement of this position, see Victor Sasson, "The Literary and Theological Function of Job's Wife in the Book of Job," *Bib* 79 (1998): 86–90 (87).

80. See, e.g., Clines, *Job 1–20*, 51; Terrien, "Job," 921.

81. See Janzen, *Job*, 49–51, for a similar interpretation of תמה.

curse.[82] Good sees the most possibilities, suggesting that her opening line, מחזיק בתמתך, might be a sarcastic question, or a statement of fact. This ambiguity means that in the second line (ברך אלהים ומת) the imperatives are also ambiguous. This command could urge a farewell (say goodbye to God and die [taking ברך as "bless"]); a rebellion (throw it in God's face and pay the consequence of death); an encouragement (go on in your integrity even until the point of death); a plea for Job to have pity on himself (curse God and be released from your suffering).[83]

As some of these interpretations suggest—and what contributes to the confusion of her statement—is that Job's wife, in urging the curse, uses the euphemism, "bless" (ברך) (a euphemism seen earlier in 1:5, 11; 2:5). But in this context, the possibility arises that ברך is to be taken literally: that Job's wife, seeing the disruption of the system of justice and how virtue leads only to calamity, urges Job to "bless" God (be virtuous) in order to hasten his death.[84] Linafelt suggests other possibilities for a literal sense of ברך: Job's wife might be saying, "Still you hold fast to your integrity; continue to bless God, though you will die"; or more sarcastically, "Still you hold fast to your integrity; continue to bless God [for all the good it has done to you] and you will die."[85]

The interpretive possibilities of a mere six Hebrew words are as impressive as they are seemingly inexhaustible. Murphy's statement rings true: "Job's wife now speaks for the first time, and the import of her words is not clear."[86] Even more impressive is that this level of interpretive ambiguity is found in what Newsom describes as a "didactic tale," which, like all didactic tales, has "a necessarily authoritarian relationship to meaning. Within the world of didactic narrative, truth is neither plural nor elusive nor contestable but is unitary, unambiguous, and absolute."[87] At first glance, this description seems to apply to every part of the Joban tale, except for Job's wife's brief, but enigmatic speech.

Upon closer examination, though, the entire unit that narrates Job's affliction (2:7–11) seems to be less than unambiguous and absolute. First of all, Job's

---

82. Newsom, "Job," 356.

83. Good, *Turns of Tempest*, 200.

84. The vast majority of commentators are loathe to concede ambiguity here. They tend to support what Linafelt calls "the standard euphemism theory," that since scribes so wanted to avoid the notion of cursing God, when they came across a text with a "curse" word next to God's name, they inserted the euphemism ברך instead of a word meaning "curse." Two commentators at least suggest that the case might not be so transparent (Cooper, "Reading and Misreading," 77; Good, *Turns of Tempest*, 196), while one traces the implications of this ambiguity throughout *Job*, which he ends up describing as undecidable in Derrida's sense (Linafelt, "Undecidability of BRK," 154–72). Van Wolde ("Text-Semantic Study," 33) also sees ambiguity, but only with the usage of ברך in 2:9. Guillaume, for his part, argues against the majority of scholars by reading "curse" in some places where most translate "bless" and vice versa. Most notable is 1:21 where he argues Job, in fact, does curse God. He does not admit ambiguity, however. See Philippe Guillaume, "Caution: Rhetorical Questions!," *BN* 103 (2000): 11–16 (11–12). Kermode maps out how this ambiguity is displayed in some works of art (Frank Kermode, "The Uses of Error," *Theology* 89 [1986]: 425–31).

85. Linafelt, "Undecidability of BRK," 167.

86. Murphy, *Job*, 13.

87. Newsom, *Contest of Moral Imaginations*, 42.

response to his wife's baffling statement pales in comparison to his non-verbal and verbal reactions to the previous news of the deaths of his children. Here Job's verbal response to disaster does not, as before, render the disaster a cause for worship. Job's more muted reaction seems to catch the eye of the narrator, whose endorsement of Job is, itself, far more muted than in the previous case. Here, the narrator merely claims, "In all this, Job did not sin with his lips" (2:10), rather than previously: "In all of this Job did not sin and ascribe to God folly" (1:10). The difference between the two is not overly astounding, but what the narrator says the second time around is as interesting as what he does not say: one surely is made to wonder whether Job did ascribe folly to God this time. Probably not, but neither did he ascribe to God praise as he did previously. Further, if he did not sin with his lips, could he have sinned another way—in his heart, as several have contended?[88] Like Job's wife's statement, the narrator's tantalizingly invites a variety of interpretive possibilities.[89]

The invitation to interpretive possibilities, however, is not a feature of didactic tales. Nor so is poetic imbalance. According to Newsom, the

> moral imagination of didactic literature prizes coherency. Aesthetically, this value is expressed in the predilection for redundancy and the elimination of extraneous detail. It also underwrites the resolutely monologic discourse of didactic fiction. Multiple voices not subject to a central controlling voice would threaten such coherency.[90]

This was seen earlier in the introduction to the prologue, where the symbolic coherence and aesthetic symmetry of the language mirrored the dominant, unambiguous world of the life/piety/relationship complex.[91] In contrast, here, the sense of interpretive ambiguity in this narrative unit is buttressed by a concomitant sense of poetical imbalance, which emerges when this unit is compared to the rest of the prologue. In the introduction (1:1–5) there were short rhythmic phrases, parallelism in description of Job's character, rhythmic order in the description of Job's children and possessions, and highly symbolically significant numbers. The two heavenly scenes (1:6–12; 2:1–6) are virtual mirror images of each other, where details of setting are identical, much of the dialogue is identical, and where each scene enacts a highly stylized conversation between God and *haśśatan*. In the first scene of Job's trial (1:13–22), the message of disaster arrives via four overlapping, and virtually identical, messengers whose reported speech follows a distinct pattern and contains shared language. Job's own spoken reaction to the disasters comes in two brief, symmetrical phrases, each one displaying typical Hebrew parallelism, followed by his own confession of praise.

---

88. See Robert W. E. Forrest, "The Two Faces of Job: Imagery and Integrity in the Prologue," in *Ascribe to the Lord: Biblical and Other Essays in Memory of Peter C. Craigie* (ed. Lyle Eslinger and Glen Taylor; JSOTSup 67; Sheffield: JSOT Press, 1988), 385–98, for an elaborate statement of this position. This interpretation dates back to the Talmud (*b. Bat.* 16a).

89. Van Wolde argues that the subtle differences between Job's two spoken responses reveals a growing sense of doubt in the second, compared to the steadfast faith of the first. See van Wolde, "Text-Semantic Study," 34.

90. Newsom, *Contest of Moral Imaginations*, 46.

91. See ibid., 42–46.

Moreover, each of these previous scenes (after the first one) opens with the identically stylized setting phrase, "One day…" (וַיְהִי הַיּוֹם; 1:6, 13; 2:1), which acts as a poetic marker to separate each scene from the others and thus maintains a sense of poetic structure. Tellingly, this poetic structure is broken with the second testing scene (2:7–11). Not only so, this scene lacks almost all of the structural order and stylization that its counterpart (1:13–21) has in abundance.[92] Instead, there is only a terse description of *haśśatan*'s affliction upon Job's body, and Job's reaction to the affliction. No poetic arrangement of four overlapping messengers whose messages build to a crescendo; only the basic facts. There is no stylized patterning of the verbal response to the affliction as there was previously. Now Job's wife speaks in short, highly ambiguous statements, and Job responds in kind. Furthermore, *haśśatan*, himself, appears out of place in this scene. Previously, human characters appeared only in earthly scenes (1:1–5, 13–21) and heavenly characters appeared only in heavenly scenes (1:6–12; 2:1–6). Here, however, *haśśatan* appears in an earthly scene, out of his normal place in the heavenly realm.[93]

Clines understands the setting phrase, "One day…," to operate as a marker of the shift from earthly scenes to heavenly ones and back. The lack of this phrase in 2:7 signals to Clines "the impingement of the divine world upon the human" paving the way for *haśśatan*'s appearance on earth.[94] In Driver and Gray's words, the heavenly scene "dissolves" into the earthly one.[95] What might really be transpiring, however, is the dissolving of the symbolic world of the authoritarian didactic tale itself. For as interpretive ambiguity opens up the tale to competing interpretive possibilities not consistent with the authoritarian, monological relation to truth, so also the highly stylized, symbolically ordered and coherent story world ceases to hold its shape.

And this sense of dissolving or collapsing is focused on the highly ambiguous statement of Job's wife to her husband: "Curse/bless God and die." Above, various interpretive possibilities were explored, all of which surrounded the sense of the words "integrity" (תמה) and "bless/curse" (ברך). I have reserved discussing the final word—מות—until now. Seemingly free of the translational ambiguities of ברך and the semantic ambiguities of תמה, the word apparently signifies the simple and obvious meaning, "death." However, as with the first occurrence of this word in the announcement of the final messenger, the word מות here reveals much more. First of all, God's restriction on *haśśatan* that he spare Job's life means that Job's only encounter with death in this second test scene comes from his wife's mouth. Unlike the previous scene, where Job encountered several reports of death that employed death euphemisms before encountering stark, literal, and desymbolizing מות—euphemisms that served

---

92. The exception might be the description of Job being afflicted from his feet until his head (2:7). This description appears to be in line with the hyperbolic description of Job's virtue, possessions, and losses previously. See Clines, *Job 1–20*, 47.

93. Ibid., 9.

94. Ibid.

95. Driver and Gray, *Job*, 1:22.

simultaneously to soften the impact of the devastating news and to direct attention away from the incoherence and incomprehensibility of the various deaths—here Job immediately encounters desymbolized מות. And this time, the desymbolizing effects of מות are felt in the very poetic coherence of the story world. For while in the previous scene desymbolized death resulted in the collapse of the life/piety/relationship complex but left the symbolic-poetic coherence of the language of that unit intact, now the encounter with מות threatens to collapse even that poetic coherence. Job's story world spirals toward the abyss.

Further adding to the desymbolizing effects of literal מות in the mouth of Job's wife is the precise formulation of her statement: ברך אלהים ומת ("bless/curse God and die"). This phrase implies a logical connection between the action of blessing/cursing and dying, as if the two were somehow related. However, the ambiguity of the sense of the signifier ברך draws attention also to the ambiguities and theological problems surrounding desymbolized מות. What reality does *this* signifier point to? Certainly to the cessation of life, but as Lifton argues (and as Job's resymbolization of literal "death" in 1:21 indicates), this "reality" requires interpretation—it requires placement in some sort of constellation of symbolic imagery in order to be made sense of. Yet if literal death does not have any place in the symbolic system of abundant life, literal death stands only for desymbolization: the paralysis of this system of symbolization leading, perhaps, to its collapse. This is the sense that מות had on the lips of the fourth messenger: the literal death of Job's children signaled the desymbolization of the world of the symbolization of abundant life.

On the lips of Job's wife, literal death has a related function. Whatever referent מות points to is obfuscated by its apparent close relation to the ambiguities of the word ברך, and more generally, to the overall ambiguity of her statement, and more generally still, to the basic sense of ambiguity and dissolution of the narrative and poetic world in this scene. On her lips, מות stands far from any symbolic system that would ground it and give it symbolic sense. Literal death is desymbolized, and paradoxically, stands for this very desymbolization.

Does Job make an attempt to resymbolize this time around? His actions (or lack thereof) and words suggest yes, but not in the same way as before. Most important is what he does not do. He rejects his wife's command (2:10a) and refuses to succumb to מות. Had he decided to curse/bless and die he would have accepted the reality of disorienting, uninterpretable, desymbolized death, and his own death likewise would have been utterly meaningless. Furthermore, *haśśatan* would have been proved right, and both the life/piety/relationship complex *and* Job's attempted resymbolization of life and death under the direction of God (1:21) would have definitively been proved farcical. Finally, the reader would be left in theological quicksand, without the firm ground of a system of symbolic immortality on which to stand. Desymbolization would have ruled the day.

This Job does not accept. Instead he resymbolizes death in a short question with massive theological ramifications. He asks his wife, "Shall we receive good from God, but not evil?" (2:10b). Although this question locates disaster and death along a similar binary scale as did his previous resymbolization, this time

around the extremes are not biological birth and death, but good (טוב) and evil
(רע). This new pair resonates in the life/piety/relationship complex where they
stand for the two extremes of abundant life, and meager life or death-in-life. In
Deuteronomy, טוב is the description of the life of obedience to the deity, and
stands for the abundant life and blessing that result from relationship to God,
while רע stands for disobedience and implies the sickness, dispossession, and
death that result from alienation from God.[96] Similarly, in the Psalms, the
extremes of טוב and רע stand for human conduct, distinguishing humans and
indicating whether one stands in relationship to the deity or not,[97] while Proverbs
uses the pair both to designate a person's deeds and as epithets to distinguish the
wise from the foolish.[98] In general, in the life/piety/relationship complex, טוב
and רע function to indicate a person's actions, describe the results of relationship or alienation from the deity, and designate a sort of ontological description
of that person, indicating whether he or she stands in relationship to the deity or
not.

In Job's resymbolization, however, טוב and רע are simply what one receives
from God, much in the same way that in his earlier resymbolization birth and
death were simply received from God. The relationship again is cast in totalitarian terms. More significantly, though, is the content of טוב and רע. In Job's
mouth טוב undoubtedly refers to the blessings recounted in the introduction to
the prologue: fertile livestock, multiple children, life, fecundity, and liveliness—
all of which corresponds to the טוב of the life/piety/relationship complex. The
term רע, on the other hand, signifies very differently in Job's mouth than in the
life/piety/relationship complex. There, even though indicating the opposite of
piety, life, and relationship to the deity, it still signified in relation to that
complex, *within* that same symbolic system. It was just the flip-side of the same
coin. On Job's lips, however, רע represents all the "evil" that had happened to
him—the desymbolized deaths of his livestock and children, the affliction that
left him just short of death. In Job's resymbolization, רע represents *desymbolized* מות with which his wife has just confronted him. It therefore stands for
that which is absolutely outside of any system of symbolic immortality—that
which cannot be interpreted and understood and accounted for theologically.
And in Job's resymbolization, God is responsible for this רע; he is the one who
gives it, despotically, to humans.

The implications of this resymbolization are potentially enormous (in both
senses of the word!). It might not simply be that Job is affirming that God brings
both blessings and harm, and that God knows what he is doing.[99] Nor might this
simply be a demonstration of Job's absolute piety, that he is willing to accept all

96. This is most bluntly stated in Deut 30:15–16: "See, I have set before you today life and
good, death and bad. I have commanded you this day to love Yawheh your God, to walk in his ways,
and to keep his commandments, laws and rules, that you may live and increase and Yahweh your
God may bless you in the land that you will enter and possess."

97. See Pss 34:14–23; 36:2–5; 37:27–29; 52:3–9.

98. See Prov 12:13–14; 14:19, 22; 15:3; 28:10. See also 15:15 and 31:10.

99. Clines, *Job 1–20*, 54.

that God dispenses.[100] Both of these explanations seem to imply that God operates within a coherent system of symbolic immortality—a coherent moral and
theological world—which, although not always obvious to humans, nevertheless
is upheld by God.[101] But this is not the case. In Job's mouth טוב and רע do not
even signify in the same symbolic system. While טוב may represent blessings,
piety, life, and relationship, רע represents desymbolized death and that which
fails to register in the symbolic system of abundant life. The terms טוב and רע
are not just a simple binary in an either/or symbolic system, but they stand for
the entire system (the טוב of the life/piety/relationship complex) *and* that which
calls this entire system into question (desymbolized, incoherent, unintelligible
רע).[102]

Further still, if in the symbolic system of abundant life God was understood
as absolutely central to the system as the partner in the hierarchical relationship
responsible for both for the design and the operation of the system, now, in
Job's resymbolization, God is also responsible for רע—for that which calls the
system into question including its center, namely God. God, therefore, is responsible both for the system in which God can be known (טוב) *and* for the collapse
of this system and the collapse of the ability to know God (רע). The implications
of this resymbolization are dizzying. And so Job sits in and astounded, death-
like silence (2:13).

2.4. *Death at the End*

This chapter began by noting a quirk in the narrative in the final scene of the
prologue (2:11–13): references to death are all over, and yet no one has died; or
rather, mourning rites, which are prompted by and point to death, are performed
in the absence of that which prompts and is pointed to by mourning rites. This
final scene is fitting for the prologue, for the plan to test unmotivated piety has
been set up as a crisis of death and as the plot has progressed emphasis has
shifted, gradually and subtly, to the symbolization of death. The deaths of Job's
livestock and children may have desymbolized death briefly in 1:13–19, but Job
quickly resymbolized death in 1:20 in terms that, while not as optimistic as the
symbolization of abundant life, maintained relationship with the deity and
explained his children's deaths. His second encounter with מות in 2:9 prompted
a new resymbolization, which, while seemingly maintaining a sense of relationship with the deity within a symbolic system, also threatened the intelligibility
of any such system. Job desymbolized even while he resymbolized.

---

100. Habel, *Job*, 96.

101. A third alternative is that in this speech Job is accepting a world of randomness, which
would seem to imply an incoherent system of symbolic immortality.

102. Though much of the literature of the HB affirms the symbolization of abundant life (what I
am describing as the טוב aspect of Job's speech), I do not want to suggest that the ancients always
assigned meaning to experiences based on this symbolic system. The ancients, rather, seemed to be
cognizant of unexplainable phenomena that could not be made to fit this predominant system. What
Job does, although in an abbreviated and suggestive fashion, is to explore the implications of what
does not fit.

Finally, the prologue ends with a last scene of death. But death does not signify properly. Death is pointed to everywhere, but death is not present—no one has died. In Job's silence, desymbolized death and incoherence rise to the fore. But Job will soon speak again. Indeed, he will speak effusively. Will he attempt to resymbolize death again? Will he flesh out the (desymbolizing) implications of his last attempt at resymbolization? To the poetic dialogues we now turn.

Chapter 3

DESYMBOLIZED DEATH IN JOB'S EARLY SPEECHES (CHAPTERS 3–20, PART ONE)

The deathly silence at the end of the prologue gives way to an explosion of talk in the poetic dialogues. Fittingly, Job's opening speech after his seven-day silence will be fixated on death—both his wish to be dead and his contemplation of Sheol (3:3–26). Death will continue to be a major theme of Job's speeches throughout the first two cycles (3:1–20:29), but eventually will recede to the background by the end of Job's speeches in the poetic sections of the book (21:1–31:40). By Job's last speech, he will become so preoccupied with his desire for vindication that he will all but abandon his previous usage of death imagery (29:1–31:40).

The contrast between Job's usage of death themes at the beginning of the poetic dialogues and his usage of them at the end of the dialogues is striking. In the former he is obsessed with the benefits of death, employing the densest cluster of death words in the entire book; whereas in the latter, when he does use death imagery—very infrequently—it is in the service of a protest that contrasts the injustice of his current situation with his great piety. Piety, indeed, becomes Job's rallying cry, invigorating and fuelling his plea of innocence (31:1–40). Job's speeches end with his recollection of all the good he once did, of his former grand standing, of his life.

Reversing the flow of the prologue, which began with a picture of life and liveliness but gave way to one of death and silence, here, the poetic dialogues begin focused almost exclusively on death, and end with an impassioned and lively cry for justice. The task now, as previously, will be to trace the movement from the one to the other. However, because the scope of material to be examined is so large, I will spread out my analysis of the poetic dialogues over the course of the next three chapters. In this present chapter I will focus on the early portions of the first cycle of speeches; the next will cover the later portions of the first cycle through the end of the second; and the last will focus of the third cycle and Job's last speech before God's response. I will include ch. 21 in my analysis of the third cycle even though most consider it to be part of the second. As Clines argues, it functions as a bridge chapter, linking the second and third cycles.[1] I will argue in the following chapter that a subtle but decisive shift occurs in Job's symbolization of death in this chapter that is carried out throughout all of Job's remaining speeches.

---

1. Clines, *Job 1–20*, 285.

3.1. *Death's Multiple Symbolizations in Job's Speeches in the First Two Cycles*

Lifton argues that in response to the threat of death, or as a reaction to surviving mass death, humans frequently respond in one of two polar opposite ways: "extreme stillness and cessation of movement, or else frenetic, compensatory activity."[2] Survivors of the A-bomb in Hiroshima demonstrated both responses. On the one hand, many exhibited a stillness, both physically and psychically, a sort of numbing which was "a temporary form of symbolic death called forth as a protective device against more absolute psychic death (the psychosis that might result if one were to experience feelings appropriate to the grotesqueness of the environment)."[3] On the other hand, many others demonstrated a sort of heightened activity, "usually of an unfocused, desperate kind," "a delayed intensification of movement after sustained cessation."[4]

While the story of the fictional character Job obviously differs from actual people who survive real traumatic experiences, it is interesting that Job's reactions to the disasters he experiences connect with those of the Hiroshima survivors in terms of the poles of stillness and activity. As examined above, the prose tale ends with a picture of absolute stillness: Job's final reaction to the disasters he experiences is shocked numbness spent in silence, sitting on the ground. With the poetic dialogues, however, Job moves from this physical (and seemingly psychical) numbness to an explosion of talk—a lively, passionate expression of his confused suffering. Like the "unfocused, desperate" activity of some Hiroshima survivors, Job's speeches swirl from topic to topic, frequently not flowing in an immediately obvious pattern. Elements of introspection, lament, defiance, accusation, fantasy, invective, and speculation all comingle in a variety of ways. Job's speeches express a sort of "intensification of movement after sustained cessation"[5] albeit an intense verbal movement as opposed to the physical movement of the trauma survivor. Nowhere is this "movement" more obvious than in Job's symbolization of death where death comes to express a panoply of emotions and meanings, at times competing and at times complementary, branching out from the death-as-hope theme in ch. 3 to variety of expressions: a wish for death (6:8–9; 7:15; 10:18–19); an exploration of death as a place of no return (7:8–9, 21; 10:21); various expressions of the deadening of life (7:1–7; 9:25–26; 14:1–6); accusations that God is his murdering foe (6:4; 7:14; 9:17, 34; 10:8–9; 13:21, 24; 16:7–17; 19:6–20); declarations of God's injustice with regard to death (9:22–23); appealing to his own near death as a cry for justice (16:18–22); and expressions of the hopelessness of death (14:7–22; 17:11–16).

Although this variety of death expressions seemingly follows no logical progression, it generally demonstrates one significant pattern: while at the start, in ch. 3, Job links death and hope, this hope gradually, but completely, vanishes

---

2.   Lifton, *Broken Connection*, 112.
3.   Ibid.
4.   Ibid.
5.   Ibid.

and death comes to mark a place of complete and utter hopelessness, even as Job continues to view life as deadening. A discussion of Lifton's writings about centering, decentering, and recentering will provide a sort of focus to Job's mixture of various death themes.

3.2. *Job's Death Themes and the Symbolization of Death*

Throughout these pages I have been referring to a "symbolization of death," both Job's and the friends'. To speak of a symbolization of death is to recognize that all of a person's experiences are truly only experienced by being recreated mentally by means of images and constellations of images, the sum of which comprise one's sense of self. As discussed earlier, according to Lifton, the basic goal of the organism is to maintain vitality, which consists of attaining a stock of vital and vibrant images and forms that enable "life": "capacities for participation in love and communal relationships, for moral and ethical commitment, and for maintaining a sense of self that includes symbolic development, growth, and change."[6] Included in this stock of vibrant images is a symbolization of death.

But this imagistic vitality depends not only on the ability to create and maintain images and forms, but to *break them down* and to *recreate them* in order to encompass new experiences and new stimuli, a process that transpires by means of what Lifton refers to as "centering" and "decentering," mediated by "grounding." Centering is the ordering of the experience of the self in three "directions"—temporally, spatially, and emotionally—each of which involves the organism's ability to mediate proximate experiences with ultimate connections.[7] Temporal centering "consists of bringing to bear upon the immediate encounter older images and forms in ways that can anticipate future encounters";[8] spatial centering consists of "unifying immediate…exposure, including bodily involvement, with 'distant' ('ultimate,' 'abstract,' 'immortalizing') meanings";[9] and emotional centering consists of "making discriminations in emotional valence between our most impassioned images and forms (what we call the 'core' of the self) and those that are less impassioned and therefore more peripheral."[10] When the organism is able to attain a level of centeredness, one "feels…'at the center of things,'"[11] which then enables the self to experience and comprehend the world in which the self is situated.

The self can only retain its centeredness through its capacity for decentering, "for sufficient detachment from its involvements to be able to make judgments upon events and principles beyond itself."[12] Decentering is the process of altering existing forms that make up the self and it allows the old forms to be applied

---

6. Lifton, *Life of the Self*, 71.
7. Or, "harmonizing immediate and ultimate obligations" (Lifton, *Broken Connection*, 144).
8. Lifton, *Life of the Self*, 71.
9. Ibid.
10. Ibid.
11. Ibid., 72.
12. Ibid.

to new types of psychic experience. Although sometimes painful and disorienting, "in decentering there is a partial suspension of close integration in temporal,
spatial, and emotional planes, with anticipation of new integrations of a more
inclusive kind,"[13] which is the anticipation of recentering. Without decentering
the self becomes static. Without centering one cannot associate new experience
with viable form. The lack of either inhibits the vitality of the self.

The mechanism that enables the process of centering, decentering, and
recentering is that of grounding, "the relationship of the self to its own history,
individual and collective, as well as to its biology."[14] Where there is grounding,
the pain and confusion of decentering can be in the service of recentering,
"achieving a new mode of still-flexible ordering."[15] For whereas "Every movement away from centeredness, every encounter with significant novelty (significant in terms of its departure from preexistent inner form), entails anxiety and
risk, often guilt, rage and a sense of inner chaos,"[16] but with grounding this
anxiety and risk result in "a more centered self."[17]

Lifton uses the terms "centering" and "decentering" quite differently than do
Piaget and Inhelder. The latter use the terms in the context of a discussion about
the child's psychological development in its movement from a focus on itself
exclusively ("centering") to its perception of itself in reference to other objects
and events in its environment ("decentering"), both at the sensory-motor level
and on the cognitive, social, and moral levels.[18] For Piaget and Inhelder decentering is a step in the natural development of the child, fully replacing the
centering phase around age eleven or twelve when the child develops the ability
to "[adopt] an imaginary center of vision outside of [its] bodily location."[19]

For Lifton, however, the terms "centering" and "decentering" do not refer to
developmental stages of the child psyche, but pertain to the human necessity
throughout life of image building and the formation of mental structures.
Whereas Piaget and Inhelder use "centering" to refer to the child's exclusive
focus on its own bodily location, Lifton uses "centering" to refer to the ordering
of experiences into constellations of coherent forms and images. Conversely,
while Piaget and Inhelder use "decentering" to refer to the child's imaginative
perception of its body in relation to other objects and events in the environment,
for Lifton decentering is the partial suspension of the constellations of forms and
images in light of novel experience.

---

13. Ibid., 71.
14. Ibid., 72. Lifton describes "grounding" elsewhere as "accountability to those most integral to
one's historical and biological roots" (Lifton, *Broken Connection*, 145).
15. Lifton, *Life of the Self*, 73.
16. Ibid.
17. Ibid., 74.
18. Jean Piaget and Bärbel Inhelder, *The Psychology of the Child* (trans. Helen Weaver; New
York: Basic Books, 1969), 94–95, 128–29.
19. Martin Buss, "Role and Selfhood in Hebrew Prophecy," in *Psychology and the Bible: A New
Way to Read the Scriptures.* Vol. 2, *From Genesis to Apocalyptic Vision* (ed. J. Harold Ellens and
Wayne G. Rollins; Westport, Conn.: Prager, 2004), 277–94.

According to Lifton, one's symbolization of death comprises one of the key constellations of the self. As argued above, the life/piety/relationship complex is a very stable, fixed, and coherent symbolic system and one might imagine it to be a sort of theological and moral "center" that anchors its symbolization of death. I will argue throughout this chapter, however, that the earlier portions of the first cycle indicate that Job's symbolization of death appears to be desymbolized and that it has shifted from the symbolic moorings it once had. Far from being positioned in a symbolic structure that allows the life and vitality of the self, it actually functions to Job's detriment.

One gains the impression that Job's articulation of death's desymbolization points to his own decentering, namely the suspension of life/piety/relationship complex in light of his novel—and painful—experiences. This desymbolization of death is evident from Job's two very opposite uses of the death theme in the early portions of the dialogues: his conception and fantasy that life is to be found in death; and his subjective experience of death in life. Although both of these death themes arise in various places throughout the first cycle, I will devote most of my analysis to chs. 3 and 7 since they are particularly good examples.

3.2.1. *Life in Death (3:11–19)*

Job's initial speech, after seven days of silence, is his most highly stylized and thematically coherent of all of his speeches (apart from chs. 29–31), and it serves to orient not only the rest of his speeches, but the entire dialogue with the friends. Significantly, Job punctuates this speech with the repeated refrain of the desire now to be dead. He voices this desire for death in all three sections of this speech: the first section consists of a curse against the day of his birth and a (now impossible) wish that he had been a stillborn (3:3–10); the second section opens with the same wish to have been dead at birth and goes on to speculate about the nature of his existence were he now to be in Sheol (3:11–19); and the final section questions why God allows sufferers to live at all—sufferers who would much rather be dead (3:20–26). This repeated return to the wish of being dead establishes it as the basic theme of the speech and the basic frame of reference for the upcoming dialogues. What makes death so attractive for Job is that he conceives Sheol to be a place of abundant life, which certainly is a unique conception.

In the middle section of this initial speech Job reveals what he envisions about Sheol that makes it desirable. His fantasy of death is based on the belief that Sheol is a place of utter rest and tranquility, which Job describes using three synonyms, שׁכב, שׁקט, and נוח. Of the three, the first is by far the most common word in the HB, whose range of meaning includes sleeping, lying down, having sexual relations, and death. The "death" sense of the word fits with the context of Job's description of Sheol, suggesting that trio of "sleep" words connote death or the sleep of death.[20]

---

20. שׁכב frequently has this sense in the HB, normally in the phrase "to sleep with one's ancestors" (Gen 47:30; Deut 31:16; 2 Sam 7:12; 1 Kgs 1:21; 2:10; 11:21, 43; 14:20, 31; 15:8, 24; 16:6, 28; 22:40, 50; 2 Kgs 8:24; 10:35; 13:9, 13; 14:16, 22, 29; 15:7, 22, 38; 16:20; 20:21; 21:18; 24:6;

The other two "sleep" words nuance this "death sleep" by indicating more precisely the nature of the sleep that Job envisions. For its part, שקט has several connotations. Most frequently, especially in the prose narratives, the word describes the peacefulness and tranquility of a people or a land, in contrast to the turmoil of war and upheaval.[21] It also stands more generally for a sense of tranquility and calm as opposed to anxiety, tension, and hyper-activity.[22] In the Psalms and Prophets the word often represents the calm and peacefulness that Yahweh provides, or is urged to provide, for his servants;[23] or it represents Yahweh's own calm and peacefulness that he is urged to break in order that he deal with his enemies.[24] Similarly, in prose narrative ישן almost always suggests a deep sleep that comes over individuals who then undergo some sort of ordeal or hardship while asleep,[25] while in the Prophets and the Writings the word frequently suggests the tranquility of sleep that Yahweh provides his servants[26] or the slumber that Yahweh is urged to rouse himself out of in order to dispatch his, and his servant's, enemies.[27]

Both of these "sleep" words link to the life/piety/relationship complex especially in poetic contexts. They stand for the peacefulness, rest, and tranquility that enables the pious to live abundant lives as God guards and protects them. The short Psalm of Lament, Ps 3, expresses this nicely. In it the Psalmist laments the foes who attack him (vv. 1–2), but then confesses that Yahweh is his protector and that Yahweh listens to his cry (vv. 3–4). Furthermore, the Psalmist announces that in the face of numerous opposing forces (v. 7) he is able to lie down (שכב) and sleep (ישן) because "Yahweh sustains me" (v. 6). The image is one of Yahweh providing life, sustenance, and rejuvenating rest to his servant even in the face of seemingly insurmountable opposition. Rest and tranquility stand for abundant life.

Job's fantasy in 3:11–19 shares this vision of peacefulness, rest, and tranquility, but with the highly significant alteration that this life-giving rest of abundant life is to be found only in Sheol, not in life. In fact, to Job, life is anything but peacefulness and tranquility (3:26). It is characterized, rather, by עמל and רגז, synonyms whose respective translations "trouble" and "turmoil" suggest the upheaval and disruption of Job's life (3:10, 26).[28]

---

2 Chr 9:31; 12:16; 13:23; 16:13; 21:1; 26:2, 23; 27:9; 28:27; 32:33). It also suggests the sleep of death in other cases (Judg 5:27; Pss 41:8; 88:5; Isa 14:18; 43:17; 50:11; Lam 2:21; Ezek 32:19, 21, 27, 28, 29, 30, 32).

    21.   Josh 11:23; 14:15; Judg 3:11, 30; 5:31; 8:28; 18:27; 2 Kgs 11:20; 1 Chr 4:40; 22:9; 2 Chr 14:1, 4, 5; 20:30; 23:21; Isa 14:7; 30:15; Jer 30:10; 46:27; 47:6, 7; 48:11; Ezek 16:49.

    22.   Ruth 3:18; Prov 15:18; Isa 7:4; 57:20.

    23.   Pss 76:8; 94:13; 32:17; Jer 30:10; 46:27.

    24.   Pss 83:1; Isa 14:7; 62:1; 47:6, 7; 48:11; 49:23.

    25.   Gen 2:21; Judg 16:19; 1 Sam 26:7, 12; 1 Kgs 3:20. See also Gen 41:5; 1 Kgs 18:27; 19:5.

    26.   Pss 3:5; 4:9; Ezek 34:25.

    27.   Pss 44:24; 78:65; Jer 51:39, 57. The word has a related sense in Pss 13:4; 121:4; Isa 5:27. The word can also have the simple sense of "deep sleep" in the Writings also (see Prov 4:16; Qoh 5:12; Cant 5:2).

    28.   For a good discussion of the semantic range of the term עמל, see Michael V. Fox, *Qohelet and His Contradictions* (Bible and Literature Series 18; Sheffield: Almond, 1989), 97. The term

This image of life-giving rest in Sheol contrasts sharply with the traditional conception of Sheol in the HB. Generally, Sheol was considered to be a place of gloom and darkness, where humans eked out a minimal existence with their life-energies severely truncated. In Liftonian terms, Sheol was a place of separation and stasis: separation, in that the dead were said to descend there upon death, separated from the realm of the living, never to return to human contact; stasis, in that existence in Sheol was thought to be marked by a lack of vitality, movement, and liveliness, being a place of no possessions, no joy, and where humans existed only at a minimal level.[29]

Job's death fantasy, however, paints the opposite picture: Sheol is a place of human connection where the dead enjoy fellowship, not just with normal human company, but with the most venerable of all company—with kings, with the earth's counselors, and with princes (3:14–15). Moreover, through a series of images describing the residents of Sheol, Job reveals that Sheol is far from a place of stasis, but is a place where stasis is overcome. There the person "sapped of strength" (3:17b) finds life-giving "rest" (נוח). Likewise, the "prisoner" (3:18)—an image of confinement and entrapment—finds life-giving "tranquility" (שאן) while being released from the confinement and control of the "taskmaster" (נגש). And lastly, the "slave is free from his master"—another image of the one who is confined in life being released in death.[30]

עמל, with its Arabic, Syrian, and Akkadian cognates, is first of all associated with "toil—arduous, wearisome work" (Fox, *Qohelet and His Contradictions*, 101). In the HB, the misery and burden of toil can detach themselves from the idea of work and stand on their own. Thus עמל can refer to trouble or misery in general (Job 7:3), or to the effects of trouble or misery that an activity has on someone else (Ps 73:16). Further, it can refer to "life's toil" in general and not simply to specific labor (Gen 41:51). Finally, עמל might be associated with evil effects (Isa 10:1; Ps 94:20). In a unique usage, in Ps 105:44 עמל means wealth. For more on the semantic range of עמל, especially its distinctive usage in Ecclesiastes, see Fox, *Qohelet and His Contradictions*, 97–107. Fox concludes that "For the speaker of [Biblical Hebrew], the notion common to the various uses of [עמל] was, approximately, 'trouble.' This could then apply in context to burdensome and troublesome work, events, behaviors, persons, situations, and more" (Fox, *Qohelet and His Contradictions*, 101).

The term רגז also connotes "trouble" or "turmoil." Poetic texts most commonly employ רגז when discussing the upheaval in the natural order at the appearance of God on behalf of Israel (see 2 Sam 22:8; Pss 18:8; 77:17, 19; Hab 3:7) or against Israel (Isa 5:25; Joel 2:1, 10). "Trouble"/"turmoil" also is caused by upheavals in the social order (Prov 29:9; 30:21) and in the cosmic order (Hab 3:16), as well as by injustice (Isa 32:10, 11; Amos 8:8). Job employed רגז in his Sheol fantasy to describe the turmoil in life caused by the oppression by dominant groups of subordinate ones. In addition, Clines notes that רגז is also used in an emotional sense to indicate fear (Jer 33:9), strong surprise (Isa 14:9), violent grief (2 Sam 19:1), or anger (Isa 28:21; 2 Kgs 19:27, 28; Job 39:24). See Clines, *Job 1–20*, 96.

For parallels between several Egyptian "Songs of the Harper" and Job's positive valuation of death in the face of life's miseries, see Blumenthal, "Hiob und die Harfnerlieder."

29. For a full description of the traditional understanding of Sheol, see Tromp, *Primitive Conceptions*, 21–213 (especially pp. 91, 95, and 167 for separation images, and 154–56, 187–90 for stasis images). See also Johnston, *Shades of Sheol*, 69–123; Brian B. Schmidt, "Memory as Immortality: Countering the Dreaded 'Death after Death' in Ancient Israelite Society," in Avery-Peck and Neusner, eds., *Judaism in Late Antiquity*, 4:87–100 (88–92).

30. Images of activity in Sheol (as opposed to stasis) might also be understood from the actions of the kings, counselors, and princes in 3:14–15. Although the sense of these verses is disputed, it is possible to interpret these verses to mean that the kings and rulers are engaged in purposeful activity:

The upshot of this fantasy of Sheol is that many of the traditional valences of life and death have been swapped. Job locates the attributes of abundant life on the other side of the grave, in Sheol, making death, not life, desirable.

3.2.2. *Death in Life (3:20–23; 7:1–6)*

But this is not all that Job has to say about death in the earlier portions of the first cycle. If death comes to represent life for Job, it is also true that life comes to represent death. Job indicates this sense of the invasion of death into the realm of life by his frequent characterization of life as stasis, separation, and disintegration. The first of such jarring images comes in the latter portions of Job's opening speech (3:20–26), though the initial verses of ch. 7 (vv. 1–6) also contain a flurry of such images.

3.2.2.1. *3:20–23*. In these verses Job questions the deity regarding why he gives life to certain humans, whom Job identifies using three descriptors, each marked by the preposition ל: "to the troubled/sufferer" (לעמל; 3:20a), "to the bitter of spirit" (למרי נפש; 3:20b), "to the man whose way is hidden" (לגבר אשר דרכו נסתרה; 3:23a).

The first two descriptors refer to groups of people of whom Job is a part, while the last one seems to refer to Job himself because it switches to a singular form of expression from the plural ones of 3:21–22 and because it uses גבר to describe the one whose way is hidden—a term Job used earlier to refer to himself in his mother's womb (3:3). Furthermore, the first two descriptors suggest a situation of deep distress and extreme emotional bitterness,[31] while the third functions to focus the previous two and reveal the exact cause of Job's sorrowful status: he is "the man whose way is hidden."[32]

The choice of the word דרך to describe what is hidden is also significant. The term דרך is the concrete image of the path on which one walks, and symbolically, it is an important image in the Wisdom literature for moral discourse,

---

"building ruins" and "filling" their houses with silver. Most commentators, however, understand these activities to be what the kings and rulers engaged in while alive. Even so, the meaning is still unclear. The line עם מלכים ויעצי ארץ הבנים חרבות למו ("with kings and counselors of the world who rebuild ruins for themselves") has been understood in numerous ways. Many believe this to be a reference to the pyramid-builders of Egypt whose tombs would have been filled with innumerable treasures (see, e.g., Dhorme, *Job*, 34–35; Driver and Gray, *Job*, 1:36–37; Fohrer, *Hiob*, 122–23, and others). Some follow Rashi and argue that this is a reference to ruined cities that kings would rebuild to perpetuate their names (Gordis, *Job*, 37; Newsom, "Job," 369; Pope, *Job*, 31). Habel argues that this is a reference to the former glory of rulers whose building accomplishments now lie in ruin. Their ignoble end in Sheol is more desirable than their glories in life (Habel, *Job*, 110). Clines argues that the line reads in parallel with v. 15 and seems to suggest the excesses of the wealthy. Together with vv. 17–19 these lines express the inexplicable inequalities in life (Clines, *Job 1–20*, 92–95).

31. The words מרי נפש occur as a construct phrase fairly infrequently in the HB, but when they do, they always suggest extremely volatile and bitter emotion, frequently due to distressing circumstances (see, e.g., Judg 18:25; 1 Sam 1:10; 22:2; Isa 38:15; see also Isa 30:6; 2 Kgs 4:27). Often the pair describes the personal and emotional state after, or in anticipation of, the death of a loved one or oneself (1 Sam 30:6; Isa 38:15; 2 Kgs 4:27). Taken together, the descriptors עמל and מרי נפש aptly convey Job's sense of bewilderment, distress, and emotional torment.

32. See Fohrer, *Hiob*, 125.

conceived along the lines of the life/piety/relationship complex. In the Wisdom tradition דרך functions as a "ground metaphor"[33] or "nuclear symbol"[34] that "organizes other perceptions and images and conveys a way of perceiving the world" (especially evidenced in Prov 1–9).[35] According to Prov 4:10–19, there are two paths upon which one can walk: one that is straight, clear, true, and open; the other evil, dark, lawless, and dangerous. To walk on the good path means to act in accordance with Wisdom, which operates as a roadmap for this journey. Wisdom teaches the way that leads to life. Further, God is the guardian and companion of one walking on this way (Prov 3:23–26), for the way of God is the way of abundant life. "The way of wisdom becomes the religious way of Yahweh. He is the companion and guardian who blesses the traveler through life and provides him with wisdom as a necessary gift for the journey."[36] Yahweh, himself, structures the cosmos with this same Wisdom, which is the "vehicle of order and stability in society" (Prov 8:1–31).[37]

In 3:23 Job describes himself as a miserable man who craves death, "whose way is hidden." The cause of his misery is not that he has deserted or abandoned this path.[38] It has simply been hidden from him. In Proverbs דרך imagery is always active: one is always *walking* rather than *being* on one path or another. Thus the righteous "walk" along and "keep to" the right path (1:5; 2:20; 3:23; 9:6; 11:5; 28:18), while the wicked "walk" along the evil path, and "forsake" the right one (1:15; 2:13; 4:14).[39] All this implies active agency—that one's actions and decisions are what determine which path one walks on.[40] Normally, given the "two paths" imagery of Proverbs one would expect that not to be walking along the path of righteousness would entail walking along its alternative, the path of wickedness. Yet, in Job's reformulation, he has neither continued along the one path, nor has he abandoned it in favor of the other. Instead, the image is of one who is utterly bewildered, not knowing anymore where a path of any sort might be. Job's image is of stasis or paralysis. It bespeaks the unavailability of the conditions of the possibility of walking (being able to see a path) or the unavailability of a functional symbolic structure in order to underpin a rational moral world. To Job, life is like the stasis of death.

To add to this sense of stasis and symbolic breakdown, Job reveals that this bewildering non-path, non-place in which he finds himself is the result not of his own shortcomings, but of the very obstructive presence of God about him. Thus

---

33. See Fox, *Proverbs 1–9*, 128–31.

34. See Habel, "Wisdom in Proverbs 1–9."

35. Ibid., 129.

36. Ibid., 145.

37. Ibid., 154. The Egyptian Wisdom literature also teaches that this way of life is synonymous with the way of God. See Fox, *Proverbs 1–9*, 128–31, and Irene Shirun-Grumach, *Untersuchungen zur Lebenslehre des Amenope* (ed. Hans Wolfgang Müller; Munich: Deutscher Kunstverlag, 1972), 14.

38. As if the Niphal verb נסחרה were active, as NJPS translates it.

39. Other path imagery in Proverbs also implies active agency. See Prov 1:31; 3:31; 4:26; 5:8; 7:8, 25; 9:15; 10:9; 21:16.

40. See further, Fox, *Proverbs 1–9*, 137–43. See also Prov 21:8 where דרך is specifically paralleled to פעל ("conduct").

3:23b specifies that Job's way is hidden because "God has hedged him about" (יָסֶךְ אֱלוֹהַּ בַּעֲדוֹ). The verb used in this line is a Hiphil of the root סכך (it also appears as שׂכך in other places), which, in *haśśatan*'s challenge to God, referred to a protective hedge that God had built up around Job.[41] In 3:23, however, it takes on a more hostile, aggressive sense, as in Hos 2:8.[42] Job's claim here seems to complete the destruction of the nuclear symbol of the two paths and reverses the terms of the life/piety/relationship complex. As discussed above, God's path was thought to be identical with the righteous path, and God was thought to be the companion and guardian of those who walked on it. Here, however, Job suggests that God's presence is far from guardianship. It is, rather, an oppressive barrier that effectively obscures the path of righteousness and causes Job's paralysis. Again, to Job, life consists of stasis and paralysis, here attributed to God's actions.[43]

3.2.2.2. 7:1–6. Whereas in ch. 3 Job alluded only briefly to his experience of death-in-life by describing it in terms of the stasis of paralysis, in the early portions of ch. 7 he is expansive, employing a rich variety of death equivalents to describe his experience of life. Job structures his statement into pairs of corresponding verses, comparing human life, in general, to hard service and hired labor (7:1–2), comparing his own life to that of a laborer with no reward and no rest (7:3–4), and then closing with two images of his own anguish and mortality (7:5–6).

Scholars frequently note two puzzling features of these opening verses of ch. 7. First, whereas the progression from the first pair of verses to the second follows the logical rule of analogy (life is hard service/my life is hard service with no reward), the link between these two pairs to the third is a bit baffling. There seems to be no logical connection of Job's life of hard labor with no reward and rest, to his statements about the corrupt state of his flesh in 7:5 ("covered with worms and clods of earth"; "congeals and oozes").[44] A second puzzling feature is that while Job's comparison of life to the toil of a laborer in 7:1–4 gives the impression of life as ceaseless drudgery, in v. 6 he laments not life's unending travail, but the *brevity* of life.

---

41. *HALOT* and BDB disagree concerning this verb. *HALOT* suggests it is a Hiphil imperfect from the root סכך. It suggests that the roots שׂוךְ and שׂכך are by-forms. BDB, on the other hand, suggests that the roots שׂוךְ/סוךְ and שׂכך/סכך are different and that examples of the verbal forms of the former only occur here, Job 1:10; 38:8; and Hos 2:8. Given that BDB's suggestion posits an extreme amount of semantic overlap between the two roots, I am inclined to go with *HALOT* and argue that they are the same root.

42. See Newsom, "Job," 370.

43. Interestingly, Isa 40:27 employs a similar expression as Job 3:23: "Why do you say, O Jacob, and speak, O Israel, 'My way (דרך) is hidden (נסתרה) from Yahweh; my justice disregarded by my God'?" Like Job 3:23, this expression is used of a situation of disaster (in Isaiah, the experience of exile), though דרך does not have the same import for moral discourse in Deutero-Isaiah as it does in Wisdom literature. Further, in the Isaiah passage God is not the cause of the way being hidden. In fact, Israel's way is hidden *from* God.

44. See below for this translation.

While scholars posit a variety of solutions to these problems, the search for a logical link between the verses seems a bit strained.[45] It appears, rather, that the pairs of verses display a progression of imagery where Job gives voice to his own experience of the deadening of his life in a series of several overlaying pictures designed to capture different aspects of this death-in-life.

3.2.2.2.1. *Stasis images in 7:1–2.* In the first such picture Job alludes to the ANE mythic tradition of humans' lot in life being that of hard service,[46] a tradition that resonates with his own experience of life. The images of "hard service" (צבא),[47] "laborer" (שכיר),[48] and "servant" (עבד) form the conceptual field with which human life is compared, suggesting that human life pertains to a situation of human bondage and/or indebtedness, or rather, that human life can be characterized by the stasis of confinement. This applies most readily to the first and third terms, but also to the "laborer," a term that refers to an Israelite or non-Israelite hired worker who is likely poor in comparison to the land-owner.[49] Each of the terms refer to humans whose lot in life is to toil in the service of others, being subject to the will of those more economically powerful than they. Their lives are "necessitous, often subject to abuse, and without security."[50]

In this picture, however, stress is not on the servitude of these people per se, but on their sense of longing anticipation: they "long for" (שאף) evening's rest; they "wait eagerly for" (קוה) their earned wage. The image of life that Job paints is that of a laborer caught in the ceaseless drudgery of life's toil, longing for the future moment of rest when toil will be rewarded. Job's comparison ("like the *days* of a laborer are his *days*") is not so much about the bliss of that future moment, but about the temporality of the present dreary moment (the *day*[51]) that

45. Clines argues that whereas the verses that discuss the ceaseless drudgery of life pertain to Job's past experience of life, the image of the shortness of life applies to his future remaining days (Clines, *Job 1–20*, 185). Habel argues the progression is from slaves who work throughout the day, which then forces the realization that Job's daily attire "is the very emblem of his threatened moral condition" (Habel, *Job*, 159). Whybray, Hartley, and Newsom argue that the description of Job's flesh serves to explain why Job can get no rest (R. N. Whybray, *Job* [Readings: a New Biblical Commentary; Sheffield: Sheffield Academic Press, 1998], 54; Hartley, *Job*, 145; Newsom, "Job," 393). Rowley argues that the complaint of the brevity of life is more a complaint that life, at its best, is short. Why ought it also be filled with suffering (Rowley, *Job*, 67)?

46. See Habel, *Job*, 157, who references the Atrahasis myth where humans are explicitly created to do the hard work that the gods would otherwise have to do. See also Leo G. Perdue, *Wisdom in Revolt: Metaphorical Theology in the Book of Job* (JSOTSup 112; Bible and Literature Series 29; Sheffield: JSOT Press, 1991), 70–71, 126.

47. The term could refer to military service as it normally does in the HB (Janzen, *Job*, 80, notes that the term refers to military service some 480 times), but it also has the sense of hard labor as in Job 14:14; Isa 40:2; and Dan 10:1. This sense fits better with the two other images.

48. Clines notes that this term also could refer to a mercenary soldier (cf. Jer 46:21), but the normal "hireling" is preferred (Clines, *Job 1–20*, 184). The comparison of life to the toil of a laborer is also found in 14:6.

49. See, e.g., Lev 25:39–40, 47; Deut 24:4.

50. Clines, *Job 1–20*, 184.

51. Although "day" can refer to the 24-hour period, in this context there seems to be a contrast between "day" (7:1b) and evening "shadows" (7:2a), the time when the laborer expected to be paid (see Deut 24:15). Similarly, the "day" of the laborer seems to be contrasted with Job's restless "nights" in 7:3b.

makes the future one so desirable. Life is like that never-ending moment of longing, never satisfied, and all consuming. It is the eternal present of hard labor and servitude that achieves no end, and does not attain the *telos* of rest and reward, which would render it meaningful.

This picture of life, in Lifton's terms, is that of stasis. While stasis can imply a lack of physical movement (which would then not apply to Job's image of a toiling laborer), it also can imply a lack of progression and purposeful activity. This latter sense fits well with Job's picture: while the future meaningful moment might be longed for, the entrapment of the eternal dreary present is never overcome.

3.2.2.2.2. Stasis image in 7:3–4. With the second pair of verses (7:3–4) Job shifts from a general picture of life (7:1–2) to his own life experience. Like the purposeless drudgery and longing of the laborer, his life is characterized by "months of emptiness" (ירחי שוא). But Job has exaggerated the comparison: whereas laborers experience the ever-present empty *day* of longing, Job experiences futile *months*; whereas the laborers long for the end of the day because it brings rest and reward, the end of Job's days bring only restlessness and agitation (7:4). So, while Job seemingly breaks out of the eternal moment of drudgery by attaining the longed-for evening, he discovers it to be worse than the day of drudgery such that he longs for day to come again (7:4). Instead of the stasis of the eternal futile present, Job's life is the stasis of the never ending cycle of futile days and nights.

3.2.2.2.3. Disintegration image in 7:5. From these two images of stasis Job layers on a new image in 7:5, that of the decaying or putrefied body. Although it is clear that Job's body is the subject of both lines of v. 5 (his "flesh" [בשר] and "skin" [עור]), scholars dispute what precisely is being described. In the first line Job claims that two objects cover his flesh, רמה and גיש, yet the sense of both is contested, as are the sense of רגע and מאס in the second line.[52] The first line

---

52. Scholars usually understand the רמה of the first line to be "worms" ("my flesh is covered with worms"; see also 17:14; 21:26; 24:20; 25:6), but some suggest that here it is a cognate of the Arabic *ramaya*, meaning "sluggish; become putrid, corrupt" ("my flesh is becoming putrid," so Clines, *Job 1–20*, 163; see also, Guillaume, *Studies in the Book of Job*, 85). Both the LXX and Jerome seem to preserve both meanings: ἐν σαπρίᾳ σκωλήκων and *putredine vermium* ("in corruption of worms"). The second disputed term, גיש, many take as a *hapax* of the *Qere* גוש ("clod"), which, itself, might have a medical sense of "scabs." However, גיש/גוש appears to be in construct with עפר, suggesting the translation "clods of earth" or, metaphorically, "dirty scabs" (for this translation, see Dhorme, *Job*, 99–100). Others understand עפר simply to be a gloss on גיש and therefore translate the two words as "scab" (Clines, *Job 1–20*, 163; Fohrer, *Hiob*, 163; Friedrich Horst, *Hiob* [2d ed.; BKAT 16; Neukirchen–Vluyn: Neukirchener Verlag, 1969], 97; likely also *BHS*). Driver understands עפר as a verb cognate to the Arabic *jafara* ("covered") and then divides the lines of the verse differently, reading "My flesh is clothed with worms and scab covers my skin, it is cracked and gapes open" (Godfrey Rolles Driver, "Problems in the Hebrew Text of Job," in *Wisdom in Israel and in the Ancient Near East* [ed. Martin Noth and David Winton Thomas; VTSup 3; Leiden: Brill, 1969], 72–93 [73]).

In the second line Job states that his skin does two things: רגע and מאס. The latter is almost universally taken as a "by-form" (Habel, *Job*, 153) or "metaplastic form" (Gordis, *Job*, 80) of מסס ("flow, drip" in the Niphal; "My skin flows"). Thus JB's colorful translation, "oozes pus." Guillaume

might read, "My flesh is covered with pus and scabs"[53] or "my flesh is covered with worms and clods of earth," while the second might read, "My skin grows firm and then oozes"[54] or "My skin has split and runs with pus."[55] Whichever of the options are preferred, the imagery is of the decaying and putrefaction of Job's flesh.

While in the second line the image is of skin racked with disease, and thus bearing the mark of death through bodily corruption,[56] the first line presents a more evocative image of the decay and disintegration of Job's flesh, especially if distant cognates are disregarded and, as I am inclined to do, the line is translated, "My flesh is covered with worms and clods of earth," which seems to be the simplest and most obvious translation. The worm, especially in the book of Job, but also elsewhere, is a death symbol, representing the decay and corruption of human flesh after death.[57] "Clods of earth," especially in connection with "worms," likewise conjures images of human burial and the decay of the body in the soil.[58] Taken together, Job uses this picture of the decaying dead body to represent his personal experience of life. To Job, life consists of being clothed in death.

The particular description of *being clothed* in death is especially expressive. Throughout the HB, the verb לבש is used almost exclusively in one of two ways. First, it describes the "putting on" of certain garments that function to denote social distinctions, whether priest or other cultic functionary,[59] king,[60] soldier,[61] mourner,[62] or others.[63] Second, it is used to describe a metaphorical quality or

---

argues that the Hebrew מאם comes from the Arabic cognate *masa*, and renders the line "'(the wound) widened,' i.e. opened up again" (Guillaume, *Studies in the Book of Job*, 86). Most understand the former to mean "harden," a cognate of the Ethiopic *raga'a* ("congeal"; see Fohrer, *Hiob*, 163). Other scholars take it to mean "crack," citing the parallelism between רגע and מחץ ("shatter") in 26:12 (see Dhorme, *Job*, 100, who cites Isa 51:15 and Jer 31:35 for support). Guillaume argues the Arabic *raja'a* ("returned") is a cognate of רגע (thus "my skin returns [i.e grows again]"; Guillaume, *Studies in the Book of Job*, 85). Kopf, relying on the same Arabic cognate and dividing the lines of the verse differently, understands רגע as "becomes" (thus, "Meine Haut wird eine Erdkruste, die auseinander-fällt"; Lothar Kopf, "Arabische Etymologien und Parallelen zum Bibelwörterbuch," *VT* 8 [1958]: 161–215 [202]).

53. Clines, *Job 1–20*, 157.
54. Ibid.
55. Dhorme, *Job*, 99.
56. The line can be interpreted as the skin healing, but with the death imagery in these verses, more likely this is an image of bodily disintegration. It is inconsequential whether the first part of the line reads "My skin hardens..." or "My skin cracks...." Either way the picture is of infection that does not heal, disease that does not abate.
57. See Job 17:14; 21:16; 24:20; and Isa 14:11.
58. The noun עפר by itself sometimes stands for human mortality (see, e.g., Gen 2:7; 3:19; 18:27) and dust also was frequently used in mortuary rites (see Josh 7:6; 1 Sam 4:12; 2 Sam 13:19; 15:32; Mic 1:10; Jer 6:26; Ezek 27:30; Lam 2:10).
59. Exod 28:41; 29:5, 8, 30; 40:13, 14; Lev 6:3, 11; 8:7, 13; 16:4, 23, 24, 32; 21:10; Num 20:26, 28; Ezra 3:10; Ezek 26:16; 42:14; 44:17, 19.
60. 1 Kgs 22:10, 30; 2 Chr 18:4, 29; Esth 5:1 (queen).
61. 1 Sam 17:5, 38; 1 Kgs 22:30; 2 Chr 18:29; Jer 46:4; Ezek 23:12; 38:4.
62. 2 Sam 14:2; Esth 4:1, 4; Jonah 3:5.

attribute that a person[64] or God[65] "puts on" or is being urged to "put on."[66] Uniquely, לבש in 7:5a seems to function in both ways. It is obviously a metaphorical clothing since Job's clothes cannot literally be worms and clods of earth, but the clothes he understands himself to be wearing also function to mark his social standing, at least in his own eyes. Just as a king decks himself out in royal regalia that identify his kingly role, or a priest in cultic vestments that establish his priestly role, so also Job is clothed in worms and clods of earth that establish him in his deathly role, as a living dead person. In a step beyond the mourner, who wears certain garments and performs certain rituals likely to identify with the dead for the period of mourning, Job wears garments that establish him as dead.

This one evocative image seems to fill in the "missing middle" of Job's resymbolization of death in 1:21 in reaction to the deaths of his children ("naked I came…"). There Job described the life cycle in terms of its beginning and ending, both experienced without clothes (naked), but made no reference to the period between the naked, non-existence of birth and the naked, non-existence of death. Presumably this missing middle would be the opposite of its boundaries: life/existence rather than death/non-existence; clothed rather than naked. Job's image in 7:5, however, reveals that life's clothes are actually nothing other than the very raiment of death. Thus, to Job, pre-birth is non-existence (and therefore something like death), life is death, and post-life is non-existence and death.

In its entirety, the verse layers a new image of death-in-life on top of the stasis images of 7:1–2 and 7:3–4, employing, instead, imagery of what Lifton would call disintegration: the diseased and decaying human body in the process of breaking down and falling apart. Bodily disintegration will become a powerful metaphor for Job as he articulates his own sense of death-in-life throughout his speeches.[67]

3.2.2.2.4. *Stasis image in 7:6.* In the last verse in this cluster (7:6), Job employs the image of the weaver's shuttle to express his sense of his life being tainted by death. The picture of the shuttle repetitively going back-and-forth recalls the earlier stasis image of the eternal drudgery of the days and nights of futility in 7:3–4. Focus in this instance, however, is more on the speed of the shuttle, than on its motion ("My days are *swifter than* the shuttle")[68] and on the inevitability of the termination of this motion when the thread runs out ("They

---

63. Gen 27:15, 16; 38:19; 41:42; Deut 22:5; 1 Sam 28:8; 2 Sam 13:18; 2 Chr 5:2; 28:15; Esth 6:8, 9, 11; Prov 31:21; Isa 4:1; 22:21; Jer 4:30; Ezek 9:2, 3, 11; 10:2, 6, 7; 16:10; 34:3; Dan 10:5; 12:6, 7; Zeph 1:8.

64. 2 Sam 1:24; 2 Chr 6:41; Job 8:22; 10:11; 27:17; 29:14; Pss 35:26; 109:18, 29; 132:9, 16, 18; Isa 61:10; Ezra 7:27. Probably also Judg 6:32; 1 Chr 12:19; 24:20 where the spirit of the Lord "clothes" a person.

65. Job 40:10; Pss 65:13; 93:1; 104:1; Isa 51:9; 52:1; 59:17.

66. It is also used metaphorically with neither God nor humans clothing themselves with something: Ps 35:26; Prov 23:21; Isa 49:18; 50:13

67. See 6:4a, b; 9:17; 10:16–17; 13:28; 16:7–9, 12–14; 19:2, 10.

68. Contra Newsom, "Job," 394.

end for lack of thread"),[69] which, by a play-on-words, also is an ending "without hope" (תקוה means both "thread" and "hope"). The issue is not so much that Job is looking ahead to his remaining days and sees that they are few,[70] but that he senses that his life is flying by, racing speedily and inevitably toward certain death. This image is perhaps not as strongly a stasis image as the previous ones, but it does suggests a certain paralyzing inability to change one's destiny in light of the overwhelming sense that life is flying by.

This image appears to be an outright contradiction of the earlier image of life as never-ceasing drudgery and futility (7:3–4). There Job experienced his life as interminable; here he experiences it as swift and short. Logically, the two images are contradictory. However, as death images they both suggest different, but related, aspects of Job's sense of death-in-life: the former of Job's sense of the numbing drudgery of meaningless and futile existence; the latter of his sense that life is tainted by the inevitability of death and that life's very speed and brevity prevent meaningful action. Both images, along with the images of disintegration in 7:5, convey the sense of the deadening of life.

Job will employ a variety of images throughout his upcoming speeches to expresses the brevity and insubstantiality of human life. Humans will be compared to the breath/wind (7:7), the fading cloud (7:9), a vapor (7:16), the flower (14:2), and a shadow (14:2).[71] In the later portions of the dialogues, the image of swift life moving ineluctably toward certain death begins to fuse with the notion that death represents hopelessness. Whereas in 7:6b Job expresses this hopelessness by means of a clever play-on-words (באפס תקוה, "without thread," "without hope"), it finds more elaborate expression in Job's later speeches (14:7–22; 17:11–16). This, of course, is in direct contradiction to ch. 3 where Job finds the hope of tranquility, rest, and peace only in death, a contradiction about which I will have more to say in the next chapter.

Before moving on, I must comment briefly about the death equivalents— images of stasis, disintegration, and separation—that Job frequently uses throughout his speeches. Many, but not all, of these are conventional images that Job adopts and then transforms to suit his purposes throughout his speeches, but most obviously in the death-in-life theme and in the soon to be examined divine murder theme. Very frequently in Psalms of Lament the Psalmist frames his own experience of distress and turmoil using the stasis imagery of having strength sapped, being worn down,[72] or being trapped;[73] the disintegration imagery of bodily corrosion and dismemberment;[74] and the separation imagery of opposi-

---

69. For this translation, see Dhorme, *Job*, 101. Clines argues that this translation is unsatisfactory because the metaphor does not reveal "the 'thread' from which life is woven" (Clines, *Job 1–20*, 163). He suggests the translation, "they have reached their end, and there is no thread left" (p. 157).

70. Fohrer, *Hiob*, 177.

71. For more on the use of these images throughout the HB, see James L. Crenshaw, "Flirting with the Language of Prayer," in *Worship and the Hebrew Bible: Essays in Honour of John T. Willis* (ed. M. Patrick Graham, Rick R. Marrs, and Steven L. McKenzie; JSOTSup 284; Sheffield: Sheffield Academic Press, 1999), 110–23 (117–19).

72. See, e.g., Pss 6:7, 8; 31:11; 38:11; 102:5, 24; 109:24.

73. See, e.g., Pss 38:14; 69:3, 14–16.

74. See, e.g., Pss 22:15, 16, 18; 31:10, 11, 13; 38:4, 6, 8, 9; 102:6.

tion and rejection by foes[75] or by intimates.[76] And as with Job's usage of such imagery, the Psalmist frequently intermixes the various images, layering one upon the other.[77]

The Psalmist, however, has a very different goal in employing such imagery than does Job. For the Psalmist this imagery forms the language of prayer, and calling the deity's attention to his plight is for the purpose of invoking Yahweh's aid so that he will come to rescue and restore the petitioner. This is not at all true in Job's usage of death equivalents, for Job's speeches lack entirely any of the elements of a Psalm of Lament (invocation,[78] complaint, affirmation of trust, plea, vow), save for the complaint itself. Most importantly, his speeches do not have as their goal the deliverance by Yahweh and the restoration to right relationship.[79] Some scholars argue that the rhetorical goal of usurping the language of complaint from the Psalm of Lament is to highlight what follows the complaint in Job's speeches, in place of the plea for God's deliverance.[80] More likely, however, is that since Job gives no indication that he is engaged in prayer, the use of Psalmic-type death imagery calls attention not to what follows, but to itself, as an authentic expression of Job's subjective experiences. By employing traditional imagery in a non-traditional manner, Job personalizes conventional images and actively disintegrates the symbols that held life together. They stand for his own sense of death-in-life.

3.3. *Life-in-Death, Death-in-Life, and the Logic of Suicide*

The logic of Job's discourse on death in the initial portions of the first cycle seems to be paradoxical. On the one hand, in the life-in-death theme, death represents what is desirable and good, and is therefore sought after. On the other hand, in the death-in-life theme, death is experienced as painful and anguishing, it is a wretched man's unfortunate experience of life. So, according to Job, death is, paradoxically, both good and bad.

Of course, the emphasis of the two themes is different. In the life-in-death theme Job's focus is on his anticipation of what life on the other side of the grave will consist of, whereas in the death-in-life theme his focus is on his own experience of life on this side of the grave. In fact, his experience of death-in-life seems to motivate his craving for life-in-death.

---

75. See, e.g., Pss 17:9–12; 25:19; 31:12; 35:11; 38:13; 41:6–9; 42:11; 56:3; 64:4–5; 69:5; 86:14; 102:9; 143:3.

76. See, e.g., Pss 22:7–8, 17–18, 23; 31:12, 14; 35:15–16, 21; 38:12; 41:10; 55:12–15, 21–22; 69:9; 88:9, 19; 109:25.

77. For good examples, see Pss 22; 31; 38; 69; 88; 102.

78. Although Habel (*Job*, 154) notices ironic addresses to God scattered here and there.

79. For more on Job's "resistance to prayer," see Newsom, *Contest of Moral Imaginations*, 136–38.

80. See, e.g., Habel, *Job*, 154, 267; Newsom, "Job," 387, 394, 458–59, 460, 475. For more on Job's usage of the lament form, see Newsom, *Contest of Moral Imaginations*, 132–50; Claus Westermann, *The Structure of the Book of Job: A Form-Critical Analysis* (trans. Charles A. Muenchow; Philadelphia: Fortress, 1981), 31–66.

According to Lifton, the purpose of the symbolizing function of humans is to ensure the vitality of the organism. But Job's death imagery in the initial portions of the first cycle is geared not at all toward the vitality of the self. In fact, it seems to operate to the detriment of the self, for the poles of life-in-death and death-in-life form for Job what Lifton describes as the logic of suicide.

According to Lifton, suicide and the contemplation of suicide relate to two inter-related components: a "universal logic" (Lifton's term), which is what one understands to be the connection between the act of killing oneself and its ultimate "meaning"; and what might be called a "proximate logic,"[81] that is, personal feelings of inner disturbance, powerlessness, despair, and a sense of being trapped or inescapability that convince a person that suicide is a desirable, if not the only available option.[82]

This latter component (suicide's proximate logic) pertains to the sense of being entrapped or cornered that those who contemplate suicide frequently feel. The person senses that he or she lacks the power to break out of this situation due to an acute sense of stasis. "Killing oneself may appear to be the only way to break out of the 'trap' or 'encirclement' and assert whatever it is one feels one wants to, or must, about one's life."[83] Lifton suggests that recourse to suicide (and, in other cases, violence) often is a quest to find relief and to recover life-energy and vitality. There is an irony here that "in suicide, one wants to die and to live"[84] or that one is able to live only by dying.

If people are drawn to suicide due to the overwhelming sense of entrapment and stasis, it is only so because the act of killing oneself necessarily is connected to "some internalized mental structure around the meaning of that act,"[85] which forms the "universal logic" of suicide. Accompanying the feelings of stasis and entrapment is the "radical absence of meaning and purpose, and of the impossibility of human connection."[86] Absent for such people is the feeling that experience can ever become significant or pleasurable, that psychic action can ever be resumed, and "that larger meaning structures can prevail"[87] unless one commits suicide. One simply cannot imagine a livable future—in fact, the future might even be worse. "More specifically, the suicide can create a future only by killing himself. That is he can reawaken psychic action and imagine vital events beyond the present only in deciding upon, and carrying through, his suicide."[88] In this sense, suicide ironically is thought to re-structure and provide form to a world in which all structure and form seems to have gone awry. Suicide, therefore, is a form of "self-completion... [It is] an expression of formative process, even as it

81. Lifton does not use the term "proximate logic." The term is my own designation for this other aspect of the logic of suicide in Lifton's writings.
82. Lifton, *Broken Connection*, 252–53.
83. Ibid., 249.
84. Ibid., 248.
85. Ibid., 243.
86. Ibid., 249.
87. Ibid.
88. Ibid.

ends that process in the individual,"[89] enabling the person to imagine a meaningful, livable future.

Job's death-in-life and life-in-death themes seem to correspond to the proximate and ultimate logic of suicide. For like this proximate logic, Job's own sense of his life is dominated by images of stasis, that his life is entrapped and he is powerless to effect change. Similarly, with his Sheol fantasy, his belief that life is to be found in death, Job re-discovers a symbolically coherent world. Whereas on this side of the grave all structure and form seem to have gone awry, leaving him with the sense that his vitality has been deadened, the other side of the grave offers the hope of the restfulness of abundant life. As with the logic of suicide, Job envisions that to live, he has to die.

This type of logic and this understanding of death, however, indicate Job's decentering. Traditional combinations of forms and images have been disrupted, especially in regards to Job's symbolization of death. And, as Lifton suggests is common for those who undergo decentering, Job experiences life as stasis and disintegration.[90] The question will now become whether Job will remain in this position or whether decentering will lead to recentering and a renewed vitality of the self.

3.4. *Job's Desire for Death after Chapter 3*

Job's conviction that death is better than life will wane after ch. 3 even though he will re-state his desire for death several more times (6:8–9; 7:15; 10:18–22). In fact, after ch. 10 Job will never again state his desire for death, despite his continued elaborate usage of death imagery. If Job's death imagery is desymbolized in the early portions of the first cycle, by ch. 10 it appears to shift ever so slightly from this bewildering position. It will be useful to compare his statement of his desire for death in 10:18–22 to that of ch. 3 to see how Job's focus alters and to set up the discussion in the following chapter regarding the shift that Job's death imagery undergoes.

In 10:18–19, Job poses a question that resembles that of 3:10, but with significant differences:

> Why (למה) did you bring me out (יצא) of the womb (רחם)? I should have perished (גוע) so that the eye would not have seen me.[91] I would be just as though I never was, carried from the womb (בטן) to the grave. (10:18–19)

> Why (למה) did I not die at birth (רחם)? Perish (גוע) as I came out (יצא) of the womb (בטן)? (3:10)

First, Job now names God as the one responsible for failing to bear him to the grave. Although the image of God "hedging" him about in 3:23 shows that Job

---

89. Ibid., 252.

90. He will also make use of images of separation extensively later.

91. Or, as Habel (*Job*, 181) reads, "Better I had expired before an eye saw me"; many others have something similar.

is aware of God's role in his plight, Job does not generally discuss God much in his death imagery in the initial portions of the first cycle. Job 10:18–22, however, mark a shift in Job's conception of God's role in his life. Increasingly Job will focus on God's activities against him or God's inaction when action is required.

A second major difference between this death wish and that of ch. 3 is Job's conception of Sheol. Earlier Job viewed Sheol as a place of peacefulness, tranquility, and, paradoxically, life. Now all such promise and optimism are gone. In 10:22 Job characterizes it as a place of utter gloom, described in terms of numerous "darkness" terms, which, although perhaps conventional terms to describe Sheol, carry an exaggeratedly ominous sense to them because of their sheer density (צלמות, חשך [×2], אפל, עיפה [×2]).[92] Previously Job thought Sheol to be a place where the disorderliness and incomprehensibility of life would be reordered, a place where the ultimate and proximate logic of life would be restored. Now, however, Sheol is a place "without order" (ולא סדרים[93]) whose light is actually darkness (תפע כמו אפל[94]), mirroring the chaotic darkness prior to creation (חשך; Gen 1:2). Job seems to have lost the ultimate logic of suicide. Choosing death would no longer be a meaningful act. He will fittingly no longer voice a desire to be in Sheol.

Job's shift to a more overt discussion of God's role in his life and his link of death with hopelessness—themes that will dominate his discussion of death in the upcoming speeches—indicate that perhaps Job's death imagery is, at the very least, moving away from its previous desymbolized state. It is no accident that as this process is underway Job also seizes upon the much discussed legal metaphor, which arises for the first time in Job's speeches in ch. 9. Before examining this more fully, however, I would like to pause and consider the death imagery in the speeches of the friends and how it acts as a response to Job's desymbolized death imagery. Specifically, I will examine Eliphaz's initial response to Job in chs. 4–5 since it utilizes many of the strategies the friends will employ repeatedly to convince Job of their point of view,[95] and since, as I will show, it has the most diverse approach to death of all the speeches of the friends.

92. See Newsom, "Job," 415. On "darkness" terms as conventional descriptors of Sheol, see Tromp, *Primitive Conceptions*, 95–98.

93. Driver proposes the Arabic *sadira* ("dazzled by glare") as a cognate to סדר, which occurs this once in the HB. He suggests "without ray of light" as a translation for the phrase (Driver, "Problems in the Hebrew Text," 76–77). Fohrer emends סדר to נוהרה ("light") and translates the phrase similarly (Fohrer, *Hiob*, 201). Clines, however, notes that the word is common enough in later Hebrew, including at Qumran (Clines, *Job 1–20*, 223).

94. Driver takes תפע from the root יפע ("show dark cloud") similar to the Arabic *yaf'u(n)* ("cloud foreboding rain"; Driver, "Problems in the Hebrew Text," 76–77).

95. Which Newsom enumerates as "[Construing] Job's experience in terms of narrative structures that integrate and ultimately transcend the present turmoil [4:3–7; 5:9–16, 17–26]…, [advocating] the specific religious practice of prayer, which…has the therapeutic capacity to enact a form of order that displaces [רגז] [5:8]…, [and offering] iconic narratives…that combine narrative frameworks with a set of generative metaphors that reassert the moral order of the world and thus deny [רגז] any ontological status [4:8–11; 5:2–7]" (Newsom, *Contest of Moral Imaginations*, 96)

3.5. Death in Eliphaz's First Speech (Chapters 4–5)

Philippe Nemo understands the friends' responses to Job in terms of the thera-peutic with an emphasis on technique. Technique views the world as immedi-ately transparent and makes a claim to universal, unified knowledge and insights. It views other claims to knowledge as deficient. The friends, according to Nemo, claim a moral technique in the face of the suffering and evil that Job has endured:[96]

> Moral technology claims to have overwhelmed what was most serious in evil. The caesura separating the moment in which the ground of the world is still firm from the moment when it falls away like rotten floorboards is regarded by moral technology as a problem that has been pinpointed, bypassed, erased. The world, almost completely transparent to knowledge, is a degree of order superior to all conceivable disorder... It dominates the whole earth.[97]

According to Nemo, technique must ultimately fail because it cannot encapsu-late excessive or radical evil, such as Job experiences and attempts to articulate.[98]

The therapy of the friends, introduced brilliantly in Eliphaz's first speech, employs the technology of the life/piety/relationship complex in order to under-stand and explain Job's experiences. Specifically, Eliphaz demonstrates death to be perfectly symbolized in this symbolically coherent world, and he asserts this powerful symbolic system in the face of Job's desymbolized death imagery and his articulation of the logic of suicide. Particularly troubling to Eliphaz, it seems, is that whereas previously Job's resymbolizations in the prologue conceded at least a modicum of meaningfulness in life, his statements about death in the initial portions of the dialogues assert the absolute turmoil and meaninglessness of life, conceiving of symbolic coherency and meaning only in death. To this paradoxical and, from the friends' perspective, problematic understanding of death, Eliphaz counters not only with the therapy of the life/piety/relationship complex and its specific attention to proper, symbolically coherent and signifi-cant death, but he also pushes the boundaries of this complex in order to offer a therapy equal (he hopes) to Job's travail.

Of the five distinct sections of Eliphaz's first speech (4:3–11, 12–21; 5:1–7, 8–16, 17–27), all but one (5:8–16) employ images of death in order to reassert his moral therapy. In three of these four sections (4:3–11, 12–21; 5:17–27), he even lingers on death, seemingly relishing its symbolic potential. And in each of these three sections, the symbolic significance of death is slightly different, revealing the full breadth of death's place in the symbolic world of Eliphaz's speech. If, in Job's first speech, a newly and paradoxically construed death is the lynchpin of his argument, in Eliphaz's therapy, death also is a locus of significance.

---

96. Philippe Nemo, *Job and the Excess of Evil* (trans. Michael Kigel; Pittsburgh: Duquesne Uni-versity Press, 1998), 43–76.

97. Ibid., 62–63.

98. Ibid., 76–80.

3.5.1. *First Technique: Death of the Wicked*

Eliphaz begins his response by reminding Job of his former stature as one who would aid those who had suffered tragedy (4:4) and by contrasting this with his current stature now that he is the one to suffer (4:5). Job likely would concur with this contrast, but for very different reasons. To Job, the contrast has to do with shattered systems of meaning, whereas to Eliphaz, Job needs first to remember how the world operates and then to locate his place in this coherent world.[99] Eliphaz, therefore, lays out for Job a coherent picture of the world. He offers Job technique:

> Is not your piety your confidence? The integrity of your ways your hope? Think back, which of the innocent has perished? Where have the upright been cut off? It is just as I have seen: those who plough evil and sow trouble reap them. By the breath of God they perish and by the blast of his nostrils they are finished. (4:6–9)

This opening speech reveals how radically different Eliphaz's symbolic universe is from Job's. It is organized into two contrasting images, that of the pious and that of the impious, mirroring the "two ways" imagery of Proverbs. Each pair re-animates for Job the life/piety/relationship complex by re-organizing key tropes and metaphors of Job's speech in ch. 3. First of all, whereas Job located his hope for life and meaning in death, Eliphaz resymbolizes death by restoring hope to its proper symbolization as the result of piety (4:6). The words Eliphaz employs to discuss Job's piety not only echo those of the introduction to the prologue (יראה, תם, נקי, ישר) and therefore reorient Job to this symbolically coherent world, but they also reorient Job's own symbolic understanding of his experiences. For whereas Job felt that "his way (דרך)" had been hidden, Eliphaz believes that the "integrity of [Job's] way (דרך)" ought to be his hope. Job's image of stasis and paralysis has been co-opted and returned to its normal symbolization.[100] To Eliphaz, Job's way continues to be intact and whole. It ought to be that in which Job has hope.

In the other half of the pair, Eliphaz co-opts one of Job's keywords to describe the devastation and upheaval of his life, עמל ("trouble"; 3:10, 20) and returns to its proper symbolization (4:8). To Eliphaz, עמל, like און ("evil"), is a moral category. It represents the impious things that people do, which inevitably result in calamity being returned to them. This view, of course, is that of the symbolization of abundant life.

But most importantly, Eliphaz re-orients Job to a proper symbolization of death in each half of the contrasting pictures of piety and impiety. First, Eliphaz asks rhetorical questions—questions that are based on the assumption of obvious answers: "Who among the innocent has perished (אבד)? [None!] Where have the upright been cut off (נכחד)? [Nowhere!]." Later, in 5:19–22, Eliphaz will fill out the details of the relation of the pious to death when he reveals that God

---

99. Newsom (*Contest of Moral Imaginations*, 101–5) describes this strategy as giving to Job a sort of "narratability" to his experience.

100. This is not so much a resymbolization, because this would imply working through the experience of desymbolization, which Eliphaz gives no indication to have done.

guards the pious from sudden and calamitous death. Although God reproves
(יכח; 5:17a) and apportions discipline (מוסר; 5:17b), it is not for the purpose of
bringing the pious to death, but to benefit the pious, to serve as a correction of
action and to further the cause of piety. Therefore, the pious have nothing to fear
from situations that would normally bring sudden and/or calamitous death:
famine (רעב), battle (מלחמה), destruction (שד), starvation (כפן), or attack from
wild beasts (חית הארש; 5:20–23).[101] God, in fact, *redeems* the pious from death
(פדה ממות; 5:20a), an image entirely consistent with the life/piety/relationship
complex where God rewards the pious with abundant life, even if abundant life
sometimes comes by way of discipline.

In fact, only the impious die early and do not experience abundant life, as
the second half Eliphaz's pair in 4:8–11 makes clear: the wicked (חרשי און,
זרעי עמל) perish (אבד) and are destroyed (כלה). Underscoring this symbolization of death, Eliphaz concludes this portion of his speech with a somewhat puzzling reference to lions (4:10–11). Although some commentators view these
verses as secondary,[102] the comparison between the wicked and lions is fairly
common in the Psalms.[103] To Eliphaz, the wicked are like lions who, although
appearing ferocious, break their teeth and die (אבד) at any moment.

An emphasis on the death of the wicked will be a point of emphasis in many
of the upcoming speeches of the friends. Normally, when they speak of death it
will be the untimely and catastrophic death that the wicked can expect. This is
especially true of the friends' speeches in chs. 15, 18, and 20 where they use a
variety of death equivalents to express the death-in-life that the wicked experience on earth, even as actual death speedily approaches. Eliphaz describes the
wicked "withering" prematurely (15:32–33), with fire and darkness consuming
them (15:23, 30, 34), as they writhe in torment (15:20). Bildad uses images of
stasis and confinement to express the quality of the life of the wicked (the net
snares them, the trap seizes them, and so on; 18:8–10) and he describes the
ephemerality of their lives with images of the failing light (18:5) and faltering
lamp (18:6). The bodies of the wicked also disintegrate (18:13) in the wake of
hunger (18:12a) and disaster (18:12b). Zophar argues that the wicked "perish"
(20:7) and go to the grave prematurely (20:11). The deity lets loose his anger
against the wicked, slaughtering them with a barrage of weapons (20:23–25),
even as their household is consumed (20:26–28).

---

101. The other image, the "scourge of the tongue" (שוט לשן) does not seem to have as obvious a
relation to death as do the other images, although many interpret it this way. For example, Habel
takes שוט as an infinitive of the root "to rove" (1:7; 2:2) and parallels this image with the שד of
5:22b, which he reads as "demon." Thus both images are references to the demonic forces of death
that rove the earth with sinister intent (Habel, *Job*, 117, 135–36). Gordis takes שוט לשן to be an ellip-
tical expression for שוט לשן אש, meaning the destruction of a blazing fire (Gordis, *Job*, 58–59).
Dhorme understands the phrase to mean gossip that sows discord, strife, and eventually, war
(Dhorme, *Job*, 70).

102. See, e.g., Fohrer, *Hiob*, 139–41; Artur Weiser, *Das Buch Hiob* (ATD 13; Göttingen:
Vandenhoeck & Ruprecht, 1951), 47.

103. See Pss 7:3; 17:12; 22:14, 22; 35:17; 58:7. See Clines, *Job 1–20*, 127, for more. See also
J. J. M. Roberts, "Young Lions of Psalm 34:11," *Bib* 54 (1973): 265–67, for Akkadian parallels.

Though much of Eliphaz's statement of the death of the wicked parallels those future ones of his friends, two aspects of these initial words of Eliphaz's response to Job are noteworthy. First, he does not accuse Job of perfidy nor of causing his own suffering. Eliphaz takes Job's piety as a given and urges Job to seek solace in it. Second, although he will elaborate on the fate of the pious in 5:17–27, in his initial words to Job in 4:3–11, Eliphaz takes more time describing the fate of the wicked by tying the wicked to death, than describing the fate of the pious. The force of this emphasis on the deadly fate of the wicked is to exclude Job's fate from theirs and to encourage Job that death emphatically is not in store for him, for he obviously does not qualify as a proper candidate.

This emphasis on the death of the wicked also serves to chastise Job for his own valuation of death in ch. 3. If, in that speech, Job conceptualized death as "the good"—as a place free from the oppressive presence of the deity and where life and meaning could be experienced—here Eliphaz takes pains to locate death properly in the symbolization of abundant life by linking it categorically with the negative fate of the wicked at the hands of a just deity. Whereas Job viewed death positively, Eliphaz counters with proper therapy and negative death. Furthermore, this emphasis on the proper symbolization of death in Eliphaz's first speech calls attention to what is at stake in the disagreement between Job and Eliphaz, and will serve to orient the dispute in the coming dialogues. The disagreement, at least at this point, is not over Job's piety, but over the meaning of death and the role of the deity in relation to death.[104] Whereas for Job death represents relief, release, and (paradoxically) life in the absence of the oppressive deity, Eliphaz counters by properly re-ordering the terms of the life/piety/relationship complex.

3.5.2. *Second Technique: Death of the Pious*
To this conventional conceptualization of death at the beginning of his response to Job Eliphaz adds another one to the end (5:26). Having established already that the wicked die early and calamitous deaths (4:7–11) and that God saves the righteous from such deaths (5:17–25), Eliphaz turns to a much less developed symbolization of death in the life/piety/relationship complex, that of the symbolic placement of the ultimate death of the righteous. For although the righteous do not die early, they do, indeed die. Death, in this case, is not an indication of wickedness or alienation from the deity, but is a crowning achievement of a life lived abundantly. To die at an old age with plenty of possessions and offspring is to die the full, virtuous death of the righteous. The model for this type of death is that of Abraham, whom God promised would die "in peace…in a good old age (שׂיבה)" (Gen 15:15), but the image of this abundant death is also found in the deaths of Moses (Deut 34:5–7) and David (1 Chr 29:28).[105]

Notable about the symbolization of the death of the righteous, however, is how muted and implicit this symbolization is in comparison to the symbolization of the death of the wicked. In the latter case, a clear, explicit, and prominent

104. By the time of Eliphaz's final speech (ch. 22), however, Job's piety will become an issue.
105. It is found less so in the death of Gideon (Judg 8:32).

connection is made repeatedly in the HB between death, wickedness, and alienation from the deity. As suggested earlier, this connection is the flip-side of the life/piety/relationship complex. In contrast, the symbolic placement of the biological necessity of death among the righteous rarely—almost never—receives overt description. It must be gleaned from various narrative and poetic details, both positive and negative. The former pertain to those model deaths mentioned above. These deaths are described using terms to connote abundance, fullness, and wholeness. So, Abraham died "in peace" (בשלם; Gen 15:15), "in a good old age" (בשיבה וטבה; Gen 15:15; 25:8), "old and sated" (זקן ושבע; Gen 25:8); Moses died with "his eyes...not dimmed and his vigor...not abated" (לא כהתה עינו ואל נס לחח; Deut 34:7); and David died "in a good old age, full of days, riches and honor" (בשיבה טובה שבע ימים עשר וכבוד; 1 Chr 29:28). The righteous are not supposed to die old and sorrowful (Gen 42:38; 44:29, 31), lifeless and unnourished (Ruth 4:15), without peace (1 Kgs 2:6, 9), or alienated from the deity (Ps 71:18; Isa 46:4).[106]

The symbolization of the death of the righteous, however, lacks any specific statement comparable to the description of the death of the wicked in, for example, the Fate of the Wicked Poems or the Psalms of Lament. Furthermore, the images used to describe the deaths of righteous ones (Abraham, Moses, David) are much less rich and fewer in number than the wealth of images and instances of imagery of the death of the wicked.

This does not deter Eliphaz. If there are no other statements of the death of the righteous in the life/piety/relationship complex, Eliphaz provides one, announcing that the righteous person, who is saved from untimely and calamitous death, "shall go to the grave at a ripe old age,[107] as a sheaf comes up in its season" (5:26). The image of the sheaf is at once an image of abundance (fertility, crops), nourishment, and fullness (completion of the full life-cycle).

Although this image of the abundant death of the righteous is more-or-less implicit in the symbolization of abundant life, Eliphaz makes it overt, and therefore offers to Job an entirely coherent and proper symbolization of "good" death. Good death is not the absence from the deity and vitality on the other side of the grave as Job has stated. Good death is abundance and fullness on this side of the grave—from birth through old age—in relation to the deity, which culminates in a full and completely satisfactory death. Once again, Eliphaz has resymbolized death for Job.

---

106. Ps 92:13–16, although not describing the death of the righteous, captures the abundant life that the righteous live in old age. They "blossom like the palm," "grow like the cedar," "are planted in the house of Yhwh," "flourish in the courts of God," "produce fruit," and "are always vigorous and fresh."

107. The exact translation of כלח is hotly debated. Suggestions range from "vigor," "strength," "freshness," "full age," "sap," and so forth. I follow Grabbe and take it as "old age" based on Arabic cognates (Lester L. Grabbe, "Comparative Philology and the Text of Job: A Study in Methodology" [Ph.D. diss., Claremont Graduate School, 1975], 56–60), while at the same time, attempting to allude to the suggestions that pertain to "vigor" and "strength." For a brief look at various possible translations, see Clines, *Job 1–20*, 118–19.

3.5.3. *Third Technique: Death and Immorality*

The third symbolization of death (4:19–21), which falls in his speech between the other two (4:7–11 [plus 5:20–22] and 5:26), stakes out new ground entirely. It is an image of death not at all found in the life/piety/relationship complex, neither explicitly, as in the death of the wicked, nor implicitly, as in the death of the righteous. Nor is it found in Job's own musings about death in the initial portions of the dialogues.

Ostensibly because of its novelty, Eliphaz introduces this topic with a rather lengthy statement of the supernatural quality of the knowledge he will impart (4:12–16). He establishes the main point of his argument through the rhetorical questions, "Can a human be righteous in relation to God? Can a man be pure in relation to his maker?" (4:17).[108] That is, because humans cannot be wholly righteous all the time, they ought to expect a measure of suffering and calamity. To emphasize the imperfection of humans, Eliphaz employs images of disintegration: human bodies as finite, corruptible, and ephemeral. They are "houses of clay whose foundation is in the dust" (4:19);[109] "they can be[110] crushed like the moth" (4:19);[111] "they can be shattered between morning and evening" (4:20); "they can be utterly exterminated";[112] "their tent-cord can be pulled up" (4:21).[113] He ends his litany with the blunt statement that humans "die" (מות; 4:21), the most literal of all statements of human mortality. This extended consideration of the frailty of the human body is in service of Eliphaz's main point that since

---

108. The words translated "in relation to God" and "in relation to his maker" are מאלוה and מעשׂהו. It is possible to read the preposition מן as a comparative ("Can a human be more righteous than God…?"), as many of the older translations do (see, e.g., KJV, RV, ASV, NEB, NIV). Many other simply translate the preposition to mean "before" ("Can a human be righteous before God?"; see, e.g., RSV and JB for something similar), but as Newsom points out, the rhetorical question clearly indicates an impossible situation, and since entrance liturgies assume moral purity and righteousness of one who comes before God, the preposition ought not to be translated as "before." Instead, one ought to go with the NAB and take מן as "in relation to" or "as against" (Newsom, "Job," 378). See BDB, 579, and *HALOT*, 536, for this sense.

109. The image here draws on Gen 2:7 and suggests "the material nature of man" (A. B. Davidson and H. C. O. Lanchester, *The Book of Job with Notes, Introduction and Appendix* [new ed.; Cambridge: Cambridge University Press, 1918], 33). It links human beginnings and endings to inanimate earth.

110. I understand the verbs to be expressing the modality of possibility. See Clines, *Job 1–20*, 113, as well as his "Verb Modality and the Interpretation of Job 4:20–21," *VT* 30 (1980): 354–57.

111. Moths normally are noted for their destructiveness in the HB (Job 13:28; Ps 39:12; Isa 50:9; 51:8), although they also can represent decay (Hos 5:12). In this case, the moth seems to represent frailty.

112. I am taking the נצח, normally meaning "forever," as a superlative following D. Winton Thomas, "Use of נצח as a Superlative in Hebrew," *JSS* 1 (1956): 106–9.

113. יתר is here rendered "tent-cord" rather than "excess" (see Driver and Gray, *Job*, 1:48; Pope, *Job*, 38; see also Job 30:11 and Ps 11:2 where it has this sense). Gordis refers to "the familiar Oriental figure of life as a tent" for which he cites Isa 38:12 and Wis 9:15 as examples (Gordis, *Job*, 51). The image of the tent-cord being pulled up is one of the ephemerality of human existence, although Clines asserts that tent-cords (יתר) are never the object of נסע (Clines, *Job 1–20*, 114). Fohrer and Pope counter that both tent-cords and tent-pegs can be "pulled up" (Fohrer, *Hiob*, 146; Pope, *Job*, 38).

God charges even the angels with error (4:18b), how much more frail humans who are given to decay and corruption anyway.[114]

So, with this argument, the symbol "death" takes on a third meaning in Eliphaz's response to Job: it stands for wickedness and alienation in the first place; for good, full, abundant life in the second place; and now, for immorality and suffering.[115] The question must be asked: What function does this new symbolization of death have? In a reading sympathetic to Eliphaz, it seems to be a concession to Job that the symbolization of death in the life/piety/relationship complex might be inadequate to the enormity of Job's experience. Or, again, given Job's piety in comparison with his recent experiences of suffering and loss, a slightly alternate conception of death's symbolization might be in order, one that normalizes human death, making it recognizable, expected, and not so chaotic. It is possible that Eliphaz has already worked through the process of centering–decentering–recentering and this theological innovation comprises part of his newly organized center. Eliphaz has reconfigured an accepted symbolization in order to account for Job's lot.

3.5.4. *Summary of Eliphaz's Moral Technique*
The three distinct aspects of Eliphaz's symbolization of death do share three common characteristics—characteristics that will also be present in all the future speeches of the friends. First, all of them, including his reconfiguration of traditional symbolizations, function as technique, viewing the world as immediately transparent and making a claim to universal knowledge. Eliphaz's moral technology has identified Job's situation "as a problem that has been pinpointed, bypassed, erased."[116] In the first case, Eliphaz offers Job a corrected account of what death is and who it is for; in the second case, he offers Job a corrected picture of "good death"; in the third case, he offers Job an innovative explanation of why he has suffered.

Second, in all of the symbolizations of death, including the reconfiguration, the relationship to the deity remains intact. This is obviously the case in the first one, where the death of the wicked by the hand of God (4:9) stands in contrast to the pious person protected from calamitous death by God (4:6–7; 5:19–22). Similarly, the statement of the "good death" makes overt what is implicit in the life/piety/relationship complex, and represents the culmination of a life protected by God from early death (5:19–22), as if God preserves the life of the pious for

114. Newsom understands the argument to involve a symbolic comparison, not a logical progression. She compares the terms of this argument (mortality/immorality) to the dual meaning of the word "corrupt," which has both a material and moral sense (Newsom, "Job," 379).

115. Eliphaz's theological novelty has caused some commentators to argue that Eliphaz did not actually utter this (see H. L. Ginsberg, "Job the Patient and Job the Impatient," *SJT* 17 [1968]: 98–107; Gary V. Smith, "Job IV 12–21: Is it Eliphaz's Vision?," *VT* 40 [1990]: 453–63; Naphtali H. Tur-Sinai, *The Book of Job: A New Commentary* [trans. Sefer Iyov; Jerusalem: Kiryath Sepher, 1957], 88–91). Other scholars who find this section problematic for a variety of reasons include Margaret Brackenbury Crook, *The Cruel God: Job's Search for the Meaning of Suffering* (Boston: Beacon, 1959), 68–69; J. C. L. Gibson, "Eliphaz the Temanite," 259–72 (265–67); Rowley, *Job*, 49.

116. Nemo, *Excess of Evil*, 62–63.

this one final moment (5:26b). And lastly, even while premising human suffering on the breach in relationship with the deity that results from inescapable immorality, Eliphaz's reconfigured symbolization of death still assumes relationship with the deity as the starting point, for mistrust (4:18a) only occurs in the context of a relationship. Further, this is a generic type of mistrust that inhabits the divine–human (and angel) relationship, and not one that singles out an individual being in a personal way.

Finally, in all of Eliphaz's symbolizations of death, piety remains a vital term. In the symbolization of the death of the wicked, piety preserves the pious from death while its lack leads to demise; in the symbolization of the death of the pious, piety leads to good, full, abundant death as a culmination of a life well lived; in the account of human corruptibility, the fact of human mortality proves the fact of the impossibility of absolute human piety, though not its existence, in general. In fact, this symbolization depends upon the notion that humans, like angels, are creatures from whom piety is expected.

These three distinct aspects of Eliphaz's speech will also be true of all of the friends' speeches. All of them function as moral technique, the relationship to the deity forms a major component of each, and each maintains an emphasis on piety.[117] Where the remaining speeches of the friends differ from Eliphaz's first speech is that they will become more personal as the dialogues progress, consisting of accusations against Job's character and explicit statements of his assumed perfidy,[118] and they will make increasingly more elaborate usage of death imagery in their symbolization of abundant life. They will open up very little new ground in the debate, however. In fact, the friends will focus almost exclusively on traditional depictions of the impoverished death of the wicked, returning only twice to Eliphaz's apparent theological innovation,[119] and not at all to statements of the abundant death of the pious.[120] Their rhetorical strategy in their dispute with Job will be persuasion by repetition.[121]

Throughout the bulk of the first cycle, Job appears to be unfazed by the friend's repeated offerings of technique. His focus remains firmly on his own experience of overwhelming suffering (excessive evil, in Nemo's terms), articulated through desymbolized death. As the speeches progress, however, Job's articulation of death undergoes subtle shifts (in the second cycle) and extensive shifts (in the third cycle)—shifts that accompany an altered perspective of his situation, and will indicate a move from decentering to recentering. I will now turn to the second cycle where these shifts begin to appear.

---

117.   The only one that might not display some of these aspects is Bildad's speech in the third cycle (ch. 25), although scholars are not in agreement regarding the scope of this speech.

118.   Bildad will blame the deaths of Job's children on their sin (8:4). Eliphaz will accuse Job briefly of immorality in 15:4–5 before doing so extensively in 22:5–9.

119.   15:14; 25:4.

120.   See 8:11–13, 22; 11:20; 15:20–35; 18:5–21; 20:5–29; 22:15–20.

121.   The friends will also use death imagery in a couple of minor ways in their remaining speeches. First, Bildad uses the image of the ephemeral nature of human life to appeal to the unreliability of personal experience in the face of the wisdom of the sages (8:9). Second, Zophar uses images of Sheol and the heavens as the limits of the universe, which God's mystery extends far beyond (11:8).

Chapter 4

SHIFTING DEATH AND THE LEGAL METAPHOR
(CHAPTERS 3–20, PART TWO)

In the preceding chapter I argued that Job's death imagery is desymbolized in the initial portions of the first cycle of speeches, demonstrated by his discussions of life-in-death and death-in-life, which form the ultimate and proximate logic of his suicidal desire for death. However, as his speeches progress, Job slowly abandons his conviction that life is found in Sheol so that by 10:18–22, while he still wishes he would have been stillborn, he sees no hope for life in the grave. From this point on in Job's speeches, subtle but significant changes occur when Job discusses death: his emphasis will increasingly be on the deity's role as the agent of his disaster and suffering; and he will develop an increasingly negative attitude toward the prospect of death. Death will soon take on new meanings: oppression and murder at the hand of the deity; the injustice and immorality of the deity; and extreme hopelessness. So, from death-in-life, Job will move to divine murder; and from life-in-death, Job will move to hopelessness-in-death. At the same time as this shift in Job's conception of death occurs, Job also begins to contemplate legal action against God. As I will argue below, the legal metaphor functions as a focusing mechanism for Job's desymbolized death imagery, allowing the recentering process to begin, although it will not be complete until the last round of speeches, to be examined in the next chapter.

4.1. *From Death-in-Life to Divine Murder*

In order to gain a better understanding of Job's increasing focus on God's role as his murderer after 10:18–22 and how this relates to the centering–decentering–recentering process, it will be useful to pause and consider what Lifton writes about anxiety, anger, and rage in the decentering process.

4.1.1. *Anxiety, Anger, and Rage in Lifton's Writings*
Concerning decentering, Lifton writes that "Every movement away from centeredness, every encounter with significant novelty (significant in terms of its departure from preexistent inner form), entails anxiety and risk, often guilt, rage and a sense of inner chaos."[1] Subjects who feel their vitality threatened—as

---

1. Lifton, *Life of the Self*, 73.

certainly happens in decentering—experience anxiety, guilt, anger, rage, and violence in varying amounts. Anxiety, according to Lifton, is "a sense of foreboding stemming from threatened vitality and anticipated breakdown of the integrity of the self."[2] When one perceives that the self's resources are inadequate to the threat, anxiety results—"the feeling of having been put adrift from ordinary manageable existence and thrust into an alien realm dominated by the threat. For nothing in the experience of the self enables it to counter the threat."[3] Anxiety is felt as a sense of "Disintegration, and its subjective equivalent ('falling apart'),"[4] while feelings of separation and stasis cause the perception of the threat to the structure of the self.

Guilt is a form of anxiety and results when one feels responsible for separation, stasis, and disintegration: "We can therefore define guilt in general as an image-feeling of responsibility or blame for bringing about injury or disintegration, or other psychological equivalents of death."[5] Guilt, however, comes in two forms: a static guilt that causes "the deadening immobilization of the self";[6] or an animating guilt, which occurs "when one can derive from imagery of self-condemnation energy toward renewal and change."[7]

Anger is similar to guilt in that it "has to do with a struggle to assert vitality by attacking the other rather than the self."[8] One feels oneself to be a victim, betrayed by one who is trusted:

> The imagery that accompanies this sense of being victimized is likely to involve one's own disintegration in the form of breakdown of moral and psychological integrity. Angry imagery or even violence is expressed in an attempt to reestablish autonomy, pride, integrity.... One feels badly used by the powers that be; the experience of anger and rage become necessary for self-definition.[9]

4.1.2. *Anxiety and Threat in Job's Speeches*

As Job's speeches progress through the latter portions of the first cycle and throughout the second, Job, as before, emphasizes his own threatened vitality and breakdown of the self with the imagery of disintegration, separation, and stasis,[10] but with the crucial difference that, like those who experience anxiety and anger, Job identifies the source of his threat, namely, God. Job's usage of death equivalents to state his experience of death-in-life prior to 10:18–22 comes to be replaced by death equivalents to express his sense of divine murder

---

2. Lifton, *Broken Connection*, 128.
3. Ibid., 131.
4. Ibid., 128.
5. Ibid., 139.
6. Ibid.
7. Ibid.
8. Ibid., 147.
9. Ibid., 149.
10. For Lifton disintegration is the "essence of anxiety," which is then experienced as a sense of falling apart (ibid., 129). He argues that separation and stasis imagery are causes of the threat to the structure of the self, not subjective experiences of the threat to the self. In Job's speeches, however, it is impossible to identify disintegration imagery as the "essence" of his anxiety. Disintegration, separation, and stasis, rather, appear to co-mingle, as examined above.

after this passage. Nowhere is this better illustrated than in 16:7–17 and 19:6–20 where Job makes abundant use of images of disintegration, stasis, and separation all geared toward expressing his threatened vitality and revealing God as the source of that threat.

In the opening verses of 16:7–17 Job uses all three death equivalents to articulate his sense of God's role in causing his subjective feelings of death. First Job claims to have been "worn out" "or wearied" (לאה; 16:7a) by God,[11] an image of exhaustion or enervation. The word suggests both the inability of physical movement due to over-exertion[12] and emotional drain or deadness.[13] It is an image of stasis—of the perceived inability of physical movement coupled with psychic and emotional paralysis—with God as the cause.

The parallel line, "you have made all my company desolate/appalled,"[14] moves from an image of God's effect on Job (stasis) to a focus on God's effect on Job's company. The exact referent of this company (עדה) is ambiguous, either being a reference to Job's family[15] who were "destroyed" or "devastated" (שמם) by God in the prologue, or to a larger group of acquaintances who certainly are "appalled" (שמם) at Job's sorry state, a sure "signal of divine displeasure."[16] Either way, Job presents an image of what Lifton would call "the death equivalent of separation"—the sense of detachment from meaningful human contact—either through the destruction of his family, or through the ostracism of his community due to his apparent divine disfavor. And again, Job identifies God as the agent of separation.

From images of stasis and separation, Job moves quickly to one of disintegration, using the metaphor of the deity as a vicious wild animal to voice his sense of bodily violation (16:9). God's animal anger (אף), depicted in the following verse as "gnash[ing] his teeth" in rage, causes him to tear Job to pieces (טרף) as a wild beast would its prey.[17] Job experiences even the enraged gaze of the beast/deity as a weapon destined to violate his body: "my enemy looks daggers at me."[18]

---

11. Although the subject is not specified here, the parallel line makes clear that it is God.

12. See, e.g., Prov 26:15; Isa 16:12; 47:13; Jer 12:5; and perhaps also Ps 68:9.

13. See, e.g., Isa 1:14; 7:13; Jer 6:11; 12:5; 15:6; 20:9.

14. Because of the apparent disparity in line length in the MT of v. 7, some emend עדתי ("my company") to רעתי ("my calamity" or "woe") and re-divide the lines to read, "Only now he hath wearied me out, (and) appalled me; and all my calamity hath seized hold upon me. It hath been a witness and risen up against me; my leanness testifieth to my face" (Driver and Gray, *Job*, 1:144; see also Pope, *Job*, 114). I agree with Habel that "the staccato effect of the [emended] poetic lines is forceful and the text makes good sense without emendation" (Habel, *Job*, 264).

15. Gordis, *Job*, 175–76. He cites 15:34 for support of this translation, where the word is parallel to אהל. NJPS therefore translates, "You have destroyed my whole community."

16. Clines, *Job 1–20*, 382. Clines offers Ezek 32:10 and Jer 49:20; 50:45 as proof of this sense of שמם in the Hiphil.

17. See, e.g., Gen 37:33; 44:28; 49:27; Exod 22:13; Num 23:24; Deut 33:20; Pss 7:2; 17:12; Isa 5:29; Jer 5:6; Ezek 19:3, 6; 22:25, 27; Hos 5:8; Mic 5:8; Nah 2:12. In the most of these examples the lion or the wolf is the animal tearing its prey.

18. As translated by NEB. Literally, "My enemy sharpens his eyes against me" (צרי ילטוש עיניו לי). The verb לטש refers to the sharpening or whetting of a plowshare (1 Sam 13:20), sword (Ps 7:2), or razor (52:2).

The remaining verses of 16:7–17 and 19:6–20 will continue to overlap various images of stasis, separation, and disintegration in a "cinematic tour de force,"[19] and the collective impact of the images will be to point God out as the cause of Job's death. This overlapping of death images, much like the overlapping of death-in-life images of 7:1–6, follows no logical progression. Instead Job uses them to express his sense of his own murder at God's hand. They are different images—stasis, separation, and disintegration—to get at different aspects of this murder. I will briefly examine these, beginning with the images of separation.

4.1.2.1. *Separation*. Job expands on his initial image of separation in 16:7 twice in the passages under consideration (16:10–11; 19:13–18). In the first case, Job indicates that an unspecified group "open[s] wide their mouths toward me" (16:10), employing a rare verb (פערו) whose sense seems to be the reproach of the jeering crowd as the parallel line suggests ("In scorn they strike my cheeks"). However, this specific verb also has echoes of the gaping mouth of Sheol long-ing to devour its victims,[20] echoes not found in the more common verbs used to express "gaping of the mouth in reproach," פצה[21] and רחב.[22] This connection between human reviling and death seems to allude to the sense that lack of mean-ingful human connection (here expressed as the revulsion and assault [v. 11]) is a death equivalent—human alienation metaphorically equivalent to being thrust into the devouring jaws of Sheol. Further, following on the heels of images of divine hostility, these images of human hostility imply that the latter are a direct result of the former.[23] Implicitly, God is the agent of human hostility.

In 19:13–19, Job expands on his earlier statement in 16:7 that God has made "his company" desolate, and will list the various members of his family and community from whom God has alienated him: "kin" (אח), "acquaintances" (ידע), "clan members" (קרוב), "friends" (מידע), "guests in my house" (גרי ביתי), "maidservants" (אמהות), "servant" (עבד), "wife" (אשה), "brothers" (בני בטני), "young children" (עבילים), "intimates" (מתי סודי), and "those I love" (זה אהבתי). This variety of terms to express social relations is matched by the variety of terms used to express Job's separation from them: they are "put far away" (רחק) from Job, they have "become estranged" (זור), they have "ceased to be" or "deserted" (חדל) Job, they have "ignored" (שכח) Job, they consider him a

---

19. Newsom, "Job," 458 (although she is referring only to the sequence of images in 16:9–11). Similarly, Alter writes of this poetic sequence that "A sense of temporal progression is thus produced in a manner analogous to the illusion of movement created in the cinema, where a series of still photographs flashes on the retina with sufficient speed so that one seems to flow into the next, each frozen moment in the visual sequence fusing into temporal flux" (Robert Alter, "From Line to Story in Biblical Verse," *Poetics Today* 4 [1983]: 615–37 [626]). Alter, however, suggests that a logical link exists between these images—a link that I am not advocating (Alter, "From Line to Story," 627).

20. See Isa 5:14.

21. Ps 22:14; Lam 2:16; 3:46, although this verb is connected to death in a different way in Gen 4:11; Num 16:30; Deut 11:6.

22. Ps 35:21; Isa 57:4.

23. See Clines, *Job 1–20*, 382–83; Gordis, *Job*, 176–77; Habel, *Job*, 272; Newsom, "Job," 458.

"stranger" (זוּר) and an "alien" (נכרי), they "do not answer" (לא ענה) him, Job is "alien" (זוּר) to them, he "is loathsome" (חנן) to them, they "despise" (מאס) him and "turn aside" (דבר) from him,[24] they "abhor" (תעב) him, and they have "turned against" (הפך) him. Job understands himself to be separated from human contact due to God's actions.[25]

4.1.2.2. *Disintegration.* Job 16:12–14 picks up the prior military imagery of 6:4 and 7:20 (the arrows aimed at their target) and elaborates on it, casting God in the role of the divine warrior attacking and killing his enemy, Job. Job's claim in 16:12 to have been "at ease" (שׁלו) sets up a comparison between his own sense of peace and tranquility before God's attack and the peace and tranquility of a city or land before invasion by an enemy.[26] More specifically, the comparison is between the battered city and Job's battered body, which was "shattered" (פרר) and "broken to bits" (פצץ) by God.[27] More descriptively, Job identifies specific body parts to have suffered the brunt of the attack. First, God has "seized" (אחז[28]) his "neck" (ערף), which Clines notes is "the most vulnerable part of one's flee-ing opponent"[29] (16:12). Second, with Job as his "target" (מטרא), God "pierces" (פלח) his "kidneys" (כליות), the body part in ancient Israel associated with the emotions (16:13). Third, God's merciless attack causes Job's "gall" (מררה) to be "poured out" (שׁפך). All in all, Job's body, like a besieged city wall, has been "breached" (פרץ) repeatedly by his attacker, God (16:14).[30]

The specific body parts Job claims God attacks are significant not only for the images of bodily disintegration they conjure, but also because of the meaning they had in ancient Israel, specifically the neck and kidneys. Aside from cultic contexts, the neck almost always is associated with the compliance or insub-ordination of subjects to their master. Thus to be "stiff-necked" means to be

---

24. Following Clines, *Job 1–20*, 429; Fohrer, *Hiob*, 308; Wilde, *Hiob*, 211; and *HALOT*, who understand the root to be a cognate to the Arabic *dabara* ("be behind"). See Ps 76:6; Cant 5:6.

25. For the relation of this passage to Psalms of Lament, see Westermann, *Structure*, 44–46.

26. See 1 Chr 4:40; Zech 7:7; and possibly also Dan 4:1. See also Judg 18:7, 27, where the people of Laish were "at ease" before they were attacked (although the verb in this passage is the synonym of שׁלו, שׁקה).

27. These verbs have a combat sense in Ps 74:13 and Hab 3:6, although the former occurs most frequently in covenant or oath contexts (i.e. "break the covenant"; see, e.g., Gen 17:14; Lev 26:15, 44; Num 15:31; 30:9, 13, 14, 16; Deut 31:16, 20; Judg 2:1; 1 Kgs 15:19; 2 Chr 16:3; Ezra 9:14). Its occurrence in *Job* is the only reduplicated (Pilpel) form.

28. A term used to describe combat situations. See Josh 22:9, 19; Judg 1:6; 12:6; 16:21. Fohrer argues that there is an allusion here to Ps 137:9 ("Happy is the one who seizes and shatters your little ones against the rock"), which also alludes to a combat context, but in a slightly different sense (Fohrer, *Hiob*, 287–88).

29. He cites Gen 49:8; Exod 23:27; and Ps 18:41 for support (Clines, *Job 1–20*, 384). For more on the military language of this passage, see ibid., 383–84.

30. He will add one more image of disintegration in 19:10, which seems to share the military metaphor: "He breaks me down on every side." Here Job compares his sense of bodily destruction to a city wall being torn down in battle (see Fohrer, *Hiob*, 313; Habel, *Job*, 300, for this interpretation). The reference also could be to a building that is demolished (Clines, *Job 1–20*, 444). Either way, it is still an image of disintegration.

obdurate and insolent, disregarding the requirements of one's lord,[31] while to present the back of one's neck, especially in the context of battle, means to cease fighting in an effort to flee, and it represents an admission of defeat and the capitulation of retreat from an overpowering foe.[32] The image of God seizing Job's neck combines both of these senses, for despite the battle context, Job does not present God his neck (capitulation and retreat), but seems to remain stiff-necked and obdurate in his appeal to God. God, however, seizes Job's neck, metaphorically seizing Job's subordination, with the literal image of God walking off with Job's neck as a prize, as one would seize booty in battle.

The kidneys, apart from cultic contexts, not only represent the seat of emotions,[33] but also suggest the "essence" of an individual, which God is frequently urged to test in order to gauge his/her sincerity of devotion to him.[34] The kidneys, therefore, come to stand for intimacy with the deity.[35] The image of the arrows of God's archers piercing Job's kidneys is a graphic picture both of Job's sense of God's murder of his "essential" being, as well as God's destruction not only of their intimacy, but of the *possibility* of intimacy (the organ of intimacy has been destroyed).

This is not the first time, however, that Job voices his experience of divine murder employing images of bodily violation and disintegration. Earlier Job also described his sense of attack by the divine warrior: his body racked with divine arrows (6:4a) whose poison attacked his spirit with malicious intent (6:4b). The difference between the images of divine murder in ch. 6 and those in ch. 16 is that previously the imagery functioned to strengthen the claim of the desirability of death, for though Job felt his suffering to be an attack by a murderous deity (6:4), his ultimate wish was for God to crush him finally and decisively (6:8–9). His experience of divine violation and violence prompted his wish that his life should end. In ch. 16, however, imagery of divine violence and murder is not at all linked to a wish for death, and, because it stands in a lengthy litany of similar death images, represents Job's subjective statements about his experience of divine murder.

4.1.2.3. *Stasis*. In ch. 19 the military imagery, which had earlier been used to express Job's sense of disintegration, now comes to stand for Job's sense of being trapped and immobilized by God. Using the imagery of the city under siege, Job claims in 19:6 that God has "thrown up siegeworks against me,"[36] a

---

31. The term "stiff-necked" almost always is applied to Israel in its disobedience to Yahweh. See Exod 32:9; 33:3, 5; 34:9; Deut 9:6, 13; 10:16; 31:27; 2 Kgs 17:14; 2 Chr 29:6; 30:8; 36:13; Neh 9:16, 17, 29; Isa 48:4; Jer 2:27; 19:15; 32:33.

32. See, e.g., Gen 49:8; Exod 23:27; Josh 7:8, 12; 2 Sam 22:40; Ps 18:40; Jer 48:39, and also probably Jer 18:17.

33. Job 19:27; Prov 23:16.

34. See Pss 7:9; 26:2; 73:21; Jer 11:20; 12:2; 17:10; 20:12.

35. Ps 139:13.

36. The word here translated "siegeworks" (מצודו) some connect with the root צוד ("hunt") and translate as "net" (a sense the word seems to have in Qoh 7:26). However, in light of the imagery in Job 19:7–12, and in light of this passage's parallels to Lam 3:5–9, it probably best has the sense of "siegeworks" as in Qoh 9:14 (see Clines, *Job 1–20*, 428; Habel, *Job*, 291).

picture that suggests Job's entrapment and inability to move, as was the case for residents of a city under siege who would be trapped inside. It is an image reminiscent of Job's claim to have been "hedged in" by God in 3:23, the difference being that previously Job's focus on death-in-life was to contrast with how desirable Sheol would be. In this stasis image, however, emphasis shifts to the agent of the stasis, God.

While the following image of Job's unanswered cry ("I cry out 'Violence' but am not answered; I cry out for help, but there is no justice!"; 19:7) likely pertains more to Job's sense of separation from human contact, the following images of Job's path being "walled up" by God (19:8), and his "glory" being stripped and "crown" removed (19:9) again seem to utilize the image of a king set under siege in his city, hemmed in on all sides by his enemy and having his capacity to rule cut off.[37]

From these "siege" images, the text moves to the image of God setting darkness (חשך[38]) upon Job's paths (19:8). Although this is not as obvious a siege image as the others,[39] it does suggest the immediate picture of inhibition of the ability to walk due to the inability to see one's way. Further, the "darkness" imagery in Job, while certainly in this context suggesting the absence of light that occludes one's path, also comprises the book's imagery of death. So this one image gives the impression both of the physical stasis of being unable to walk due to the inability to see where one is going, and, at the same time, of the metaphorical death that accompanies such stasis.[40] And again, God is identified as the cause.

The lines of v. 8 also form a neat mini chiasm:

A: *He has walled up* <u>my way</u>
B: I cannot pass
A': *He has set darkness* <u>upon my paths</u>

The simple symmetry of lines A and A' adds emphasis to the one non-paralleled line, which functions as a hinge between them. This "hinge" line is a blunt statement of immobility and stasis, while the parallel lines emphasize the agent of stasis, God.

---

37. See Habel, *Job*, 300, for this reading. Newsom also sees in these images the stripping of dignity and self-determination (Newsom, "Job," 475).

38. Guillaume takes the Arabic *hasak* ("thorn hedge") as a cognate to this noun. So, instead of the image of God laying darkness on Job's path, he suggests it is the image of God hedging in Job's road (Alfred Guillaume, "The Arabic Background of the Book of Job," in *Promise and Fulfilment: Essays Presented to Professor S.H. Hooke in Celebration of His Ninetieth Birthday* [ed. F. F. Bruce; Edinburgh: T. & T. Clark, 1963], 106–27 [114]). This recalls Job's earlier claim that God had "hedged him about" (3:23). The more obvious sense of חשך, however, is perfectly intelligible in this context.

39. Hence, Cline's argument that the image of God walling up Job's path ought not to be taken as a siege image (contra Habel; Clines, *Job 1–20*, 443).

40. The image has affinities with 3:22 where Job claimed that God had "hedged about" his way, although this time the word chosen to refer to the path is תיבה and not the highly significant word (in Wisdom circles) דרך.

Finally, after a brief image of disintegration in 19:10,[41] Job resumes the siege imagery in 19:11–12. With God's anger decisively kindled against him, God's "troops" amass (גדודים) and build a rampart (דרך) against Job and, in a grossly disproportionate image that would be amusing were it not so gruesome, they "lay siege around his tent" (יחנו סביב לאהלי), as if this massive force were necessary to topple a mere tent, which Job perceives himself to be.[42]

As with the death-in-life theme, the imagery of stasis, separation, and disintegration in the divine murder theme finds frequent parallel in the Israelite prayer tradition in the Psalms. But as with that other theme, Job's usage of this imagery here reverses some of their traditional connotations in the Psalms. Two images of disintegration, that of the divine beast tearing Job apart and the divine warrior violating his body with various weapons, are particularly revealing. The Psalmist frequently uses lion imagery to express a sense of assault and danger, or ravaging attacks of his foes.[43] The Psalmist then calls out to God for deliverance from this situation—a plea based on the Psalmist's piety and relationship with the deity—with the goal being the restoration of abundant life. Job, however, casts God in the role of the attacking lion, tearing his body apart, an image that makes death, not life, the consequence of any sort of relationship—indeed, any sort of contact—with the deity.

The Psalmist also uses war and weapon imagery either to describe his experience of attack by his foes[44] or as a plea to call on God to use his divine weapons to defeat the wicked.[45] Again, the goal is for God to intercede on behalf of the pious Psalmist and to restore him to abundant life.[46] For Job, however, as in the wild beast imagery, God is the one who unleashes weapons against Job, violating his body. Again, death, not life is Job's experience of relationship with the deity.[47] This is expressed best in the image of God piercing Job's kidneys, organs which, as mentioned above, stand for intimacy with the deity. To Job, relationship with God is the destruction of intimacy and the experience of death.

The other stock Psalm of Lament imagery that Job employs in the divine murder theme (wasting away, growing weak, pursued by foes, shunned by intimates, and so forth) functions in similar ways to the lion and war/weapon

---

41. Chapter 19:10a certainly is an image of disintegration. Verse 10b is debatable.

42. Habel's statement is apt: "God's grand assault is a bitter example of divine overkill" (Habel, *Job*, 301).

43. See, e.g., Pss 17:12; 35:17. See also 22:21–22; 59:7–8, 15–16, where the lion and other animals represent a general assault on, or danger to, the Psalmist. For a comparison of these passages in *Job* to the Lament Psalms, see Westermann, *Structure*, 50–58.

44. See, e.g., Pss 17:9–11; 42:16; 55:19; 64:4–5. See 22:21 for a similar usage.

45. See, e.g., Pss 7:13–14; 35:2–3; 64:8.

46. Newsom ("Job," 459) also notes the theme of the Divine Warrior is used in a similarly positive way throughout the HB where God fights on behalf of his people (Exod 15:3–4; Isa 42:13).

47. Some Psalms do use the imagery of God attacking the Psalmist, but the assault is either understood as warranted due to sin, which is then confessed (Ps 38), or the assault gives the Psalmist cause to plea for divine salvation (Ps 88). Similarly, in Lam 3:20 divine violence is for the purpose of turning Israel back to God. Job, however, neither confesses sin as the cause of his assault, nor does he seek divine salvation and renewal of relationship.

imagery, in that it inverts the terms of life, piety, and relationship with the deity, to make death the experience of God's relationship of terror.[48]

4.1.3. *Anger and Threat in Job's Speeches*

Job's imagery of stasis, separation, and disintegration after 10:18–22 clearly identifies God as the agent who brings his death. God is the one singled out as Job's threat. While the friends urge Job to examine himself in order to find the cause of his real and perceived threat—a type of self-blame that would manifest itself in guilt—Job rejects their pleas, instead turning outward for the cause, an outward move that those whose anxiety develops into anger frequently make, according to Lifton. Job blames God. He is God's victim, betrayed in the intimacy of their prior relationship, a fact that leads to Job's anger, which manifests itself in his speeches as a protest against God's unjust, immoral ways. Job voices this angry protest in several places throughout his speeches.

4.1.3.1. *7:20–21 and 10:20.* Job arrives at his specific form of angry protest by considering his own death and God's responsibility for it. In the earlier stages of the portion of the dialogues presently under consideration, Job voices this angry protest only implicitly. He does this first in 7:20–21 when he uses the image of his imminent death ("for soon[49] I shall lie in dust") to urge God to forgive his sin and desist from his attacks. Job's entreaty, however, plays upon Ps 8:4–5, in which the Psalmist confesses that God has "remembered" (זכר) and "cared for" (פקד) humans, even though they are less exalted than the moon and the stars. This Psalm is a grateful confession of the relationship between God and humans in which God showers humans with blessings, and it is a perfect statement of the symbolization of abundant life.

In Job's parody, however, the salubrious image of God as caretaker becomes the oppressive image of God as vigilant "Watcher of humanity" (נצר אדם; 7:20), over-eager to pounce on any wrongdoing, ever-ready to inflict suffering on humans. The Psalmist's God who "cares for" humans (פקד; Ps 8:5) is to Job the God who enthusiastically "inspects" (פקד; 7:18) humans for fault. The effect is that God makes Job his "target" (מפגע), a military term designating the object of assault.[50]

---

48. For more on the relationship between Job 16:7–17 and 19:6–12 to Psalms of Lament, see Tryggve Mettinger, "Intertextuality: Allusion and Vertical Context Systems in Some Job Passages," in *The Voice from the Whirlwind: Interpreting the Book of Job* (ed. Leo G. Perdue and W. Clark Gilpin; Nashville: Abingdon, 1992), 257–80 (269–74). Westermann argues that Job's usage of the lament form in ch. 7 gets absorbed into his accusations against God (Westermann, *Structure*, 46–48).

49. The words עתה כי here can also be read to say, "for then," as Fohrer suggests. This would make Job's death a consequence of God's forgiveness: "Und warum nimmst du meine Schuld nicht weg und übersiehst meine Sünde nicht? Ja, dann könnte ich mich in den Staub hinlegen, und suchtest du nach mir, so wäre ich nicht mehr" (Fohrer, *Hiob*, 160). According to Newsom ("Job," 396), this reading suggests that death would be a consequence of God's forgiveness so that when God attempts to renew his oppressive surveillance of Job (7:17), Job will be safely out of reach.

50. For more on the intertextual relations between these two texts, see Mettinger, "Intertextuality," 266–69.

Job's rhetorical question, "If[51] I have sinned, what have I done to you?," berating God for the apparent incommensurability of the paltry sin of a near-dead man compared to the absurd punishment God has inflicted, is the context in which his lament-parodying plea is to be understood. For the sake of the parody, Job has assumed the moral world of the Psalmist, that of the symbolization of abundant life, and worked back from the reality of his overwhelming suffering to the supposed sin that is at its root. His plea in 7:21, "Why do you not forgive my transgression, bear away my iniquity?," need not be an admission of inadvertent sin,[52] but is an angry protest against the injustice of a God who, apparently, has concocted charges of wrongdoing against Job, for which he is now exacting vengeance.[53] The plea for God to "forgive," as in the Psalm of Lament, is a plea for God to relent from his anger. Only this time, God has no reason to be angry.

Further, the reason Job gives for God to relent from his anger is not a confession of sin and renewed vow to seek God (as might be the case in a Psalm of Lament), but because death is imminent: "when you seek me, I shall be no more" (7:21).[54] As Habel argues, normally, in the language of prayer, the verb "to seek" (שׁחר) is used of supplicants seeking Yahweh's aid. Here, however, the verb has a more sinister tone—that of God, "The Watcher," searching out humans for faults.[55] Job's plea, then, is an indictment against a God who relentlessly pursues Job with torment so oppressive that soon God will inevitably murder Job. Job urges him to desist now, before he has committed this final, awful, and completely unwarranted act.

Job's usage, and parody, of the psalmic death language here is therefore both a plea for God to desist from his relentless oppression, and a tacit claim about the injustice of a God who punishes for no reason. In this way Job reverses Eliphaz's attempted link of mortality and morality in 4:7–21. There Eliphaz attempted to argue that to be a human who faces the inevitability of death means

---

51. The "if" must be supplied here, as the LXX, Syriac, and the vast majority of commentators do. The virtually identical line in 35:6 does include the אם. Andersen, however, seems to be the lone voice arguing that one ought not to supply the "if" because it gives Job "a quite undeserved air of self-righteousness" (Francis I. Andersen, *Job: An Introduction and Commentary* [TOTC; Downers Grove, Ill.: InterVarsity, 1976], 139 n. 1).

52. As argued by Driver and Gray, *Job*, 1:74; Fohrer, *Hiob*, 181–82; Rowley, *Job*, 70. Indeed, Job bases his arguments with the friends and with God on the supposition of his innocence throughout the book (see 6:10; 9:20, 21; 12:4; 27:2–6; 31:1–40).

53. Or, as Clines translates the question, "'Why do you not pardon any sin of mine?' sc., assuming I have committed some sin" (Clines, *Job 1–20*, 195).

54. Although, the "you" can be understood not as God, but as an impersonal "anyone" (so Gordis, *Job*, 83). This, however, would be a strange shift in addressee—God has been the exclusive addressee from 7:11 onward.

55. Or, "God seeking out humans as victims" (Habel, *Job*, 167). See, also Newsom, "Job," 396. Others, however, argue that the verb implies a more loving intent: God will eventually seek out Job in order to renew relations with him, but Job will be gone forever (see, e.g., Driver and Gray, *Job*, 1:75; Rowley, *Job*, 70). This view of a loving God would be quite a shift in Job's characterization of God, compared to the rest of the book. It makes more sense to understand the verb "to seek" along the lines of God, "The Watcher," seeking out his prey.

also inevitability to be sinful. Here, Job takes the image of his own inevitable death and suggests it reveals not his own immorality, but God's.

Job makes this link between his own death and God's immorality in several other places in the first two cycles. In 10:20, key verses in which Job's understanding of Sheol shifts from abundant life to gloomy death, Job briefly employs the image of his impending death as an angry cry for God to relent from his oppression. Like 7:21, here the charge that God is acting immorally is at least implicit in these verses, especially falling on the heels of 10:1–17, in which Job accuses God of unmotivated aggression toward him.

4.1.3.2. *9:21–24 and 16:18–22.* Two passages make the link between Job's death and God's immorality explicit. In ch. 9, Job contemplates the difficulties of a trial with God. Though Job knows himself to be "in the right" (צדק; 9:15, 20) and "blameless" (תם; 9:20) a trial would be useless: God "increases [Job's] wounds for no cause" (9:17) and he would somehow "declare [Job] perverse" (9:20). In light of the disparity between his own innocence and the suffering he endures, Job declares angrily that "both the innocent and the guilty he destroys! When a scourge brings death suddenly, he mocks the despair of the innocent" (9:22b–23). Sudden death, reserved for the wicked according to Eliphaz (4:7–11), actually demonstrates the injustice of God.

In 16:18–22, Job also speaks in legal terms to decry the injustice of God, all the while employing death imagery. This time, however, the legal metaphor is that of the blood avenger, who vindicates a murder upon seeing spilled blood[56] (16:18), and the legal counsel who will argue his case (16:19).[57] In this instance, Job envisions himself as already dead, having had his blood spilled (16:18), *and* as speedily approaching imminent death (16:22). Either way, the prospect of his death—his murder at Yahweh's hand—prompts Job's angry cry for God to be found guilty of injustice. Again, Job links his mortality with God's immorality.[58]

The link of forensic categories with the claim that his death is unjust is significant. I will examine it in more detail below. Before I do, however, I would like to comment on the shift in Job's earlier statements of life-in-death from ch. 3. For just as Job's articulation of his experience of death-in-life shifts to the agent of his death-in-life, God, so also his fantasy of life-in-death shifts to a sense that death is hopeless.

---

56. See Gen 4:10; 37:26; Isa 26:21; Ezek 24:7–8.

57. Debate rages over who this witness would be. Some think it to be God testifying against himself (see, e.g., Dhorme, *Job*, 239; Driver and Gray, *Job*, 1:148; Fohrer, *Hiob*, 291–92; Gordis, *Job*, 178; Hartley, *Job*, 264; Franz Hesse, *Hiob* [2d ed.; ZBK 14; Zürich: Theologischer Verlag, 1992], 116–17; Rowley, *Job*, 120–21; Whybray, *Job*, 86), another heavenly being or intermediary of some sort (see, e.g., George Herbert Box, *Judaism in the Greek Period, from the Rise of Alexander the Great to the Intervention of Rome [333–63 B.C.]* [Clarendon Bible Old Testament 5; Oxford: Clarendon, 1932], 128–30; John B. Curtis, "On Job's Witness in Heaven," *JBL* 102 [1983]: 549–62; Sigmund Mowinckel, "Hiobs go'el und Zuege im Himmel," in *Vom Alten Testament* [ed. Karl Budde; BZAW 41; Giessen: Töpelmann, 1925], 207–12; Newsom, "Job," 460; Pope, *Job*, 117–18), an unknown witness (Janzen, *Job*, 125), or Job's own spoken testimony that, by articulating it, ensures that it will be on record in the heavenly court (Clines, *Job 1–20*, 390).

58. 14:5–6 might also be included. Here Job uses the fact of his mortality to urge God to relent.

4.2. *From Life-in-Death to Hopeless Death*

As argued previously, by 10:18–22 Job's fantasy of life-in-death develops into an increasingly negative conception of Sheol. After 10:18–22, Job will move to the seemingly logical conclusion that Sheol is utterly hopeless, and he therefore abandons his wish for death. When Job now ponders Sheol it will only be in the bleakest, direst terms. This sense emerges in two passages, 14:7–22 and 17:11–16.[59]

4.2.1. *14:7–22*

In 14:7–22 Job contrasts the hope that he observes trees to have (14:7) and the corresponding hopelessness that humans have (14:19). The comparison is based on the prospect for the renewal of life after death. In tree terms, "death" consists of being "cut down" (כרת),[60] with "roots grow[n] old" (יזקין שרשו), and having a dead stump (ימות גזעו); while images of renewal include "sprout[ing] again" (חלף), "bud[ding]" (פרח) and "put[ting] out branches" (עשה קציר), "shoots [that] will not cease" (יונקת לא תחדל). This picture is the arboreal equivalent to his own Sheol fantasy in ch. 3, that is, that death, far from being the termination of life, actually results in the renewal of life.

This renewal to life of the dead tree—its "hope" (תקוה)—contrasts starkly with the fate of humans. Humans are more like the extinct waters of a vanished lake or of a permanently dried up stream:[61] "mortals die and languish" (חלש).[62] In contrast to the tree, which, after death, has its life-forces renewed, humans die and are stripped of their life-power in Sheol.[63] Unlike the tree, which sprouts branches again, when humans die, "they do not rise again" (לא קום) for as long as the heavens remain (14:12b). From Job's earlier fantasy of Sheol with its images of activity, liveliness, and other life equivalents, Job now reverts to a more traditional conception of Sheol, which he describes in terms of stasis imagery: the enervation of life's energies.

---

59. Death and hopelessness might also be linked in 13:15, which can be translated "See, he will kill me; I have no hope" (NJPS) or "Yea, though He slay me, yet will I trust in Him" (AV), depending on whether one reads the *Kethib* לא ("I have no hope") or the *Qere* לו ("I hope to [in] him").

60. In addition to the obvious sense of "cutting down" a tree, the root also commonly has the sense of death, as in "to be cut off [from life]." Since the comparison is between the tree being cut down, and the death of humans (7:10), it is likely that this sense of כרת is also present here.

61. Some interpret this reference to the lake and stream differently. They argue Job is using another impossible situation like 14:12b (the heavens vanishing), for although the sea or mighty river might dry up it is impossible that humans should live after death (see, e.g., Dhorme, *Job*, 200). As Clines notes, however, this reading is dubious due to the *waw* at the start of v. 12, which is the "and" of comparison (Clines, *Job 1–20*, 329).

62. Some have emended this verb to חלף ("passes on, away"); see, e.g., Driver and Gray, *Job*, 1:128; also, Alfred Guillaume, "The Use of חלש in Exod. XVII. 13; Isa. XIV. 12, and Job XIV. 10," *JTS* 14 [1963]: 91–92).

63. Contra Gordis who argues that the sequence of ימות ויחלש in reference to humans must be an instance of *hysteron proteron*: "but man dies and grows faint, i.e., man grows faint and dies" (Gordis, *Job*, 149).

Further, humans cannot anticipate the same hope as trees, for human hope suffers the same erosion as do mountains, rocks, stones, and earth, which are worn down by relentless exposure to the elements (14:18–19). As much as humans can fantasize of life after death (14:13), such hopes are mere chimera. God obliterates all such hope by being the agent who brings death (14:19). God "overpowers [humans] once for all; [they go] away;[64] [God] changes [their] appearance[65] and dispatches [them]." The reality of the finality of death obliterates all hope.

4.2.2. *17:11–16*

The theme of the hopelessness of Sheol finds expression again in 17:11–16, although here several verses have severe translational problems. The exact sense of vv. 11–12 is very obscure,[66] but v. 13 begins with an "if" clause (lasting through to the end of the section) whose subject is Job's hope in the face of impending death ("If[67] I should hope for Sheol as my home…").[68] The idea of Job hoping for Sheol at least has faint echoes of his earlier hope for Sheol in ch. 3 where Sheol represented the place of tranquility, rest, and life. This time, however, the prospect of death renders hope futile (17:15), which Job articulates with the image of hope, itself, dying similarly to how he dies ("Will it descend with me to Sheol?").[69]

Even more interesting is how Job articulates his own sense of his impending death employing kinship terms. Sheol is to be his "home" (ביח), the domicile where he "makes [his] bed" (17:13). Although the notion of Sheol as a house

---

64. The verb הלך is likely a euphemism for death (see Job 19:10; Ps 39:14).

65. It is possible that משנה פניו refers here to *rigor mortis* (Gordis, *Job*, 152; Gordis follows Ibn Ezra), but it also could simply be understood as the "ravages of old age" (Clines, *Job 1–20*, 335; Crenshaw, "Language of Prayer," 121). For another proposal, see Baruch Halpern, "Yhwh's Summary Justice in Job XIV 20," *VT* 28 (1978): 472–74.

66. For a brief look a the interpretive possibilities, see Clines, *Job 1–20*, 374–75, who notes that the LXX even omits v. 12, which is supplied by Theodotion.

67. The אם here has also been understood as an interrogative ("Can I hope again? [Certainly not! since] Sheol is my home"; Dhorme, *Job*, 253), and as an emphatic particle like the Arabic *'inna*, which would normally make the statement negative ("I have nothing to hope for"; see Fohrer, *Hiob*, 279; Wilde, *Hiob*, 191, 198). See also Gordis, *Job*, 172, 184.

68. Some find the verb קוה ("hope for") to be problematic, since Job will soon suggest he has no hope (17:15–16). Gordis, for example, taking אקוה as a diminutive form of קו ("line"), translates "I have marked out my home in Sheol" (Gordis, *Job*, 172, 184).

69. This verse has a host of fairly minor translational problems, none of which affect the sense of the verse, that hope is descending to Sheol. First, תרדנה appears to be a feminine plural verb, which seems to have no apparent feminine plural subject (although see Clines, *Job 1–20*, 375, for a solution). Some, therefore, revocalize it to be a feminine singular verb with an energic *nun* (see, Gordis, *Job*, 185; Pope, *Job*, 122). Second, some follow the LXX and emend בדי ("bars of Sheol") to הבידי ("with me"; thus "Will they descend with me to Sheol"—see Clines, *Job 1–20*, 369, 375; Driver and Gray, *Job*, 1:156; Fohrer, *Hiob*, 279, 282). Others argue בדי is a contraction of בידי ("into the hands of"; Mitchell Dahood, "Northwest Semitic Philology and Job," in *The Bible in Current Catholic Thought* [ed. John L. McKenzie; Saint Mary's Theology Studies 1; New York: Herder & Herder, 1962], 55–74 [62]; Pope, *Job*, 122). Lastly, most revocalize נחת to read "we shall descend."

seemed to be a conventional description,[70] בית also suggests the household and the intimacy of one's family.[71] This connection to the family—a life equivalent—is made more firm with the reference to the father, mother, and sister in v. 14. To Job, however, kinship ties are exclusively with death: Sheol is his household, the Pit is his father, worms are mother and sister. The familial intimacy he experiences is with personified death. This, therefore, is anything but an expression of the life equivalent of connection. It is, rather, a heightened and startling image of the death equivalent of separation: connection not with the living, but with death. And this fact spells the destruction of hope.

4.3. *The Repositioning of Death and the Legal Metaphor*

After 10:18–22, the two themes examined above dominate Job's death imagery: God is responsible for Job's murder and therefore is unjust; and the prospect of death ends all hope. But this shift in Job's conception and articulation of death occurs simultaneously with the rise of what scholars refer to as "the legal metaphor"—Job's contemplation of the possibility of a trial before God. Job first muses with the possibility of a trial with God at the start of ch. 9, although by the end of the chapter he writes off such a trial as an impossibility unless God would relent from his oppression (9:32–35). At various points throughout his successive speeches Job will return to the legal metaphor in order to frame his experiences and to voice his own sense of what he needs to do (e.g. 13:6–28; 16:19–21; 19:25; 23:4–7).[72] Significantly, at almost the exact moment that Job's conception of death seems to shift and Sheol begins to be conceived of negatively (10:18–22), Job employs the legal metaphor for the first time (ch. 9).

I do not believe the concurrence of the shift in the conception of death and the rise of the legal metaphor to be mere coincidence. Forensic categories are rational and clarifying and they seem to provide a sort of focus to Job's conception of death. To understand how or why this happens, it will be useful to return to Lifton's discussions of centering and grounding.

Centering, as discussed previously, is the process of ordering the experience of the self in order to mediate proximate experiences with ultimate connections. The purpose of centering (along with decentering and recentering) is to enable the organism to maintain vitality by attaining a stock of vital and vibrant images

70. See Job 30:23; Ps 49:12; Qoh 12:5, and Tromp, *Primitive Conceptions*, 77–79.

71. See, e.g., Gen 7:1; 12:1, 17; 35:2; 42:33; 50:22; Lev 16:6, 11, 17; Deut 6:22; Josh 22:15; etc.

72. For full examinations of the legal metaphor, see Michael B. Dick, "Legal Metaphor in Job 31," *CBQ* 41 (1979): 37–50; J. B. Frye, "The Legal Language of the Book of Job" (Ph. D. diss., University of London, 1973); Berend Gemser, "The *rib*- or Controversy-Pattern in Hebrew Mentality," in Noth and Winton Thomas, eds., *Wisdom in Israel*, 120–37; Habel, *Job*, 54–57 (and throughout the commentary); Newsom, *Contest of Moral Imaginations*, 150–61; Heinz Richter, *Studien zu Hiob: Der Aufbau des Hiobbuches, dargestellt an den Gattungen des Rechtslebens* (Theologische Arbeiten 11; Berlin: Evangelische Verlagsanstalt, 1959), 20–132; J. J. M. Roberts, "Job's Summons to Yahweh: The Exploitation of a Legal Metaphor," *ResQ* 16 (1973): 159–65; Sylvia Huberman Scholnick, "Lawsuit Drama in the Book of Job" (Ph.D. diss., Brandeis University, 1975).

and forms that enable life: "capacities for participation in love and communal relationships, for moral and ethical commitment, and for maintaining a sense of self that includes symbolic development, growth, and change."[73]

Legal imagery and forensic categories seem to comprise a set of stock images that functioned this way in ancient Israel. On a grand, societal level, the law codes provided a guide to social relations both between Israelites and their neighbors and among Israelites themselves. They functioned to organize the complex relations between the various strata of society: gender, class, social function, sexuality, and so on. Optimistically, such social organization enabled individuals to identify themselves and others and to negotiate successfully the complexities of human interaction in society. At its best, Israelite legal regulations provided a structure "for participation in love and communal relationships."[74]

Simultaneously, legal regulations provided standards of ethical commitment by stipulating which types of activity were acceptable in society and which were not. Hence, Israelite law codes provided regulations for such diverse behavior as eating, going to war, sexual habits, and sacrifice. Occupying a central place within these standards of ethical commitment were the regulations concerning death: who may kill whom and for what reasons.[75]

Most importantly, Israelite law established itself on ultimate grounds, tracing its origins, and its importance, to the deity. Thus the HB depicts legal provisions as being delivered straight from God.[76] This is significant for three reasons. First, the law stipulated provisions for correct relations with the deity, including which avenues to go through in order to propitiate the deity, and which kinds of religious actions were acceptable and which were not. Second, by grounding legal stipulations on ultimate grounds, the more "mundane" or "secular" of such stipulations then took on a much more "religious" importance. To act ethically in any area of life was to maintain not only a communal relationship with fellow Israelites, but a communal relationship with God. In Liftonian language, the mundane, proximate experiences of life suddenly gained an ultimate importance, allowing the "harmonizing [of] immediate and ultimate obligations."[77] Legal stipulations, therefore, functioned to organize the life/piety/relationship complex, for piety, in legal categories, represented obedience to the law, which simultaneously determined one's relationship to the deity, who then granted or rescinded life based on obedience.[78]

---

73. Lifton, *Life of the Self*, 71.

74. Ibid. At their worst, legal regulations are a means of social control that reify such differences as class, gender, and sexual orientation, ensuring the hegemony of certain elites.

75. See n. 79 for a full list of the types of crimes punishable by death.

76. See, e.g., Exod 20:1, 19; 21:1; 25:1; Lev 1:1; 4:1; 5:14; 6:1, 12, 17; 7:22, 28; 8:1; 11:1; 12:1; 13:1; 14:1; 15:1; 16:1; 17:1; 18:1; 19:1; 20:1; 21:1, 16, 24; 22:1, 17, 26; 23:1, 9, 23, 26, 33; 24:1, 13, 15; 25:1; 26:26; 27:1; Num 5:1, 5, 11; 6:1, 22; 15:1, 17, 37; 18:1, 8, 25; 19:1; 28:1; 30:2; 35:1, 9; Deut 5:1, 19; 10:1; 12:1.

77. Lifton, *Broken Connection*, 144.

78. Of course, the life/piety/relationship complex does not need to be defined in forensic terms, as is the case in Psalms and Proverbs, as discussed above.

Third, the establishment of legal stipulations on ultimate grounds meant that even death fell into the realm of divine sanction. And this, indeed, is what Israel's legal material demonstrates, for death repeatedly is presented as being the prerogative of God alone. Humans are not allowed to kill other humans intentionally, except when given a divine commission to do so in order to exact punishment on someone who has committed a grave offense, in which case the killing of the transgressor is indispensable for the healthy operation of society.[79] God's prerogative over death is also obvious in cultic contexts, where disobedience to divinely given cultic stipulations was understood to result in a divinely appointed death, whose model seemed to be that of Nadab and Abihu in Lev 10:1–2.[80]

Part of the power of legal discourse to function as a vibrant set of images is demonstrated by how forensic categories get adapted by different sorts of discourses and become useful images to explain different types of experiences. This is most obvious in prophetic discourse, which frequently adopts legal forms, such as the *rîb* dispute. Another prominent example is the Deuteronomistic History or the Chronicler's History whose respective recountings of "history" are driven by the legal categories of obedience to legal stipulations.

As I suggested above, I do not think it coincidental that Job's discourse about death shifts at the same moment he adopts the legal metaphor in his third speech in the first cycle (chs. 9–10). Legal stipulations supply a rational order to the world and are able to organize the infinite world of experience into coherent systems of meaning. Thus, while Job's speeches from ch. 9 onward are perhaps not dominated by an obsession for a trial before God, the legal metaphor, which Job considers from time to time, does provide Job an ordered symbolic system with a coherent and rational understanding of death in which to begin to understand his sense of his own death. The legal metaphor enables the transformation of his desymbolized death imagery in two ways. First of all, because death is God's prerogative in Israel's legal discourse, Job's sense of death-in-life must amount to God's killing of Job or divine murder, a claim with implicit legal

---

79. For laws pertaining to the killing of a murderer, see Exod 21:12, 14; Lev 24:17; Num 35:16–21, 30–31; Deut 19:11–12. Other offenses were grave enough to warrant death: striking (Exod 21:15), cursing (Exod 21:17; Lev 20:9), or disobeying one's mother or father (Deut 21:21); kidnapping (Exod 21:16; Deut 24:7); bestiality (Exod 22:18; Lev 20:15–16); profaning the Sabbath (Exod 31:14, 15; 35:2; Num 15:35–36); giving one's child "to Molech" (Lev 20:2, 4–5); committing adultery (Lev 20:10; Deut 22:22); having sex with the wife of your father (Lev 20:11) or with your daughter-in-law (Lev 20:12); a man having sex with a man (Lev 20:13); being a wizard, medium, or false prophet (Lev 20:27; Deut 13:6; 18:20); blaspheming God's name (Lev 24:16); committing idolatry (Deut 13:10–11; 17:5–7); disobeying a priest (Deut 17:12); being found not to be a virgin when married (applicable to women; Deut 22:21); fornicating (Deut 22:24); and rape (Deut 22:25–26). Unintentional killing was a different story. In some cases one who committed manslaughter was considered a murderer, and therefore had to be put to death (Exod 21:12; Num 35:16–21; Deut 19:11–13), in other cases this person was not considered a murderer, depending on the intent (Num 35:22–28; Deut 19:4–10). In the latter case the person would not be put to death because the murder was unintentional. Further, killing one's slave was not considered murder (Exod 21:20) nor was beating to death a thief caught in the act (Exod 22:1).

80. See Exod 28:35, 43; 30:20–21; Lev 8:35; 16:2, 13; Num 18:3, 7, 22.

ramifications. Second, in light of the negative connotations associated with death in legal discourse, that it is a punishment reserved for certain nefarious miscreants, Job reconsiders his fantasy of death/Sheol as "good" because death now takes on more negative connotations and can no longer be considered "good."

But I do not want to give the impression that Job is consciously calculating the implications of the legal metaphor on his own conception of death. That only seems to be the case in two passages, 9:21–23 and 16:18–22, in which Job's contemplation of legal matters leads him to consider the legal ramifications of his own death. In both cases Job draws an analogy from what would be the case between humans to what he constructs for the divine–human relationship. And in both cases he concludes that God is acting unjustly. More frequently, the legal metaphor simply provides Job a framework or symbolic universe that shifts the valences of his conception of death, even if unconsciously.

But Job does not arrive at a resymbolization of death at this point in the dialogues for two reasons. First, despite Habel's claim that the legal metaphor is the central literary device that "integrates narrative progression and theological motif,"[81] Job's actual usage of it is more sporadic and halting than Habel suggests. As Newsom argues, "legal language [is] a medium of exploration, by which Job can configure and reconfigure his situation, though explicitly legal speech actually occurs rather infrequently."[82] The legal metaphor is more of an experiment for Job at this point rather than a fully articulated symbolic system in which he resymbolizes death. The halting use of this metaphor only provides a degree of focus to Job's conception of death.

Second, at this point in the dialogues, Job still is fixated on the meaning of his *own* death. He is not yet ready to speak of death *in general*.[83] The difference is crucial. General death is the language of symbolic systems. In Nemo's words, it is the language of technique. General death knows what death signifies and knows how to place any particular death into its symbolic universe. The friends speak about general death, but Job does not yet speak in generalities. He still is focused exclusively on the meaning of his own death, even though the legal metaphor provides him a degree of focus for discussing it.

Perhaps the best example of exactly how the legal metaphor functions to organize Job's sense of desymbolization occurs in 16:18–21 where Job explicitly connects death and the legal metaphor. The short passage picks up on the prominent theme of divine murder, but casts that murder in an explicitly legal context. While Job's shift from an emphasis on death-in-life to divine murder implies a certain forensic claim in that "death" now becomes "murder," in 16:18–21 Job begins explicitly to think through these forensic implications in a way that allows him to conceive of his own death in a rational and symbolically coherent system.

---

81. Habel, *Job*, 54.

82. Newsom, *Contest of Moral Imaginations*, 154. See her analysis of the actual extent of legal language on pp. 150–61.

83. Even his brief general statement about death in 9:22 is motivated by his own experience of death.

First of all, Job articulates his death as a murder that requires satisfaction. He does so by alluding to the general forensic principle that spilled blood needs to be avenged:[84] "O earth, do not cover my blood! Let there be not be a resting place for my cry!" (16:18). Specifically, the symbolism of the blood of the murdered crying out in protest is drawn from the story of Cain and Abel (Gen 4:8–12). There, the blood of the murdered innocent sibling cries out to God, who, accordingly, acts as advocate of the murdered, as he punishes the murderer. As in legal contexts, God here is depicted as the only one with authority to apportion death. Humans, when they do kill others, overstep their boundaries and must face punishment.

In Job's usage of this imagery, however, one key component has been altered. It is not that a human has overstepped his boundary. God has. The deity has played the role of Cain and spilled Job's innocent blood. The legal metaphor then provides for Job the means to envision the consequences of this murder as he confesses confidence that "my witness is in heaven, my defender is on high." Just as the cry of Abel's innocent blood reached God who acted as his advocate, avenging Abel's innocent death, so also Job envisions his spilled blood receiving a similar heavenly advocate who will argue Job's case before God as one might argue in a human court (16:21).

By employing explicitly legal language to describe his experiences, Job is able to provide a context or vantage point from which he can identify his particular situation, which allows him to envision a resolution where he is vindicated. But in 16:18–21 Job is just beginning to explore the possibilities of the resymbolization of his experiences—he is not yet ready to conceive of a complete symbolic system. Though the legal metaphor provides a modicum of order to his experiences, and though it enables him to grasp his experiences as part of a greater whole, his usage of the metaphor also contains a paradox that ultimately undermines the symbolic power of the legal metaphor.

This paradox has to do with his conception of the deity, whom Job symbolizes simultaneously as murderer and advocate. Though Job does not name God explicitly as his murderer, it is obvious that Job considers God to be so, both because of the connection of this passage to the elaborate divine murder imagery employed earlier and because God clearly is the defendant in the legal scenario Job envisions in 16:21. Less obvious is that Job's heavenly advocate ought to be identified as God (16:19). Many scholars make this connection,[85] but some dispute it on the basis of, among other things, the logical inconsistency of a deity who is both murderer and avenger of the murder.[86] Job, however, is drawing on the legal metaphor that conceptualizes God as the only one with prerogative over

---

84. See, e.g., Gen 9:5–6; Num 35:16–21.

85. See, e.g., Andersen, *Job*, 182–83; Dhorme, *Job*; Fohrer, *Hiob*, 291; Gordis, *Job*, 178–79; Rowley, *Job*, 120–21.

86. Clines argues that the witness is a personification of Job's outcry (Clines, *Job 1–20*, 390). Zuckerman argues that the witness is an imaginary "counter-deity" that Job imagines (Zuckerman, *Job the Silent*, 115). Pope argues that the witness is the same character as the Mediator (19:21) and Redeemer (19:25), who is a figure who is not God (Pope, *Job*, 117–18; cf. Newsom, "Job," 460).

death, who punishes and/or commissions others to punish those who take life wrongfully. Given the parallel to the Cain and Abel story where God acts as advocate on behalf of the slain Abel, one would also expect God to be the advocate to whom Job cries.

But this is where the legal metaphor breaks down. For though the legal metaphor seems to provide a secure symbolic universe from which Job can articulate and understand his experience, at this point it is only at the expense of symbolic and logical consistency: God cannot relate to Job both as his unjust murderer and simultaneously as his just advocate. Such a symbolization does not supply an ordered, symbolically coherent account. And so as quickly as Job experimented with the legal metaphor in 16:19–21, he abandons it, and continues to articulate his own subjective experience of death as divine murder and hopeless death.

This will soon change, however. In ch. 21 Job will begin to speak more and more in the idiom of technique, progressively abandoning the personal, subjective position that has fuelled most of his speeches to that point. By the time of his last speech in chs. 29–31, Job will transform the legal metaphor and blend it with other traditional images and forms into a new, fully symbolized account of his life and suffering. And there Job will arrive at a resymbolization of death and will, himself, be recentered.

Chapter 5

GENERALIZED SPEECH AND RESYMBOLIZATION
(CHAPTERS 21–31)

In the first two cycles a series of themes emerge around which Job's symbolization and imagery of death converge. Death does not maintain a consistent conceptualization for Job, but vacillates in symbolic resonance, even as it begins to stabilize around the legal metaphor. In Lifton's terminology, death is desymbolized for Job. In the remainder of the speeches attributed to Job in the poetic sections of the book, death tends to recede from Job's discourse, only appearing in a few key places, to be examined below. When Job does employ death imagery, it seems to operate differently from how it did previously, no longer as desymbolized imagery in the articulation of the personal experience of life, but ultimately as stabilizing imagery anchored in a resymbolized discourse. In this chapter I will attempt to demonstrate how death's symbolization shifts in Job's remaining speeches. If death imagery was part of a coherent symbolic system in the introduction to the prologue and in the speeches of the friends, and if it was desymbolized in Job's speeches in the first two cycles, in the remainder of Job's speeches in the poetic sections it is increasingly resymbolized, indicating a movement toward Job's own recentering.

But interpreting Job's usage of death in these sections—indeed interpretation, itself—is extraordinarily difficult due to several severe interpretive quandaries, in addition to the more expected grammatical and syntactical issues, which are quite acute in some places (24:18–25, for example). In fact, the majority of the book of Job's major interpretive problems occur in the scope of material bracketed by the start of the third cycle and the end of the Divine Speeches. Decisions about how to handle these problems radically affect one's sense of what Job and the friends are attempting to argue.[1]

---

1. For good discussions of many of these issues, see George A. Barton, "The Composition of Job 24–30," *JBL* 30 (1911): 66–77; P. Dhorme, "Les chapitres XXV–XXVIII du livre de Job," *RB* 33 (1924): 343–56; A. Regnier, "La distribution des chapitres 25–28 du livre de Job," *RB* 33 (1924): 186–200; Henning Graf Reventlow, "Tradition und Redaktion in Hiob 27 im Rahmen der Hiobreden des Abschnittes Hi 24–27," *ZAW* 94 (1982): 279–93; Raymond Tournay, "L'ordre primitif des chapitres 24–28 du livre de Job," *RB* 64 (1957): 321–34; Westermann, *Structure*, 131–34. For a list of how many scholars have attempted to reconstruct the third cycle, see Robert Henry Pfeiffer, *Introduction to the Old Testament* (New York: Harper, 1948), 671–75; Markus Witte, *Vom Leiden zur Lehre: der dritte Redegang (Hiob 21–27) und die Redaktionsgeschichte der Hiobbuches* (BZAW

The major issues, well known to critics, center on the breakdown of the structure of the dialogic sequence, coupled with the inconsistencies and incoherence of Job's purported speeches. I will comment briefly about both of these in turn. The dialogic sequence of the first two cycles (a speech by one of the friends followed by a speech by Job) seems to break down in the third cycle: Bildad's final speech (25:1–6) is extremely short compared to both his and all the other speakers' prior speeches, while Zophar does not speak at all. One inordinately long speech is attributed to Job in their stead (chs. 26–31). But this long speech seems also to be interrupted in two places, indicated by the headings that "Job *again* took up his discourse" in 27:1 and 29:1, as if what preceded the heading were an addition even though Job supposedly is still the speaker. Chapter 28 is perhaps most obviously an addition: it has a unique literary form, tone, content, and perspective quite unlike what precedes and what follows it.[2] The vast majority of scholars take this chapter as a later addition.[3] Similarly, the hymn that precedes 27:1 (26:5–15) also has a tone and perspective different from what surrounds it, and although Job has included hymns about God's creative power in his earlier speeches (9:2–10; 12:13–25), here there is no hint of irony in the hymn as there is in the previous ones. Some scholars suggest that this unit forms part of Bildad's last speech, as many of its themes seem to coincide with ch. 25.[4] In short, neither 26:5–15 nor ch. 28 is consistent with Job's previous arguments and they do not seem to fit into the flow of his speech.

But this is also true of portions of chs. 24 and 27 (vv. 18–25 and 13–23, respectively) where Job seems to expound the position of the friends, employing their very arguments as his own. For this reason, not a few scholars argue that these verses originally were part of the speeches of one of the friends,[5] although

230; Berlin: de Gruyter, 1994), especially his nice synopsis on pp. 239–47 of scholarship on the division of speeches in the third cycle.

2.   However, for the similarities of this chapter to other passages in the poetic dialogues and Divine Speeches see Stephen A. Geller, "'Where is Wisdom?': A Literary Study of Job 28 in its Settings," in *Judaic Perspectives on Ancient Israel* (ed. Baruch A. Levine, Jacob Neusner, and Ernest S. Frerichs; Philadelphia: Fortress, 1987), 155–88 (177 n. 1); Habel, *Job*, 392; Terrien, "Job," 1099–100.

3.   A handful of scholars have attempted to understand it as part of Job's speech. See, e.g., Good, *Turns of Tempest*, 290–93; Janzen, *Job*, 187; Pieter van der Lugt, *Rhetorical Criticism and the Poetry of the Book of Job* (OtSt 32; Leiden: Brill, 1995), 526–29. The majority, however, view it as a poetic interlude between the end of the poetic dialogues and the final exchange between Job and God. See, e.g., Dhorme, *Job*, xcvii; Habel, *Job*, 38–39; Hartley, *Job*, 26; Newsom, "Job," 528; idem, *Contest of Moral Imaginations*, 169; Westermann, *Structure*, 137. Some scholars even distinguish two distinct additions: 28:1–27 and 28:28 (see, e.g., Geller, "Where is Wisdom?," 174; Jean Lévêque, *Job et son Dieu; essai d'exégèse et de théologie biblique* [EBib; Paris: Gabalda, 1970], 595–96, especially p. 595 n. 3, where he lists the scholars who hold this view).

4.   See, e.g., Gordis, *Job*, 535; Habel, *Job*, 38; Newsom, "Job," 516; Pope, *Job*, xviii. But see Newsom, *Contest of Moral Imaginations*, 167, who takes these verses as Job's "strategy of taking the friends' words into his own speech." Fohrer, *Hiob*, 381–85, suggests these verses are an independent poem like ch. 28.

5.   See, e.g., Dhorme, *Job*, xlvi; Pope, *Job*, *xviii*; Rowley, *Job*, 175–76; Samuel L. Terrien, *Job: Poet of Existence* (Indianapolis: Bobbs-Merrill, 1957), 163, who all take these verses to comprise

some attempt to interpret them as Bildad's or Zophar's words pre-empted by Job.[6]

Finally, many scholars note that the content of Job's speech in chs. 29–31 resembles that of the friends because it contradicts aspects of his own previous speeches. Some attribute these chapters to a different author.[7] I will discuss the problems of this unit more fully later.

Obviously a decision about these issues greatly affects one's interpretation of this section of *Job*. A quick glance through the commentaries shows that there are a wide variety of ways to understand this section, many of which are quite persuasive. Certainly Newsom's words, although true in general of the interpretive process, have a special ring of truth in regard to these chapters: "Given the teasing nature of the text, more than one interpretation is possible."[8]

Fortunately, because of how scant is the emphasis on death in most of these disputed chapters, I am able to remain safely non-committal regarding many of these interpretive quandaries. Brief references to death do occur in every one of these problematic sections[9] (except for Bildad's truncated speech in ch. 25), but death is prominently in view only in three places: chs. 21:21–34; 27:8–15; and 30:12–31. These three will receive the bulk of attention in the analysis below. Although the arguments for assigning sections of Job's speeches to one or the other of the friends are cogent, they are more often than not based on arguments about their inconsistency in relation to Job's earlier arguments with his friends. Inconsistency, however, should not be an issue. As I argued about death in the first two cycles, Job's conceptualization and imagery of death *is* inconsistent and contradictory in places and does shift in symbolic resonance. That it should also be so in chs. 21–31 should occasion no surprise. What should give one pause, however, is that Job seems to challenge his friends utilizing the same argument his friends have espoused all along. Of the passages I am about to examine this is especially a problem in ch. 27. Some scholars, however, instead of simply reassigning this speech to one of the friends, suggest that here Job might be parodying their words. Whether or not this is parody, I am inclined to accept the attribution of speeches in the MT and interpret this speech as Job's.[10] As I will

---

Zophar's missing speech, whereas the NAB assigns them to Bildad. Rowley notes that as early as 1780 Kennicott assigned these verses to Zophar (Rowley, *Job*, 175; see Rowley for a fuller listing of scholarly opinion about these verses).

6. See, e.g., Good, *Turns of Tempest*, 9, 288–90; Gordis, *Job*, 533 (who argues that 27:13–23 is Zophar's, while 24:18–24 is Job's presentation of the friends' perspective); Janzen, *Job*, 174, 179–86; Newsom, "Job," 522. Some even argue that these verses can be understood as Job's own perspective (Andersen, *Job*, 219; Newsom, *Contest of Moral Imaginations*, 167–68; David Wolfers, "The Speech-Cycles in the Book of Job," *VT* 43 [1993]: 385–403 [386–94]). Some also argue that these verses comprise an independent poem (see, e.g., Snaith, *Job*, 62, and perhaps also Norman C. Habel, *The Book of Job* [London: Cambridge University Press, 1975], 126).

7. See John C. Holbert, "The Rehabilitation of the Sinner: The Function of Job 29–31," *ZAW* 95 (1983): 229–37 (229 n. 1), for those who make this argument.

8. Newsom, *Contest of Moral Imaginations*, 162.

9. 24:14, 19; 27:13, 15; 28:22; 29:18; 30:12–14, 16–19, 23, 27–31; 31:12, 30.

10. The headings in 27:1 and 29:1 do give me pause, however. They seem overtly to draw attention to the fact that what precedes them is an interruption. Nevertheless, since the text indicates

argue below, in chs. 21 and 27 Job is not so much parodying the words of the friends, but mimicking their *way of speaking*. In these chapters Job experiments with a different way of talking about the world, which eventually leads him to a different way of seeing and understanding the world in chs. 29–31.

5.1. *Chapter 21: A Parody of Generalized Discourse*

I understand ch. 21 as a bridge chapter that both closes out the second cycle of speeches and introduces the third. The attribute of this speech that makes it a bridge chapter has to do with Job's unique articulation of the desymbolizing effects of his previous experiences. The specific content of *what* Job says is a continuation of what he previously said, but the manner in which he speaks— *how* he articulates his sense of the operation of the world—contrasts with his previous speeches. Job discovers a new way of speaking.

5.1.1. *Chapter 21 as a Conclusion to the First Two Cycles*
Throughout the previous speeches Job and the friends had engaged in very little true dialogue. Aside from the opening addresses of each speech, none of the speakers showed much inclination to engage the specific arguments of each others' speeches, but, instead, articulated their own perceptions of the operation of the world (the friends), or their own experiences of suffering (Job). The friends presented a picture of a symbolically coherent and morally satisfying world, whereas Job articulated his own bewildering relationship to a symbolically confusing world. The difference between the two, as I argued previously concerning their respective usage of death imagery, is the difference between symbolization and desymbolization.

Chapter 21 is no different in that Job continues to articulate a picture of a bewilderingly incoherent world where patterns of shared meaning fail to cohere. This time, however, in expressing his bewilderment, Job finally addresses the specific arguments of the friends.[11] Habel lists the many ways Job responds to his friends' assertions: his emphasis on the happiness of the wicked (vv. 7–16) contradicts Zophar's statement about their fleeting joy (20:5–11); his emphasis on the peace and tranquility of the household of the wicked (21:8–12) contradicts Eliphaz's picture of their torment (15:20–27); whereas Bildad comments on the failure of the lamp of the wicked (18:5–6), Job counters that it never fails (21:17a); whereas Zophar declares that the wicked are reserved for a day of wrath (20:28), Job responds that they do not meet this destiny (21:17c); although all of the friends maintained that the abodes of the wicked would be destroyed

that neither of these "interruptions" comes from a character other than Job, I think the interpreter ought to read them *as* Job's, regardless of when they were penned in relation to the rest of the speeches. This is what Good seems to attempt (*Turns of Tempest*, 280–93 [293]).

11. The following comment by Whybray (*Job*, 101) is typical: "[Job] picks up and comprehensively rejects the assertions that [the friends] have made about the fate of the wicked." See also Fohrer, *Hiob*, 339; Habel, *Job*, 323; Hartley, *Job*, 310; Newsom, "Job," 491; Westermann, *Structure*, 87.

(15:28, 34; 18:15–21; 20:26–28), Job suggests that the wicked will receive a lavish funeral with well-protected and maintained graves (21:27–34).[12]

Job's usage of death imagery, in particular, functions as a response to the friends' usage of death imagery, especially Eliphaz's careful distinction between the deaths of the pious and wicked in chs. 4–5. Recall that the symbolization of death in Eliphaz's first speech was the most complex out of any other speeches of the friends. Eliphaz alone attempted to "contain" Job's heterodox musings about the desirability of death (ch. 3) by offering Job moral technology: the technique of the impoverished death of the wicked; the technique of the abundant death of the pious; and the innovative technique of the link between human mortality and human immorality.

Job's speech in ch. 21 functions as a response to Eliphaz's technique by reconfiguring the relationship between the two contrasting deaths of the pious and wicked that Eliphaz described in ch. 4. Like Eliphaz, Job also presents a picture of contrasting deaths of two people in 21:23–26. One dies a symbolically abundant death, while the other dies a paltry one. The former death is "in full vigor"[13] or "in full maturity"[14] (בעצם תמו), an abundant death Job describes with two images of abundance, milk, and bone marrow.[15] The latter death is the pathetic death of the one who dies never having tasted goodness (21:25),[16] "in bitterness of soul" (בנפש מרה), a phrase Job twice used to characterize his own miserable existence (7:11; 10:1).

The usage to which Eliphaz and Job put these pictures of contrasting deaths, however, is quite different. For Eliphaz, who was engaged in re-integrating death into its proper context in the symbolization of abundant life, emphasis was clearly on which type of death one could expect to die: the abundant death belonged to the pious (5:17–27), while the impoverished death belonged to the wicked (4:8–11). To Job, however, what is important at this point is not the

---

12. Habel, *Job*, 325–26. Habel gives many more examples.

13. Janzen, *Job*, 317.

14. Habel, *Job*, 321.

15. Unfortunately, the exact referent of the milk image is occluded by the *hapax*, עטין, which many, following the versions, take as a body part ("his loins full of milk"; so the NRSV. LXX and Vulgate have "intestines," while the Targum has "breasts" and the Syriac, "sides"). BDB, based on a late Hebrew usage of עטין as a term for laying olives in a vat, translates it as "pails," although some also identify an Arabic cognate that also may have the sense of "pails" (see the nice discussion in Grabbe, "Comparative Philology," 109–11). Based on Akkadian and Aramaic cognates, Pope, *Job*, 146, translates it as "solid part, flank, haunches." Finally, Gordis, *Job*, 232–33, takes the "olive" sense of עטין to be a euphemism for "testes." However this word is understood, its connection with milk (חלב), whose symbolic resonance includes abundance, excess, and luxury, fills out the picture of abundant, full life (see Gen 18:8; 49:12; Prov 27:27; Isa 7:22; 55:1; Joel 3:18, and the common description of the abundance of the Promised Land as "a land of milk and honey" in Exod 3:8, 17; 13:5; 33:3; Lev 20:24; Num 13:27; 14:8; 16:13, 14; Deut 6:3; 11:9; 26:9, 15; 27:3; 31:20; Josh 5:6; Jer 11:5; 32:22; Ezek 20:6, 15). The following image of his "juicy" (שקה) bone marrow also suggests abundance and excess. This person experienced in life the "ease" and "tranquility" (שלאנן and שליו; 21:23b) that to Job earlier comprised the essence of life that he lacked (3:26).

16. This image builds on Zophar's rich imagery of the wicked man who is not allowed to enjoy the "streams of honey and curd" and who could not swallow the fruit of his toil (20:17–18).

piety of the ones who died, but the *fact* that they died. It is unimportant *who* died the abundant death and *who* died the impoverished death. What matters is that both "lie in the dust, covered with worms" (21:26). The *fact* of death makes a mockery of piety. The same fate awaits everyone.[17]

But Job is not finished with Eliphaz's careful distinction between the deaths of the pious and wicked, for the bulk of ch. 21 is concerned with shuffling the elements of the life/piety/relationship complex upon which Eliphaz's technique is based. This Job does by engaging the one topic the friends repeatedly presented, the fate of the wicked. Job, however, presents to his friends a unique "fate of the wicked" picture, one that ends not in the impoverished and sudden death of the wicked as the friends repeatedly claimed, but with the abundant death of the type that Eliphaz had earlier described as belonging to the pious.

Job sets up this picture of abundant death with an elaborate description of the life of the wicked beginning in v. 7, in terms of its liveliness and fecundity: "the wicked live on" (רשעים יחיו), "grow old" (עתק), and "become mighty in power" (גברו חיל). Life equivalents—images of connection and movement—then fill out the picture of the wicked. Their *connection* to their family establishes their abundance and fecundity ("Their offspring [זרע] are established before them,[18] their issue [צאצא] before their eyes"),[19] a statement resembling Eliphaz's description of the righteous ("offspring [זרע] are many; issue [צאצא] like the grass of the earth"; 5:25) and directly contradicting the friends' claim that the offspring of the wicked meet disaster.[20] Abundance extends to the livestock of the wicked, which breed without fail (v. 10), as they did for Job in the introduction to the prologue. But in contrast to Job in the prologue, the household of the wicked "is at peace, free from fear" and does not experience "the rod of God" (v. 9).

Images of movement give the impression of liveliness and celebration, reminiscent also of the introduction to the prologue. Like the celebratory movement and vitality of Job's children, the children of the wicked are full of movement and vitality, being "let loose like sheep" and "skipping about" (v. 11). Like Job's children, they celebrate, although not with festivals, but by singing to the tambourine and lyre (v. 12)[21]—instruments associated with joyful festivities[22]— and by making merry to the sound of the flute (v. 12).

---

17. Contrast this to Zophar's description of the wicked as the ones "lying in the dust" (20:11), which, as Eliphaz had described earlier, emphasizes the *who* of death, and not the *fact* of death.

18. Many, following the LXX, delete the עמם, which seems redundant after the לפניהם (see, e.g., Fohrer, *Hiob*, 336–37; Gordis, *Job*, 224, 229; Habel, *Job*, 321–22; Hartley, *Job*, 312). Tur-Sinai, *Job*, 325, attempts to translate both words ("Their seed is established in their sight, with them") while Mitchell J. Dahood, "Hebrew–Ugaritic Lexicography IV," *Bib* 47 (1966): 403–19 (411) understands לפניהם to refer to the ancestors ("their progenitors are with them").

19. NJPS understands the antecedent to "their issue" to be "offspring" ("And they see their children's children"), a reading that bolsters the picture of abundance and fecundity.

20. See 18:12, 19; 20:10, 26, 28.

21. The antecedent to "they" is ambiguous. It could either refer to the children, in which case the connection to the merry-making of Job's children is even stronger, or it could refer to the wicked. Either way, the image is of one of movement.

Clearly the images that Job uses to describe the wicked belong to the symbolization of abundant life previously discussed. The crowning achievement of abundant life, as in Eliphaz's earlier description,[23] is abundant death, described in terms of fullness and wholeness: it is the full completion[24] of one's number of days "in prosperity/happiness" (טוב), and is a descent[25] to Sheol "in peace" (רגע; 21:13).[26]

Job then will expand this description, making his symbolization of abundant death the most comprehensive in the entire HB, far outdoing even Eliphaz's attempt, which, itself, was a unique explicit statement of abundant death. In 21:32–33, Job describes the lavish funeral of the one who dies an abundant death. Such a one is spared sudden and calamitous death (21:30, as Eliphaz suggested earlier in 5:19–22), only to die the honorable death of the revered. Death does not erase the memory of this person as Prov 10:7 says happens to the wicked,[27] but others "conduct (יבל)[28] him to the grave" while "a watch/wake is set (שקד) over [his] tomb," an image likely of someone tending the tomb and keeping it from damage, a custom "designed to guarantee the continuation of the honor of the deceased" (21:32).[29] Moreover, the deceased does not come to the grave alone, but in the company of an absurdly massive throng, who accompany the funeral procession ("*every* person follows after him; before him proceeds a crowd *without number*"; 21:33).[30] Virtually every living human accompanies this dead person to the grave—an image emphasizing the intrusion on, and overwhelming of, the imagery of death with the imagery of life and liveliness. With these two images (the watch and the throng), Job's description of abundant death manages to mute the reality and finality of death by employing images of connection—a life equivalent—to describe the funeral. Even in death this person experiences the vitality of human connection.

---

22. See Gen 31:27; Exod 15:20; Judg 11:34; 1 Sam 10:5; 18:6; 2 Sam 6:5; 1 Chr 13:8; Pss 81:2; 149:3; 150:4; Isa 5:12; Jer 31:4.

23. See 5:26.

24. Reading the *Qere*, יכלו, instead of the *Kethib*, יבלו ("wear out"). Although the latter is not incomprehensible in this context (NJPS: "They spend their days"), the former is a repeated idiom for death in *Job* ("finish the days"; see 7:6 and 36:11) and makes sense given the parallel line of 21:13.

25. The root of the verb יחתו is best understood as נחת rather than as חתת ("to destroy"; see Hartley, *Job*, 313).

26. This term normally means "in a moment" (see Job 7:18; 20:5; 34:20; see Driver and Gray, *Job*, 1:184; Hartley, *Job*, 312–13; Pope, *Job*, 144), but can also mean "peacefully" as in Isa 34:14; Jer 31:2; 50:34 (see Gordis, *Job*, 229–30 [who suggests that both meanings might be present here]; Dhorme, *Job*, 313; Fohrer, *Hiob*, 337; Habel, *Job*, 321). Because of the particular symbolization of abundant life that Job is painting here, it seems best to take the term to mean "peacefully," rather than "in a moment," which would be an image of sudden death more appropriate in a typical death of the wicked poem.

27. Newsom, "Job," 494.

28. Gordis's reading (*Job*, 226), "he is borne in pomp to the grave," is perhaps a bit exaggerated.

29. Hartley, *Job*, 321.

30. Some interpret 21:33b, c, to mean that all will follow him to the grave, i.e., death, even as many have preceded him (see, e.g., Hartley, *Job*, 321; Rowley, *Job*, 153). I agree with Gordis that "this idea is not appropriate in the context here nor a sufficiently powerful presentation of Job's standpoint" (Gordis, *Job*, 235).

Furthermore, the plural usage of the word for "grave" (קברות) suggests "the elaborate character of [the] sepulchre,"[31] an image confirmed by the elaborate funeral procession, which simultaneously shows the utmost esteem in which this person was held. And even in death, this person's capacities of enjoyment are not diminished: the pleasantness of abundant death is compared to the pleasantness of the taste of something sweet ("The clods of the wadi are sweet to him").[32] Abundant death is shown to be full and lavish, the perfect accompaniment to abundant life.

Job's description of abundant death is an expansion of Eliphaz's earlier such description, except for the crucial fact that Job takes the elements of Eliphaz's symbolization of the death of the pious (life/piety/relationship) and death of the wicked (death/impiety/alienation-from-the-deity) and shuffles them. So instead of abundant death being reserved for the pious who are in relationship with a caring and disciplining deity (Eliphaz), for Job abundant death is reserved for "the wicked" (רשעים; 21:7, 17, 28) or "the evil" (רע; 21:3) who reject the deity and so alienate themselves from God (21:14–15). Job's speech in ch. 21, therefore, is a fitting response by Job to the claims of the friends, in general, concerning the fate of the wicked, and to Eliphaz, in particular, concerning abundant death. Its content is consistent with Job's previous attempts to articulate the experience of desymbolization, even if this time he deals head-on with the arguments of the friends.

5.1.2. *Chapter 21 as an Introduction to the Third Cycle*
But more than a simple response to the argument of the friends, Job's speech in ch. 21 functions as a parody of their arguments. There has been much analysis on the book of Job for its use and reuse of traditional forms of address,[33] sometimes described as being parodic.[34] Although the reuse of traditional forms can be identified in ch. 21,[35] my argument is that here Job is not so much parodying traditional forms as can be identified in the Psalms or the Prophets, for example; rather, he is parodying their *way of speaking*. Job is parodying the manner in which the friends articulate their sense of the symbolic coherence of the world. I will outline the distinction I am trying to draw by revisiting Nemo's arguments about the friends' usage of technique in their dialogues with Job.

Nemo's insightful analysis of the speeches of the friends understands them to operate as moral "technology" or "technique" whose purpose is to interpret and

31. Gordis, *Job*, 235, who cites 2 Chr 21:20; 24:25; and 35:24 for support.
32. רגב refers to the sweetness of food or drink in Exod 15:25; Judg 9:11; Job 20:12; 24:20; and Prov 9:17.
33. See, e.g., Aage Bentzen, *Introduction to the Old Testament* (6th ed.; 2 vols.; Copenhagen: Gad, 1961), 1:118–201; Georg Fohrer, "Form und Funktion in der Hiobdichtung," in *Studien zum Buche Hiob (1956–1979)* (ed. Georg Fohrer; BZAW 159; Berlin: de Gruyter, 1983), 60–77; Hartmut Gese, *Lehre und Wirklichkeit in der alten Weisheit: Studien zu den Sprüchen Salomos und zu dem Buche Hiob* (Tübingen: Mohr, 1958), 74–78; Westermann, *Structure*.
34. The most extensive analysis of parody in *Job* is by Katharine J. Dell, *The Book of Job as Sceptical Literature* (BZAW 197; Berlin: de Gruyter, 1991), 109–57.
35. See Fohrer, "Form und Funktion," 63–66, 69, 74.

explain Job's disaster, to render it in terms that "contain" its evil in the fixed, natural order of "the world."[36] So, where Job articulates an evil that seems to obliterate every order, every law (desymbolization), technique claims he is not in a position to perceive the order that actually contains him.[37] According to Nemo,

> We may call the world in which Job has his experience: *Scene I*. The friends appear and tell him that the cause of the evil under which he suffers is a set of events belonging to an Other Scene, a *Scene II*, which he does not see, but which they see and master. Together, the two scenes belong to the world and convene under a unique logic, that of the Law. But, by his exhaustive refutation of his friends' arguments, Job shows that nothing of significance takes place in Scene II. The evil that he suffers is independent of the sins imputed to him, or at least it is, by any standard, infinitely disproportionate to such sins. The alterity of evil that Job wants to discuss is really other than Scene II in relation to Scene I, but must be yet more *other*, an "other Other Scene," a *Scene III*.[38]

This "alterity of evil" that Job experiences reveals a certain truth: it "discloses itself precisely in not allowing the individual who is caught in its vertigo to exit the vertigo and rejoin the world in its stability."[39]

Nemo's analysis offers a brilliant understanding of the interplay of the speeches of the friends and Job. Specifically, it interprets the miscommunication between Job and the friends and their inability and/or unwillingness to engage each others' arguments directly in the first two cycles as an integral element of the discourse on evil that the book of Job is said to provide. What Nemo fails to do, however, is to interpret Job's explicit engagement and rebuttal of the friends' arguments in ch. 21: for the first time in the book, Job speaks in the same manner as his friends as he engages their arguments head-on. If, using Lifton's terms, the Job of the first two cycles articulated his experience of desymbolization (what Nemo might call the vertigo of a world rendered unstable by the excess of evil), while the friends articulated a highly symbolized world that explains disaster (what Nemo calls "moral technique"), in ch. 21 Job engages and rejects the symbolization of the friends, and offers, instead, what appears on the surface to be an alternative symbolization. For the first time Job seems to speak the language of technique.

Job signals a possible shift to the language of technique by the manner in which he engages the symbolization of abundant life, shuffling the elements of Eliphaz's conception of the death of the wicked and death of the pious. While previously Job certainly has alluded to this symbolization, it has been in order to play off of or parody certain elements in order to articulate his *own* acute experience of suffering, as I argued above. So, for example, he employed traditional Psalm of Lament imagery to show his own experience of death-in-life and murder at God's hand. As Newsom argues, "Job's attempt to express his own truth about the violence he has experienced...require[d] him to dislocate and

---

36. "Technique transforms all things into objects which are integrated into the world" (Nemo, *Excess of Evil*, 69).
37. Ibid., 77.
38. Ibid., 79.
39. Ibid., 40.

remold words, metaphors, and genres through which traditional language had constructed a world of meaning."[40] Even Job's burgeoning exploration of the language of legal action against God, which Newsom rightly identifies as his "constitution of an alternative rhetorical world"[41]—something that approximates a resymbolization—directly pertains to *his own* subjective experiences of being wronged and *his own* desire for vindication.

In ch. 21, however, Job abandons the subjective position upon which all of his earlier usage of traditional motifs was based and presents a generalized position—one similar to the technique of his friends. Job abandons the subject position of the "I" that so dominated his earlier speeches and does not address the vertigo of his *own* experience of desymbolization, but describes a *general* picture of a world where the wicked live abundant lives and die abundant deaths. His description of contrasting deaths (21:23–26) is not for the purpose of protesting this injustice to God, it is merely to state a *fact* of human existence.

Job's abandonment of the subjective position in favor of a generalized position is even clearer when his statements about death in ch. 21 are compared to those in 9:21–23, a previous statement about death that, on the surface, seems to be of a similar, generalized kind as that in ch. 21. In 9:21–23, Job declares that God "destroys both the blameless and wicked," a statement that, like 21:26, both comments on the troubling ramifications of death's democratic quality, and is a general statement meant to encompass all of reality. The difference between the two, however, is that Job utters the former only after a consideration of his *own* experience of inordinate suffering and his *own* blamelessness. The general statement about the destruction of the innocent and guilty is a broader application of his own experience of suffering and divine injustice. For Job, human mortality—specifically his own—demonstrates divine immorality.[42]

In ch. 21, however, Job has abandoned a mode of address that speaks from his own subject position. He will not address his own experience of suffering or his own impending death, as he had previously. He will only speak in broad strokes of the general operation of the world.

Nevertheless, Job's shift to generalized discourse is *not* an articulation of a resymbolized symbolic world. It is rather a parody of a resymbolized world. For Job, the symbolic world of his generalized discourse is not the symbolically coherent and comprehensible one of his friends. Rather, as he suggests about the deaths of the pious and wicked, the world is coherent only insofar as its operations are predictably incoherent. Job parodies technique: where the friends claim that wickedness results in impoverished death—a coherent world with predictable results—Job claims that wickedness results in abundant death—an incoherent world with seemingly arbitrary results.

---

40. Newsom, *Contest of Moral Imaginations*, 131–32. See her analysis of Job's resistance to narrative and prayer on pp. 132–50.

41. Ibid., 132.

42. The only other place where Job seems to abandon the subjective position in favor of the general is ch. 12. This chapter, however, is not so clearly a response to the arguments of the friends (although one could see it as a response to 5:8–16) and it is not explicitly about death.

Though Job's speech in ch. 21 approximates the generalized discourse of the friends, it fails to arrive at a resymbolization of death. Instead, Job uses generalized discourse to articulate his sense of the collapse of shared patterns of meaning. Desymbolization continues to characterize Job's sense of the operation of the world. However, the shift from the articulation of desymbolization as the subjective experience of the "I" to its articulation through generalized discourse does signal a shift in Job's speaking patterns. Chapter 21 marks a turning point of sorts in that Job will increasingly abandon the usage of "personal" language in favor of the generalized discourse of the friends.[43]

What does he have to gain by this shift in speaking patterns? In Nemo's words, generalized discourse offers the possibility of the containment of the "excess of evil." Whereas the focus in Job's "personal" language is on his own subjective experiences of incomprehensible disaster and on the incoherence of a shattered symbolic world in which disaster happens, generalized discourse claims that disaster is not incoherent, but is part of a much larger symbolic system that provides a logic to disaster, and supplies a comprehensible meaning to that which, on the surface, seemed incomprehensible. This is the type of "containment of evil" that the friends attempted to convince Job of throughout the dialogues.

But Job, in ch. 21, has not made the transition to authentic generalized discourse—he only parodies it. By ch. 27, however, Job will make this transition.

5.2. *Chapter 27: Generalized Discourse without Grounding*

Earlier I demonstrated why scholars dispute whether 27:13–23 is actually part of Job's speech. These verses form an obvious fate-of-the-wicked poem similar to those the friends have been fond of employing in their speeches (4:8–11; 8:13–19; 15:20–35; 18:5–21; 20:4–29; 22:15–20). My own sense is that the poem ought to be interpreted as it stands in the MT, that is, as Job's words, though ones that have a peculiar relationship to those of the friends. Having parodied the mode of generalized discourse in ch. 21, Job now gives himself over entirely to this mode, not so much as an attempt actually to "contain the evil" that has happened to him, but as an attempt to demonstrate to his friends how utterly inappropriate this type of generalized discourse is in his mouth. Job will speak as one propounding a symbolically coherent universe, but it will all sound so wrong. Nevertheless, in speaking this way, Job will (perhaps inadvertently) stumble upon the missing element that separates generalized discourse from a resymbolization of death.

5.2.1. *The Generalized Discourse of 27:13–23*
In ch. 27 Job begins by declaring an oath concerning the uprightness of his ways (vv. 2–6), before announcing to his friends that he will teach them the true ways

---

43. Though ch. 23 contains much "personal" language, in chs. 24, 26, and 27 Job speaks almost exclusively in generalities.

of God (v. 11). In v. 12 he accuses the friends of speaking nonsense before seemingly repeating the same type of argument in vv. 13–23 that he accuses them of supporting. Some scholars argue that by repeating the arguments the friends have been making Job here is parodying them.[44] Whether this is parody or not, all readers seem to sense the absolute inappropriateness of this type of generalized discourse on Job's lips.

The specific generalized discourse that Job repeats is the fate-of-the-wicked poem. As in the traditional topos, Job's focus is heavily slanted toward revealing the *ultimate* end of the wicked, death. Job gives this topic pride of place: it is both the first and the last topic of consideration (vv. 14–15 and 20–23, respectively), bracketing the only other topic, the wicked person's wealth and possessions (vv. 16–19). Of the ten verses that deal with the fate of the wicked (excluding v. 13, which acts as an introduction) six are concerned with death, both the death of the wicked person's progeny (vv. 14–15) and the wicked person's own annihilation (vv. 20–23).

Initially, Job emphasizes death by foregrounding in vv. 14–15 what many commentators note is the threefold disaster pattern: war, famine, and pestilence (with "death" standing here for plague as in Jer 15:2; 43:11).[45] As in a typical fate-of-the-wicked poem, this disaster is reserved for the wicked. What goes unnoticed by scholars is the degree to which death is symbolized here to *intrude* on life. As noted earlier, in Chapter 2, part of the symbolization of abundant life included an emphasis on life, liveliness, and fecundity, which, as in the introduction to the prologue, included the birth and health of progeny, and the abundance of robust livestock who give birth without fail. An abundance of progeny and livestock equals the abundance and multiplication of life. Here, however, while the wicked person seems to have an abundance of progeny (ירבו בניו, "his children multiply/are abundant") by a number of different wives (v. 15b),[46] this abundance of life is cancelled by an equal abundance of death: his children "are marked for the sword." Although the theme of the punishment of children for the sins of parents is fairly common in the HB,[47] Job's threefold repetition of the demise of the wicked person's progeny ("children," "issue," "the ones who survive him"[48]) in terms of complete and utter annihilation by the traditional agents of disaster (sword, famine, plague) demonstrates the complete intrusion of death into the realm of abundant life.[49] The symbolic world of the

44. See, e.g., Good, *Turns of Tempest*, 288–90; Janzen, *Job*, 174, 179–86; Newsom, "Job," 522.

45. See, e.g., Dhorme, *Job*, 394 (who cites Lev 26:25–26; 2 Sam 24:13; Jer 14:12; 24:10, for support, as well as evidence from the Amarna texts); Gordis, *Job*, 386; Janzen, *Job*, 359 n. 14; Newsom, "Job," 524.

46. אלמניו is a plural noun with a third masculine singular suffix. The LXX and Syriac, however, read "their widows," referring to the widows of the wicked person's "survivors" who had died, and not to the wicked person himself (see also, Driver and Gray, *Job*, 1:230). Fohrer suggests that this reading arose in order to combat the implication of polygamy in the MT (Fohrer, *Hiob*, 387).

47. See, e.g., Jer 18:21.

48. Reading the plural form of the *Qere* (שרידיו) over the singular form of the *Kethib* (שרידו), since this fits with the plural form of v. 14. Driver and Gray (*Job*, 1:230) argue that this refers to the children of the wicked person who, while surviving the sword and famine, will die by the plague.

49. This is typical of a fate-of-the-wicked poem. See 18:12; 19; 20:10, 20, 26.

wicked that Job paints here is the counterpart of the symbolic world of the pious depicted in the introduction to the prologue.

This dominance of death over abundant life also is implied in the echo that v. 15 has with Job's prior description of the funeral of the wicked person in 21:32–33. The reference to "the ones who survive" the wicked person, and to "his widows" imply the death of the wicked person here, although his death is not overtly described. This time, however, in the place of a throng of survivors from his community bearing him to the grave, an image of the connection and the intrusion of the living into the realm of the dead (21:33), here, his survivors are also dead (27:15), buried by Death itself,[50] an image of separation and lack contact with the living. Both the wicked man and his survivors die impoverished deaths, with no connection with the living, not even the widows performing proper mourning rites (27:15b). Thus, the image in ch. 21 of the wicked being borne to his lavish "tomb" (קברות) that was then tended by the living is replaced in ch. 27 with the death and burial (קבר) of those who should have borne him and tended to the tomb.

From the deaths of the wicked man's progeny, Job discusses briefly the destruction of his possessions (vv. 16–19), before returning to the image of the annihilation of the wicked man (vv. 20–23). The last destruction of possessions image (v. 19), however, seems to morph into a death image, indicating Job's extreme emphasis on death imagery in this sequence. Verse 19 can read, "He goes to bed rich, but for the last time; he opens his eyes and nothing is left,"[51] fitting nicely with the prior possession imagery; or because of the ambiguous antecedent to the last adverb אֵיננּוּ, the second line can also be a reference to his death: "he opens his eyes and he is no more,"[52] a reference to the wicked man's death, fitting for this passage so fixated on this topic.

Finally, Job describes, with awful ferocity, the death of the wicked man at the hand of three deadly forces. First, Job picks up on Bildad's prior reference to the "Terrors" (בלהות), which represented the personified forces of death, terrifying the wicked man on every side, chasing him at his feet (18:11, 14). For Bildad, the titles "King of Terrors" (מלך בלהות) and likely also "Firstborn of Death," had a specific chthonic referent, namely the Ugaritic god Mot, ruler of the netherworld, the personification of death *par excellence*.[53] According to Job, these

---

50. Taking מות literally in this case, and not as a reference to the plague.

51. So, Hartley, *Job*, 358. This reading requires the לֹא יֵאָסֵף to be emended to לֹא יֹוסִף ("not do again"; Hartley, *Job*, 358–59), which Dhorme (*Job*, 396) suggests is a defective form of the former. The LXX and Syriac seem to understand it this way, as do many commentators (e.g. Fohrer, *Hiob*, 387; Gordis, *Job*, 295; Hartley, *Job*, 358; Rowley, *Job*, 178). If one follows the MT, it appears to be a reference to being gathered for burial (Ezek 29:4). Blommerde, based on the Ugaritic *l'y*, takes the לֹא as a reference to "the Mighty One." He translates the verse, "Rich he lies down, but the Mighty One takes him away, He fixes his gaze and annihilates him"; see Anton C. M. Blommerde, *Northwest Semitic Grammar and Job* (BibOr 22; Rome: Pontifical Biblical Institute, 1969), 28, 105.

52. See, e.g., Dhorme, *Job*, 396 (who calls this "the last look of the dying man"); Driver and Gray, *Job*, 1:231; Habel, *Job*, 383; Pope, *Job*, 169.

53. For this interpretation, see John Barclay Burns, "The Identity of Death's First-Born (Job 18:13)," *VT* 37 (1987): 362–64; Clines, *Job 1–20*, 417–19; Nahum M. Sarna, "Mythological Background of Job 18," *JB* 82 (1963): 315–18; Tromp, *Primitive Conceptions*, 162–66. For the inter-

forces of death perform their deathly goal and overtake the wicked man "like a flood" (27:20)—the deluge image itself being one of death and destruction.[54]

Job parallels these demonic terrors to the "storm-wind" (סופה) and the "east-wind" (קדים), both also known agents of death. The storm-wind represented calamity, disaster, and the ultimate destruction of the wicked,[55] as well as the judgment of God,[56] while the latter represented the withering and drying up of life,[57] as well as sudden calamity and destruction.[58] Together, these three forces team up to destroy the wicked person, who is described as "going away" (הלך; v. 21a), which is not only a euphemism for dying, but also suggests the image of departure from human contact and connection to Sheol, the land of the dead. The deadly forces cause the death equivalent of separation.

The image of separation is carried through the last verses of this unit, although the subject of the action of these verses is disputed—whether people in general,[59] or the east-wind just mentioned.[60] If the image is of humans hurling themselves at the wicked man, indicating their scorn by clapping their hands and whistling,[61] it is an image of derision and exclusion, of the separation of the wicked man from the rest of society. If the image is a continuation of a description of the actions of the east-wind, it extends the image of separation by describing the ferocity of the east-wind's power over the wicked man in delivering him to death and separating him from the living. A third possibility is that the subject is God who is depicted as attacking the wicked man,[62] which would not be a separation image like the other two. More likely all of these potential subjects of the action are implied, creating an image that vacillates between all three, but ultimately functions to depict the complete and utter destruction of the wicked.

5.2.2. *Generalized Speech and Resymbolization*
Job's articulation of the death of the wicked, like his speech in ch. 21, is a generalized statement that abandons the mode of the subjective address of the speaking "I." The difference between Job's generalized discourse in chs. 21 and 27 is striking, however. Earlier, Job parodied generalized discourse in order to articulate his sense of symbolic breakdown and desymbolization. Although he employed a generalized mode of discourse, the content of what he said was authentic to his experiences. In ch. 27, however, Job is not so much parodying

---

pretation that "Firstborn of Death" is a reference also to Mot, see Habel, *Job*, 287–88; W. L. Michel, "The Ugaritic Texts and the Mythological Expressions" (Ph.D. diss., University of Wisconsin, 1970), 406–7.

54. Newsom, "Job," 525, who cites Pss 18:16; 32:6; and Isa 28:17 for support. See also 2 Sam 5:20; Hos 5:10; Amos 5:24; Jonah 2:2–6.

55. See Job 21:18; Ps 83:16; Prov 1:27; 10:25.

56. See Isa 5:28; 17:13; 29:6; 66:15; Jer 4:13; Hos 8:7; Amos 1:14.

57. See Gen 41:6, 23, 27; Ezek 17:10; 19:12; Hos 13:15.

58. See Exod 10:13; Ps 48:7; Ezek 27:26.

59. See, e.g., Dhorme, *Job*, 397–98; Gordis, *Job*, 292, 296 (although Gordis understands v. 22 to have the east-wind as its subject).

60. See, e.g., Habel, *Job*, 383–84; Pope, *Job*, 169, 173.

61. See Jer 49:17; Lam 2:15; Zeph 2:15.

62. See, e.g., Andersen, *Job*, 222.

generalized speech as he is giving himself over completely both to his friends' mode of discourse and their very arguments in order to demonstrate convincingly how utterly inappropriate these words are in his mouth. In contrast to his parody of generalized discourse in ch. 21, his repetition of the generalized discourse of his friends is absolutely inauthentic to his experience.

What Job demonstrates is that generalized discourse is not identical to resymbolization or the recentering of the self, for Job's speech in ch. 27 lacks the key Liftonian ingredient of "grounding" in the decentering–recentering process— "the relationship of the self to its own history, individual and collective, as well as to its biology."[63] As discussed earlier, grounded individuals are those who are able to maintain their connection to their unique and highly personal forms and images, while at the same time experimenting with new combinations of images and forms in order to account for new stimuli. Job's speech, however, appears to be ungrounded because it fails (intentionally) to connect his own personal experience of disaster along with its related desymbolization of forms and images due to this experience, with the general symbolic system he articulates here in ch. 27. In fact, his speech works to demonstrate the inappropriateness of the speech of the friends only because it is *not* grounded in his personal combination of forms and images that he articulated earlier with his desymbolized death imagery. Job's speech has the character of a fantasy or an illusion entirely inappropriate to Job's life experiences, which seems to be Job's point in articulating the generalized words of his friends.

Mimicking a different way of speaking, however, has a way of drawing the speaker into a different way of seeing and understanding the world. Job's earlier parody of the friends' way of speaking in ch. 21 articulated a generalized statement of the desymbolization of the friends' symbolic universe. His speech in ch. 27 articulates a generalized statement of the symbolic wholeness of the universe, which Job suggests does not apply. Whereas the first generalized statement did not articulate a coherent symbolic universe, but did connect with Job's experience of the world, the second articulates a coherent symbolic universe, but does not connect with Job's experience of the world. The question now is, given that Job seems to be employing generalized speech, will this *new way of speaking* lead to a *new way of understanding* the world such that Job will articulate both a coherent symbolic universe that also is true to his life experiences? If so, Job will have passed through the process of recentering and his death imagery will show evidence of being resymbolized. I believe that Job's final speech (chs. 29–31) demonstrates this process.

5.3. *Chapters 29–31:*
Symbolic Wholeness and Resymbolized Death

The Job who speaks in the last section attributed to him in the poetic sections of the book does so with a voice that scarcely resembles the Job of the previous dialogues, a fact frequently noted by readers. Scholars have identified several

63. Lifton, *Life of the Self*, 72.

ways that this speech contrasts with the previous ones. First, the introductory words of this speech are different, only bearing resemblance to those of 27:1. Job does not direct this speech at the friends—no addressee is specified. Indeed, the whole speech is marked by a glaring absence of the type of anticipatory argumentation that characterizes Job's earlier dialogue with the friends.[64] Second, throughout the speech Job envisions himself in a "settled agricultural community with walled settlements,"[65] an environment hardly represented at all earlier. Third, in contrast to Job's extensive usage of parody and irony in his earlier speeches, this speech notably lacks these rhetorical devices. Fourth, as Newsom notes, although this speech does contain a number of traditional images, topoi and genres, Job makes no attempt either to bolster his own position by appealing to tradition or to undercut the traditional voice. Instead, Job speaks directly, and simply: "the ease and fluency with which Job speaks projects an audience deemed capable of understanding him, one with whom he shares a language of meaning and value, to whom his claims and complaints would be intelligible…"[66] Fifth, the perspective of Job in this speech approaches that of the friends, typically referred to as "retributionist position."[67] For these reasons and others many historical critics suggest that the author of chs. 29–31 is different from the author of the rest of the speeches[68] or at least that the mood or tone of Job's last speech differs greatly from the previous ones.[69]

5.3.1. *Symbolic Coherence in Chapters 29–31*

The "strange" Joban voice that readers identify in chs. 29–31 is one that articulates a coherent self-narrative that grasps the significance of the experience of disaster and renders it both comprehensible and meaningful, demonstrating Job to be "in control" of the suffering that once seemed to render the world incoherent. The best way to demonstrate the uniquely coherent nature of this final speech is to compare it to his previous speeches and to Psalms of Lament in terms of their narrative, structural, and symbolic coherence.

Earlier I compared the usage of traditional death imagery in Job's speeches with its usage in Psalms of Lament. I argued that in these Psalms death imagery forms part of the complaint in the language of prayer with the specific goal of deliverance by Yahweh and restoration of right relationship. In Job's earlier speeches, however, death imagery is not invoked in order to petition for God's deliverance, but as an articulation of his own subjective experience of death-in-life and murder at God's hand.

---

64. Newsom, *Contest of Moral Imaginations*, 184.

65. Snaith, *Job*, 35.

66. Newsom, *Contest of Moral Imaginations*, 184. See also, Holbert, "Rehabilitation of the Sinner," 231–34, who argues for what he calls "deironization."

67. Good, *Turns of Tempest*, 317. See also Holbert, "Rehabilitation of the Sinner," 234.

68. For a list of scholars who make such an argument, see Holbert, "Rehabilitation of the Sinner," 229–30 n. 1.

69. For a list of scholars who make such an argument, see ibid., 229–30 n. 2. See also the nice discussion in Newsom, *Contest of Moral Imaginations*, 183–85.

This is to say that Job's previous usage of traditional death imagery does not form part of a larger rhetorical narrative with a rhetorical goal, as it does for the Psalmist. By "rhetorical narrative" I mean that death imagery in Lament Psalms comprises the stock language of complaint in the Lament Psalm, and this language performs an identifiable function in the prayer. For the Psalmist the Psalm of Lament narrates an experience of distress and turmoil, with the goal of motivating Yahweh to alleviate the suffering. Thus, the characteristic form of this Psalm begins with an invocation to God as the addressee of the prayer, followed by the complaint of the supplicant's experience of suffering, followed by an affirmation of trust in God's abilities to deliver the supplicant, followed by the plea that God, in fact, do so, followed by a vow of obedience and praise to God.[70] This prayer has a coherent narrative structure (from present misery to anticipated future deliverance) and a coherent rhetorical form (entreaty to God for deliverance). Furthermore, and most importantly, the prayer assumes a coherent symbolic world that imbues the prayer with meaning. Specifically, this symbolic world is the symbolization of abundant life, with its correlation of abundant life, piety, and relationship with the deity. In the Psalm of Lament this symbolic world is evident in the assumptions the supplicant makes, namely that the experience of death (complaint) is overcome by deliverance from God who restores to life (plea), and that deliverance and life entail right relationship with God (vow of obedience).

Job's earlier usage of traditional Lament Psalm death imagery, however, lacks any of this narrative, rhetorical, or symbolic coherence. First of all, it lacks the same narrative coherence. This is not to argue that his speeches are incoherent and therefore nonsensical, but that they lack the same clear narrative drive as the Lament Psalms. This is evident in Job's second speech (chs. 6–7), for example, whose traditional death imagery (7:1–6) appears immediately following a speech addressed to his friends (6:14–30) and immediately before an address to God (7:7–21). The death imagery seems to have no immediate structural tie to his address to his friends, and while it may connect with his address to God,[71] it is not in a manner as immediately obvious as in the Psalm of Lament. The sense of structural "messiness" of the speech is demonstrated by browsing through the commentaries where each scholar seems to understand the structure and thematic sequence of the speech differently, sometimes quite differently.[72] The same could be said for death imagery in Job's speeches in chs. 16–17 and ch. 19, which I examined above.[73]

---

70. For the classic articulation of the form of the Lament Psalm, see Hermann Gunkel and Joachim Begrich, *Introduction to Psalms: The Genres of the Religious Lyric of Israel* (trans. James D. Nogalski; Mercer Library of Biblical Studies; Macon, Ga.: Mercer University Press, 1998), 152–86. Although many specific Psalms of Lament lack one or several of these elements, the basic goal of such prayers is the deliverance of the Psalmist by Yahweh.

71. As Clines (*Job 1–20*, 167) notes, the imperative "remember" in 7:7, directed to God, seems to indicate that vv. 1–6 were spoken also to him.

72. For example, Clines, *Job 1–20*, 167, argues for three units: a monologue (6:2–13), an address to the friends (6:14–30), and an address to God (7:1–21); Murphy, *Wisdom Literature*, 25, argues for two units, 6:2–7 (which contains a complaint, justification for the complaint, affirmation of loyalty,

This structural "messiness" results in a related messiness or lack of immediate obviousness of the rhetorical goal of Job's usage of traditional death imagery. Above I suggested that while many scholars believe that Job's usage of the language of complaint draws attention to what follows the complaint in Job's speeches (frequently a declaration of innocence), I also argued that Job used this death imagery because it is an authentic expression of his subjective experiences. However, unlike the Psalm of Lament, where death imagery and the language of complaint is an integral piece of a larger rhetorical goal that dominates the whole prayer, Job's traditional death imagery does not seem to share in a greater rhetorical thrust that dominates the whole speech. Indeed, it is frequently difficult to identify a *single* dominant rhetorical goal of many of Job's speeches.[74]

Above all, however, Job's speeches lack the sense of a coherent symbolic world that the Lament Psalms assume. This is mainly because the dialogues are structured by the contrast between the friends for whom the symbolic world of the Lament Psalms remains intact, and Job, for whom it has crumbled. The life/piety/relationship complex has been disrupted and Job attempts to articulate his experiences in unique ways that parody, invert, and even contradict that complex. As Newsom argues, "the resources of traditional language for framing suffering and rendering it meaningful have utterly failed. [Job's] alienation from received language is reflected in his extensive use of irony, parody, and other means of subverting traditional speech."[75] The sense of structural and rhetorical "messiness" that one senses in Job's speeches likely has to do with the fact that Job's symbolic world has fallen to pieces and Job is groping toward a unique articulation of his experience amid the shattered patterns of meaning.[76]

In chs. 29–31, however, Job seems to have rediscovered a certain rhetorical, structural, and symbolic wholeness, albeit one that differs from that of the Lament Psalms. First of all, Job narrates a structurally coherent narrative, although not the Lament Psalm's movement from present suffering to future restoration. Job, rather, relates his own *self*-narrative told as a tale of the honorable leader in the context of "village patriarchy." The tale is one of his past position of honor amid his social circles (29:2–29) contrasted to his present experience of dishonor by those outside his social circles (30:1–25), concluding with an extended oath concerning his own past honorable conduct and an implied plea that his present dishonor is unmerited (31:1–40). The thematic vehicle of the tale is the fiction of Job's social circle whose scope increasingly widens:

and motifs from the complaint) and 6:28–7:21 (which contains Job's charge that his friends listen to him and a complaint to God); Fohrer, *Hiob*, 165 argues for four units: 6:2–13, 15–30; 7:1–11, 12–21; while Habel, *Job*, 141, argues only for two: an address to the friends (ch. 6) and an address to God (ch. 7).

73. Regarding the former, Clines (*Job 1–20*, 375) writes that "the structure of this fifth speech of Job is not so clear...."

74. Of all of Job's speeches from the first two cycles, the one that is most structurally and rhetorically coherent is his first in which he articulates his desire for death. Above I argued this speech demonstrated the proximate and ultimate logic of suicide.

75. Newsom, *Contest of Moral Imaginations*, 183.

76. Newsom offers such an analysis in ibid., 130–68.

from the domestic sphere (29:2–6), to the village among his peers (29:7–11), to those who live along margins of society (29:12–17), to those who live beyond the margins of society (30:1–18), and ultimately, to God (30:19–31).[77]

The discourse of honor and shame provides Job's self-narrative a symbolic grid that enables him to re-conceptualize his present and past life experiences. Honor is the key term that defines his past experience of life. In his previous days Job would relate to those in his social circles as a man of honor among other honorable people. As one to whom respect was due, others would show him deference by "withdrawing" (29:8a), "rising and standing" (29:8b), with-holding words (29:9), and being silent (29:10). Job demonstrated his honor by using his power and influence on behalf of the marginalized in society (the poor, orphan, widow, blind, lame, and needy; 29:12–16) and by righting injustice (29:17). Job's honor, therefore, was evidenced by his piety, which then earned him more respect and acclaim from those in his society (29:11) and the blessing and gratitude of the marginalized (29:13).

To live in a society organized by the code of honor is, for Job, to live an abundant life, as evidenced by his usage of life imagery in connection with his description of an honor-based society. Two initial life-images demonstrate this. First, Job states that his "steps"[78] were "bathed in curd" (29:6a), a descriptive image of his life, where his "steps" metonymically substitutes for his life. "Steps" is also an image of the life equivalent of movement, and it fittingly sug-gests that previously Job's experiences were marked by a sense of life and live-liness. Furthermore, "curd," in ancient Israel symbolically represented abun-dance and luxury, adding to the picture of Job's experience of abundant life. Here curds are in such excess as to be commonplace, bathing Job's very steps. The second initial image of abundance, oil flowing from rocks (29:6b), recalls the story of Moses drawing water from a rock in Exod 17:6, except that Job exaggerates the image, replacing water with oil, a product that, like curds, represented both nourishment and luxurious abundance.[79]

Linked with these images of luxury are images of connection. Job was surrounded by hosts of people who related to him in appropriate ways: children (נַעַר) who surrounded him (29:5b); youths who revered him (29:8a); elders who honored him (29:8b); nobles and princes who deferred to him (29:9–10); and the destitute of society who looked to him for aid (29:12–16). The symbolic world Job describes is one both of abundance and meaningful human connection. Job "dwelled like a king among his troops" (29:25a) in a world of abundant life.

If, in Job's recollection of his former days, the symbolism of honor structured his experience of life, in his articulation of his present days, the symbolism of shame comes to structure his experience of death-in-life. In his earlier speeches, Job relied on the traditional imagery of stasis, separation, and disintegration of the Psalms of Lament in order to give voice to his own subjective sense of death-in-life and murder by the hand of God. That is, as he articulated his

---

77. For a good analysis of this movement, see ibid., 187–99.

78. The *hapax*, הֲלִיךְ, has also been translated "feet" (e.g. Habel, *Job*, 402–3).

79. See, e.g., Gen 27:28; Deut 8:8; 32:13; 33:24; Ps 23:5; etc.

unique life experiences, he grounded them in traditional forms, even as he used these forms to express his own sense of desymbolized death.

In Job's usage of death in his last speech, he grounds his subjective feelings of death-in-life in the same traditional images of separation, stasis, and disintegration even as he connects these with the symbolism of shame. First, Job describes, in graphic detail, his sense of separation from meaningful human contact (30:9–14). Previously, in 16:7, 10–11 and 19:13–18, Job described his estrangement from kin, household members, and friends as an expression of the death equivalent of separation similar to what is found in Psalms of Lament. Here, however, Job expands this sense of separation by describing his sense of being driven out and estranged not simply from his social group, but from those who themselves have been driven away from his social group. Such ones have already been "driven out of society"[80] and reviled "like a thief" (30:5). Their residence is no longer in human social circles, but in the "wastelands" (משואה; 30:3) separated from civilization—"in the gullies of the wadis, in holes in the ground, among the rocks" (30:6); "among the bushes…under the nettles" (30:7) —all places "symbolically associated with divine punishment, with the chaotic, and even the demonic."[81] These are the outcasts of society, the dishonorable who know not how to live by the rules of decorum that govern a well-structure society. They have been "stricken[82] from the earth" (30:8b), a description that simultaneously suggests separation from meaningful human contact, and the sense of death that accompanies separation.[83] They, therefore, live beyond the borders of society, in the wastelands.

Job, however, is alienated and reviled by these. He is the target of their "mocking," a "byword"[84] to them; they "abhor and keep far" from him, while spitting in his face (30:9–10). He is separated by the separated, twice removed from the life equivalent of connection.

To live among the dishonorable outcasts is to experience death-in-life. As he did previously (16:14; 19:6–12), Job compares himself to a city under siege to depict his subjective sense of death while living among them. Thus, the same people who have abhorred and alienated him are pictured as "building up roads of destruction against [him]" while "tearing down[85] [his] pathway" (30:12b), an

---

80. Gordis, *Job*, 331, argues for the translation of גו as "society" or "community" from its use in the Syriac ("church") and Phoenician ("corporation"). See also Dhorme, *Job*, 433; Fohrer, *Hiob*, 411, 413; Habel, *Job*, 415; Pope, *Job*, 194. Alternatively, Dahood takes גו from the Ugaritic meaning "voice" and so translates this line "with a shout" (see Dahood, "Northwest Semitic Philology," 318–19).

81. Newsom, *Contest of Moral Imaginations*, 190, who cites Isa 13:19–22; 34:8–15; Hos 2:3b; Zeph 2:13–15; Ps 107:33–34.

82. Most take נכא as an Aramaized form of the common Hebrew root נכה ("strike" or "smite"). Gordis, however, argues for the meaning "bring low, depress" based on the sense of the adjectival forms of נכא (Gordis, *Job*, 332; see also Hartley, *Job*, 397).

83. A common meaning of נכה is "smite" as in "kill."

84. מלה here (normally simply "word") probably has the sense of "byword" as most commentators understand it.

85. Most take נתס to be a cognate of נתץ, although Gordis (*Job*, 333–34) finds an Arabic cognate meaning "thorns" and therefore takes נתס to mean "to place thorns."

image similar to that employed in 19:12, both of which suggest the stasis of a city under siege. As previously, this stasis image gives way to the disintegration image of Job's body as the breached city wall: "As through a wide breach they come in; amid devastation they roll on" (30:14). Job experiences this attack not simply as an offensive by the alienated humans he earlier identified, but by the "Terrors" (30:15) discussed earlier, namely, personified Death, king of the underworld. His experience of separation, stasis, and disintegration is the force of Death on him, causing his body to waste away (30:17), his life to "drain away" (שׁפך; 30:16), and giving him the sense that he amounts to little more than "dust and ashes" (30:19), symbols of death.[86]

5.3.2. *The Resymbolization of Death*
Job connects his experiences of life and death, therefore, with the symbolism of honor and shame. To live abundant life is to live a life of honor in a society of the honorable. To experience death-in-life is to inhabit the realm of the wastelands of the dishonorable and not to know the intimacy of human connection in a well-structured society. By plotting his experiences of life and death onto the grid of honor and shame, Job achieves a level of symbolic wholeness that had eluded him previously. Further, this symbolic wholeness, unlike those displayed in chs. 21 and 27, exhibits the key element of grounding in the process of resymbolization.

As discussed above, Lifton argues that humans live in and through mental forms and images that provide shape and coherence to the world. The vitality of these forms and images depends on their being centered along temporal, spatial, and emotional planes so that one can feel "at the center of things"[87] and be able to interpret and understand the self and the world. Vitality, however, equally depends on the ability to decenter, to break down centered form, if only temporarily, in order to account for novel experience. "In decentering there is a partial suspension of close integration in temporal, spatial, and emotional planes, with anticipation of new integrations of a more inclusive kind,"[88] with anticipation, that is, of recentering. Without decentering, the self becomes static; without recentering, one cannot associate new experience with viable form. Vitality, therefore, depends on the movement from centering to decentering and back.

The manner in which Lifton discusses recentering suggests that two closely inter-related elements are necessary for the swing from decentering to recentering to be complete. First, as discussed briefly above, this process must be grounded. According to Lifton, grounding is "the relationship of the self to its own history, individual and collective, as well as to its biology."[89] Grounded individuals are those who are able to maintain their connection to their unique and highly personal forms and images, while at the same time experimenting

---

86. For oppression at the hands of enemies in Psalms of Lament, see, e.g., Pss 22:17–19; 31:12; 35:11–16; 59:2–8; 70:3–4.
87. Lifton, *Life of the Self*, 72.
88. Ibid.
89. Ibid.

with new combinations of images and forms in order to account for new stimuli. Where there is grounding, the pain and confusion of decentering can be in the service of recentering, "achieving a new mode of still-flexible ordering."[90] Without grounding, that is, with "insufficiently anchored images,"[91] decentering is replaced by uncentering, "the breakdown of the ordering or centering process,"[92] as is demonstrated by schizophrenic patients, whose confusion over self and non-self causes fantasies and illusions regarding the source of one's life experiences. Such people have "a radical absence of grounding."[93]

Job's articulation of the present experience of death-in-life in ch. 30 marks a significant change from his earlier speeches. In the first two cycles Job was very much focused on his own personal and subjective experiences, and his discussions of death therefore attempted to articulate the experience of desymbolization. By chs. 21 and 27, Job moved from the articulation of the personal to the articulation of a generalized discourse that abandoned the mode of personal address. Now, however, Job returns to the highly personal mode of address, but for the first time, Job is able to embed personal speech into a complete and coherent narrative organized by the symbolism of honor and shame. Job links life to honor and death to shame, recollecting his former days as days of honor, and his present ones as days of shame. This symbolic structure empowers him to envision a return to life as he appeals to his peers concerning his honor and the injustice of his present shameful situation (ch. 31). So, while honor and shame provide the symbolic grid that enables him to re-conceive his symbolic universe, Job's discourse is simultaneously grounded in traditional images and forms (lament death imagery) that come to express his highly personal and subjective sense of death-in-life.

But, as Lifton writes, because recentering is grounded in personal forms and images, successful recentering involves the creative ordering of these forms and images into unique combinations. A recentering of the self does not simply involve a return to the previous symbolic system before its desymbolization, but it involves an innovative organization of the forms and images of the previous symbolic system in light of novel experience. According to Lifton, the decentering–recentering process "may entail continuity without sameness—the viable ordering of temporal and spatial dimensions and of emotional valence, even as the content of images and forms undergoes significant alteration."[94] This constitutes the second element in the movement from Job's decentering to recentering.

Chapters 29–31 display a variety of the new combinations that Lifton discusses. Perhaps the most interesting, however, is how Job conceives of his relationship to the deity in this symbolic world of life/honor and death/shame.

First, in his narration of his past days, Job envisions the deity behaving as an honorable member of society. Just as Job looked out for the lesser members of

90. Ibid., 73.
91. Lifton, *Broken Connection*, 27 n. 1.
92. Ibid.
93. Ibid., 417.
94. Lifton, *Life of the Self*, 74.

society and received deference from those below him, so also the deity, as Job's superior, "guarded" Job (שמר) and "shone his lamp over [Job's] head" (30:2–3). Just as Job's actions on behalf of those whose station was below his enabled them to overcome obstacles and experience life (he saved the poor and orphan, helped the blind and lame, aided the needy and stranger), so also God's actions on behalf of his inferior, Job, enabled Job to live: God's light allowed Job to "walk in the dark" (30:3b) (the life equivalent of movement).

While in his earlier days God related to Job honorably, in his present situation God relates to Job shamefully, in a manner similar to the outcasts. Even as Job experienced death at the hands of dishonorable humans, so he also experiences the cruelty (אכזר; 30:21a) and animosity (שטם; 30:21b) of a deity who brings him to death. In the symbolic grid of honor and shame, the deity's present treatment of Job falls in the category of shame.

The grid of honor and shame supplies for Job a symbolic map upon which he can locate and articulate his relationship with the deity. Previously, when Job was working through the experience of the shattering of traditional symbolic systems, the deity's actions seemed to be devoid of meaning and utterly capricious. Now, however, by plotting his experiences of life and death-in-life on the grid of honor and shame, Job is able also to locate and articulate his relationship with the deity: God's actions also fall into the realm of the honorable and the dishonorable. But to conceive of the deity in this manner is to envision a new type of relationship with the deity, one where both Job and the deity are accountable to a code of honor. While this accountability implies a certain egalitarianism of accountability, the relationship does retain a sense of hierarchy in that the relationships mediated by the code of honor are experienced by those that occupy different levels of the social ladder and therefore command more or less respect. While Job occupies a level higher than nobles, princes, and elders, it is a level lower than God's.

The full force of Job's re-conception of his relationship to the deity is felt in the climactic oath with which Job ends his speech (ch. 31). Here Job appeals to his own honorable actions within his social circles, which, at the same time, is an implied appeal to how undeserved is his own present dishonor. Although Habel probably goes too far in suggesting that Job's speech is a specifically "legal challenge"[95] where "Job is demanding the equivalent of a covenant court trial,"[96] the speech does have a certain forensic feel. Job's case for his innocence seems to be directed more toward "the court of public opinion" than toward any formal legal court,[97] what Newsom argues are "the revered moral values of his culture by which he has defined himself."[98] Moreover, Job does not address either his oath in ch. 31 or his entire speech in chs. 29–31 to God,[99] as one would

---

95. Habel, *Job*, 431.

96. Ibid., 428. He lists Mic 6:1–8 and Jer 2:4–13 as parallel examples.

97. Habel (*Job*, 430) seems to back off from his argument for an explicit forensic context by noting that the focus of the speech "is not primarily on sins against the letter of the law, but on the motivations and attitudes of the person taking the oath."

98. Newsom, "Job," 551.

99. However, God is directly addressed in 30:20–23. I will treat this section more fully below.

expect if this were Job's legal challenge.[100] Rather, the speech has a public character and is geared toward an audience "with whom he shares a language of meaning and value, to whom his claims and complaints would be intelligible…"[101] The rhetorical goal of the speech is to persuade his audience that he is a man of honor that has done nothing to merit the dishonor he faces. Simultaneously, Job's rhetorical goal implies an understanding of his experience of death-in-life, namely, that as an honorable man it does not rightly belong to him.

And yet the manner in which God is inscribed in this appeal assumes a unique understanding of Job's relationship to the deity. The forensic nature of the oath is key as it builds on the legal metaphor encountered earlier, for this metaphor assumes a relationship between plaintiff and defendant as a relationship of equals. Regardless of their social standing, both parties are to be judged by the standard of the law. In a legal context, then, Job theoretically could voice his accusations and offer his defense without worry of the power imbalance that exists between him and his accused.

In his earlier speeches, though Job toyed with the idea of a legal challenge, his inability to conceive of a trial among equals dissuaded Job of the viability of pursuing his case. In ch. 9 the power imbalance between himself, a mere human, and God, who created the world, deflated his enthusiasm for a trial. Though he knew he was in the right under the law, he knew he could not challenge so powerful an opponent (9:2–20). In ch. 13, although Job had a case prepared to present to God, his knowledge of the power imbalance between himself and the deity rendered his case feckless (13:17–28). Though Job found in the legal metaphor a means to articulate his sense of the injustice of the situation, his knowledge that an actual trial between himself and the deity would not be a trial of equals under the law prevented him from pursuing the legal metaphor to its fullest.

In chs. 29–31, however, Job's conception of his relationship with the deity is built on a new model, one quite different from that of symbolization of abundant life. In that previous symbolic system the deity stood not only as one element of the complex, but also as the guarantor of the entire system. God upheld the system and ensured its proper functioning. Fittingly, relationship to the deity was certainly conceived on hierarchical terms: one obeyed God by acting piously, and so was rewarded by God for proper behavior.[102]

In Job's resymbolization in chs. 29–31, although it assumes a hierarchically organized society with defined social stations, the individuals within society relate to each other as dictated by the code of honor. Significantly, God also relates to Job as one man of honor to another. By re-invoking the legal metaphor in his oath in ch. 31, Job now appeals to the mutually shared code of honor as that to which unequal members of a hierarchically organized society can be judged by on equal terms. The scenario Job envisions is one where God can be

---

100. Despite Holbert's claim ("Rehabilitation of the Sinner," 235) that, paralleling the Lament Psalm, Job's speech contains a formal invocation of God in 29:2–5.

101. Newsom, *Contest of Moral Imaginations*, 184.

102. For more on this system, see Chapter 2.

judged based on the code of honor to which both he and God (as well as society in general) uphold. Job, therefore, does not envision God as defendant as he did previously (chs. 9 and 13), but depicts God as one who shares the principles of honor to which Job appeals: God's concern is for righteousness (31:6) and the cause of the lowly (31:14–15). Such actions, Job argues, he, himself, has been in the habit of doing: he has been moral (31:1–12), has acted justly in his social obligations (31:13–23), has had proper social relations (31:29–34), and even acted honorably toward his land (31:38–40). As judged by the code of honor, Job must be found innocent and God must be in the wrong. God ought not treat him shamefully—with cruelty and animosity, bringing him to death (30:20–23). God ought to side with Job and reject the experience of death-in-life as belonging to this man of honor. That is, God ought to restore Job to abundant life.

Job's final speech marks his return to symbolic wholeness. Job articulates a working symbolic world in which he can narrate his own past experience of life and liveliness, his present experience of suffering and death, and his anticipated future of vindication. The discourse of honor and shame provides for Job a grid onto which he can plot his past and present experiences, and which organizes his energies in the anticipation of future actions.

From a Liftonian perspective, the action of the book in complete: Job has moved from symbolic wholeness to the experience of desymbolization and back to symbolic wholeness. The book itself, however, is far from complete. One more friend will answer Job's resymbolization (chs. 32–37), and then God, himself, will respond. The Divine Speeches are particularly intriguing, for in the HB the divine voice is the final, authoritative voice that puts an end to all speech. Will the deity validate Job's new symbolic world? Will he accept Job's resymbolization of their relationship and his implied judgment of the deity's actions? Or will God, like the friends, command a return to the symbolization of abundant life? Or perhaps God will offer something entirely new. To the Divine Speeches we now turn.

Chapter 6

THE DIVINE SPEECHES: SYMBOLIC FLUIDITY
AND THE PROTEAN SELF (38:1–42:6)

By the end of the poetic dialogues the book of Job seemingly attains a level of closure. The book began with the narration of a symbolically coherent world, which was disrupted by the various disasters that occurred to Job. For Job this disruption gave rise to a sense of desymbolization as he articulated his own bewilderment in the face of the critiques of his friends for whom the symbolic universe remained intact. However, by the end of the dialogues Job was able to interpret his sufferings and locate them symbolically in his construction of a new symbolic system where the code of honor and shame served to organize society into the civilized and uncivilized, with order and life corresponding to the former, and disorder and death to the latter. The start of the book through the end of the dialogues demonstrates the movement from symbolization to desymbolization to resymbolization, corresponding to a plot progression of beginning, middle, and end.

But what kind of end does Job's last speech provide? At the basic story level of the book, Job's speech in chs. 29–31 is far from the ending. Rather, the closure that Job's resymbolization seems to provide becomes a new opening as two more voices respond to his resymbolization: Elihu in chs. 32–37 and God in chs. 38–41. Although the narrative arc of the book seems to progress from beginning to middle to end, the continuation of the book after the apparent end calls into question not only the effectiveness of this apparent ending, but also the entire narrative arc. Perhaps the narrative movement of the stability of symbolic wholeness to the crisis of desymbolization and back to the stability of symbolic wholeness is *not* the story that the book of Job attempts to tell. In this chapter I will examine the Divine Speeches and argue that they problematize the plot progression of a simple return to symbolic wholeness in Job's last speech in chs. 29–31. The Divine Speeches, rather, demonstrate that resymbolization does not entail closure and shutting down, either at the level of the narrative arc (namely, the ending the book), or at the more important symbolic level (namely, the stability of symbolic wholeness). The type of symbolic "order" proffered in the Divine Speeches is not neat, not complete, and not final.

The Divine Speeches do not overtly engage the issues raised in Job's resymbolization. Neither do they address the issues and topics discussed earlier in the poetic dialogues. In fact, the Divine Speeches seem so unrelated to what precedes them that readers have a difficult time understanding just what they are about. Scholarly work reflects this bafflement as opinions abound regarding the interpretation of these speeches. Newsom has divided scholarly opinion into two very broad camps:[1] some argue that chs. 38–41 offer a reconstruction of relationship between God and humans,[2] while others argue they explore the character of God and creation in relation to the existence of evil and chaos.[3] Even within these two broad camps there is wide disagreement.[4]

I understand the refusal of the Divine Speeches to engage the issues and accusations Job presents in his last speech to be not so much a "problem" of interpretation, but a strategy that functions to draw attention to the alternate symbolization articulated by the deity. Moreover, the deity articulates this alternate symbolization *from a whirlwind*—traditional theophany imagery of the divine appearance in a storm.[5] This point is of great importance: in these chapters God appears before Job to deliver divine revelation, just as God did to certain key Israelite figures such as Noah (Gen 9:1–17), Abraham (Gen 12:6–8; 15:17; 17:1–27; 18:1–14), Moses (Exod 3:2–21; 19–24; 33:17–23), and Elijah (1 Kgs 19:9–18). Such events were momentous encounters with the divine, which frequently marked significant moments in the lives of individuals and in the collective life of Israel. Before I examine the symbolic world articulated in the Divine Speeches, however, I will pause and consider the implications of this theophany imagery from a Liftonian perspective. For the issue of the possibility of a simple return to symbolic wholeness after desymbolization is of importance not only for the Divine Speeches, but also for Lifton's own writings about resymbolization.

6.1. *Theophany as Experiential Transcendence*

The divine voice from the whirlwind (here סְעָרָה) is a typical image for a divine theophany in the HB. Theophanies, by their nature, are unique events that address situations of such import that they merit the divine presence.[6] In fact, the

---

1. Newsom, "Considering Job," 109.

2. See, e.g., Athalya Brenner, "God's Answer to Job," *VT* 31 (1981): 129–37 (136); Janzen, *Job*, 229–30; Jürgen van Oorschot, *Gott als Grenze: Eine literar- und redaktionsgeschichtliche Studie zu den Gottesreden des Hiobbuches* (BZAW 170; Berlin: de Gruyter, 1987), 207–9; Wilde, *Hiob*, 42.

3. See, e.g., J. C. L. Gibson, "On Evil in the Book of Job," in Eslinger and Taylor, eds., *Ascribe to the Lord*, 399–419 (415–18); Habel, *Job*, 35; Tryggve N. D. Mettinger, "The God of Job: Avenger, Tyrant, or Victor?," in Perdue and Gilpin, eds., *Voice from the Whirlwind*, 39–49 (45–46); Perdue, *Wisdom in Revolt*, 196–240.

4. For more on the allusiveness of the Divine Speeches and the corresponding plethora of interpretations, see Newsom, "Job," 595–56; idem, "Considering Job," 107–11.

5. For theophanies being accompanied by a storm, see, e.g., Exod 19:9–20; Judg 5:4–5; Hab 3:5–6; Pss 18:8–16; 77:18–19; Ezek 1:4; Nah 1:3; Zech 9:14.

6. For more on theophanies in the HB, see James Barr, "Theophany and Anthropomorphism," in *Congress Volume: Oxford, 1959* (ed. G. W. Anderson et al.; VTSup 7; Leiden: Brill, 1960), 31–38; Frank Moore Cross, *Canaanite Myth and Hebrew Epic: Essays in the History of the Religion of Israel* (Cambridge, Mass.: Harvard University Press, 1973), 147–86; Theodore Hiebert,

depiction of theophanies in the HB—the encounter with the deity, the unnatural or out-of-wordly features of the encounter, the transformation that results from the encounter—corresponds in particular ways to Lifton's description of the mode of symbolic immortality he calls "experiential transcendence."

6.1.1. *Experiential Transcendence*

Lifton's discussion of experiential transcendence occurs amid a larger discussion of the human capacity to comprehend death. As mentioned earlier, Lifton argues that humans do not grasp any sense perception or receive any bit of information "nakedly," but that the "process of perception is vitally bound up with the process of inner re-creation, in which one utilizes whatever forms are available in individual psychic existence."[7] Humans must re-create stimuli mentally, interpreting and ordering everything according to the psychic patterns of the self. This includes the understanding of death and the continuity of life, an approach to death Lifton calls the "formative-symbolic" approach. We have a "middle knowledge" of death: we know that we will die, but our actions and expressions belie that awareness. "We, in fact, require symbolization of continuity—imaginative forms of transcending death—in order to confront genuinely the fact that we die."[8]

To this continuous symbolic relationship Lifton gives the name "symbolic immortality" and he outlines five such modes that have been utilized by various societies in a variety of ways throughout history. The particular mode relevant to the Divine Speeches is that of "experiential transcendence." According to Lifton, this mode is classically that of the mystic, for whom time and death seem to disappear. "Characteristic of the ecstatic state…is a sense of extraordinary psychic unity, and perceptual intensity, and of the ineffable illumination and insight,"[9] which is a sense of perfect centering, the "ideal blending of immediate and ultimate involvements."[10] Stated slightly differently, ecstatic experience "is…characterized by extraordinary immediacy and 'presentness'"; a harmony or "inner coherence within the originally symbolized adult psychic universe."[11] The self feels alive in a special way, and the negative side of the death symbol (separation, stasis, and disintegration imagery; meaninglessness; impaired

---

"Theophany in the Old Testament," *ABD* 6:505–11; Jörg Jeremias, *Theophanie: die Geschichte einer alttestamentlichen Gattung* (WMANT 10; Neukirchen–Vluyn: Neukirchener Verlag, 1965), 7–164; John Kenneth Kuntz, *The Self-Revelation of God* (Philadelphia: Westminster, 1967), 17–231; Johannes Lindblom, "Theophanies in Holy Places in Hebrew Religion," *HUCA* 32 (1961): 91–106; Thomas W. Mann, *Divine Presence and Guidance in Israelite Traditions: The Typology of Exaltation* (JHNES; Baltimore: The Johns Hopkins University Press, 1977), 1–23, 120–230; James Muilenburg, "Speech of Theophany," *Harvard Divinity Bulletin* 28 (1964): 35–47; Jeffrey Jay Niehaus, *God at Sinai: Covenant and Theophany in the Bible and Ancient Near East* (Studies in Old Testament Biblical Theology; Grand Rapids: Zondervan, 1995), 17–332; H. W. F. Saggs, *The Encounter with the Divine in Mesopotamia and Israel* (JLCRS 12; London: Athlone, 1978), 125–52.
    7.   Lifton, *Life of the Self*, 27.
    8.   Lifton, *Broken Connection*, 17.
    9.   Ibid., 25.
    10. Ibid., 26.
    11. Ibid.

symbolic immortality) is eliminated. The experience of transcendence is found not only in the expected place of mysticism, but also in cultural rites brought on by drugs, starvation, sleep deprivation, and so forth, and in unexpected places such as song, battle, sex, childbirth, and athletic effort.[12]

While psychic unity and perfect centering characterize the ecstatic state, this intense sense of centering and unity must be preceded by a radical decentering of the self's form and images, which then leads to this reintegration and recentering.[13] But one never returns to the same inner symbolic structure one had before: one's old forms are broken during decentering and then reordered, a process that results in an inner change. Marghanita Laski describes this change as "improved mental organization, whether this takes the form of replacing uneasiness and dissatisfaction with ease and satisfaction, or of appearing to confirm a sought belief, or of inspiring to moral action or of enabling the expression of a new mental creation."[14] Interestingly, Lifton describes this inner transformation with a biblical allusion: "one can by 'losing the self' (radical uncentering) regain…a more centered self."[15]

6.1.2. *Theophanies and Experiential Transcendence*

Theophanies are not the same thing as experiential transcendence, nor are they simply literary representations of experiences that correspond exactly to the mode of experiential transcendence. Rather, the theophany as depicted in the HB has an identifiable literary form that seems to repeat, with some variation, suggesting that the theophany is more a stylized device, rather than a description of a religious or a psychological experience.[16] It functions as a literary motif to advance the plot or to draw attention to a particular theological issue.

Despite these differences, the type of experience that the theophany *Gattung* represents functions on a literary level in a manner that parallels Lifton's description of the ecstatic experience. First of all, at a very general level, both involve the personal encounter with the "divine" (however the divine is defined).

---

12. Ibid., 24–25.

13. Lifton (*Broken Connection*, 25) cites research into LSD users to back his claims.

14. Marghanita Laski, *Ecstasy: A Study of Some Secular and Religious Experiences* (Bloomington: Indiana University Press, 1962), 371.

15. Lifton, *Life of the Self*, 74.

16. Kuntz has argued that the form of the theophany contains the following elements: an introductory description; the declaration of the name of the addressee by the deity; the response of the addressee; the deity's self-asseveration; the deity's quelling of human fear; the deity's assertion of gracious presence; the holy word addressed to the current situation; the inquiry or protest by the addressee; continuation of the holy word; and the concluding description (Kuntz, *The Self-Revelation of God*, 60). This, of course, is an ideal form. Many do not have all the elements. Even one of the examples that Kuntz analyzes, Gen 26:23–25, does not contain all the elements. Furthermore, many of the theophanies in the J/E epic sources seem to be stripped down to a bare minimum, with emphasis falling almost entirely upon the divine word (see, e.g, Gen 12:7; 15:1; 26:23–25; 28:13–15; 31:11–13; 46:2–4). Muilenburg, whose analysis of the form of the theophany resembles Kuntz's closely, has suggested that in the original *Vorlage* these theophanies were likely fuller, but were stripped down by the epic authors for specific purposes (Muilenburg, "Speech of Theophany," 37–38).

For Lifton, the primary exemplar of experiential transcendence seems to be the mystic who experiences "absolute union with God."[17] He cites Sir Thomas Browne's description of Christian mystical experience as an expression of the state he is describing:

> And if any have been so happy as truly to understand Christian annihilation, ecstasies, exhaltation, liquification, transformation, the kiss of the spouse, gestation of God, and ingression into the Divine shadow, they have already had a handsome anticipation of heaven; the glory of the world is surely over, and the earth in ashes unto them.[18]

While the theophany in the HB is not identical with this type of mystical experience, it shares the absolutely crucial feature of the personal encounter with the deity in a moment of extreme significance. This point ought not to be downplayed.

Second, both the theophany and the mode of experiential transcendence stress the "unnatural," "otherwordly" or "out-of-time" features of the encounter with the divine. Some biblical theophany narratives emphasize the disruption of normal time by linking the encounter with the divine to symbolically significant time units that emphasize the perfection or completeness of the moment, marking it off from normal time. Thus, for example, Moses is on the mountain in God's presence for forty days (Exod 24:18), and Ezekiel sits in stunned silence for seven days (Ezek 3:14–15). More frequently, however, this "otherworldly" quality is presented as the disruption of "normal" time by unexpected and violent meteorological phenomena that accompany the divine appearance. The deity often appears in a thunderstorm, where the storm cloud may represent God's chariot or throne,[19] the thunder may represent God's voice,[20] and the lightning bolt may represent God's weapons.[21] In the ancient world the thunderstorm "represented absolute power which could be both malevolent and beneficient."[22] It was essential to the sustenance of life, but could also threaten life if it raged out of control. In the theophany "normal" time is interrupted by the explosion onto the scene (both literal and figurative) of the life-giving, but terrifying deity/storm.[23] In addition, the deity could be manifest in fire, as in Exod 3, where Moses is drawn to the "supernatural" bush that is on fire but is not consumed.[24]

The most elaborately described theophany scenes, however, come from the prophetic corpus, which emphasizes the "otherwordly" nature of the encounter with the divine by presenting dazzling pictures of disorienting imagery, demonstrating these encounters as momentous occurrences outside of "normal" time.

---

17. Lifton, *Broken Connection*, 25.

18. Quoted in ibid., 25–26. Lifton does not give a citation for the quotation.

19. Hab 3:8; Ezek 1.

20. Exod 19:16, 19; Ps 18:14.

21. Hab 3:11; Ps 18:15.

22. Hiebert, *ABD* 6:509.

23. Other examples of theophanies that include a storm are Exod 15:7–10; 19:16, 19; 24:15–20; 40:34–38; Deut 1:33; 4:9–40; 33:2–3, 26–29; Ps 18:14; Isa 24:17–25:8; 28:2; 29:6, 30; 27–33; Ezek 1; 10; 43; Joel 3; Amos 1:2; Nah 1:2–4; Zeph 1:14–16; Zech 9; 10:1–2.

24. For other examples of theophanies involving fire, see Gen 15:17; Lev 9:24; Num 11:1–3; Deut 9:3; 1 Kgs 18:38–39.

Isaiah's theophany, for example, involves an image of Yahweh seated on a throne, flanked by heavenly creatures with six wings, one of which touched Isaiah's tongue with a hot coal taken from the altar (Isa 6:1–7). In Ezekiel's theophany he sees the heavens rent open, a storm approach, clouds and fire, and a variety of bizarre creatures (Ezek 1).

While Lifton's description of experiential transcendence does not include storms and bizarre visions, he does emphasize the strangeness of the experience in terms that emphasize it as a unique event that, although occurring in the present, actually is a "transcendental reaction"[25] that occurs outside of "normal" time. This type of experience, "like all experience, takes place only in the present [but] is indeed characterized by extraordinary immediacy and 'present-ness.'"[26] Time seems to evaporate as the self experiences "a state of pure focus, of inner unity and harmony."[27] One actually feels oneself to "travel outside one-self" or outside the normal pattern of existence in which one has come to abide. So abnormal and seemingly otherworldly is this experience that, as mentioned above, Lifton turns to the religious experience of the immediacy of the deity in the mystical experience as the benchmark for this particular category of experience. That is, Lifton turns to the personal encounter with the divine, described also in the theophany texts of the HB, to illuminate what is involved in experiential transcendence.

Third, the theophanies of the HB share with Lifton's description of experiential transcendence the notion of a reordering or change in the individual who undergoes this experience. Lifton describes this change as the temporary breaking of one's old mental forms through the experience of unity and wholeness in the mystical encounter, which then lingers as "a still active image-feeling of intense inner unity"[28] after the mystical experience. "One never 'returns' to exactly the same inner structure of the self"[29] but one experiences the symbolic reordering that results in psychological change.

The phenomenology of the encounter with the deity in the biblical theophany, however, does not emphasize the experience of wholeness or harmony—in fact, the encounter with the deity is most frequently terrifying and disorienting. On the other hand, like Lifton's experiential transcendence, the biblical theophany frequently emphasizes the change that the theophany effects in the life of the addressee. In most theophanies emphasis falls on the content of the theophany— the message that God directs at the particular circumstances of the individual, providing this person new direction and new focus for future actions. For example, Moses' life undergoes a radical change in his encounter with the deity. God reveals that Moses is to assume leadership of the Israelites and bring them out of slavery in Egypt, a post Moses then assumes and a task he sets out to

---

25. Lifton, *Broken Connection*, 25. Lifton is quoting Donald D. Jackson, "LSD and the New Beginning," *Journal of Nervous and Mental Disease* 135 (1962): 435–39 (438).

26. Lifton, *Broken Connection*, 26.

27. Ibid., 25.

28. Ibid., 26.

29. Ibid.

accomplish (Exod 3). In Gideon's encounter with the deity he is commissioned as leader of Israel in order to deliver them from the Midianites (Judg 6:11–24). Elijah is moved to commission a new king (1 Kgs 19:9–18). Isaiah and Ezekiel are inspired to prophesy in the name of God (Isa 6; Ezek 1). The visions of Ezra and Daniel clarify the coherence of the world (4 Ezra; Dan 7–12). Even when the individual does not receive a commission to a new vocation in a theophany, the content of the divine revelation still carries enormous import. God appears several times to Abraham revealing his promise of land and progeny—a promise that will drive the narrative of the Pentateuch and beyond (Gen 12:6–8; 17:1–27; 18:1–14). Similarly, God's appearance to Hagar causes her to reverse her plans and return to her mistress where Ishmael grows and flourishes (Gen 21:17–19).

Perhaps the most noteworthy of all theophanies, however, is the appearance to Moses at Sinai (Exod 19–24). Here, God reveals to Moses the Law, the document that is to guide Israel throughout its corporate life. In this case, the theophany not only changes the direction of Moses' life, but the entire life of the people of Israel.

Finally, both the biblical theophany and the mode of experiential transcendence share a concern for issues pertaining to death and life. In experiential transcendence the feeling of intense wholeness and unity is what Lifton describes as the sense of "near-perfect centering."[30] Centering, it is worth recalling, is the sense of coherence and connection of the self, both of inner forms and images, and of these forms and images to the outside world. Centering enables the sense of human connection and what Lifton describes as symbolic immortality—the self's ability symbolically to overcome death by placing the self in a symbolic relationship to what came before and what will come after the person has died. The mode of experiential transcendence, therefore, enables the symbolic continuation of life in the face of death.

The theophanies of the HB share with the mode of experiential transcendence a greater concern for matters of life and death. Overcoming a sense of death's immanence is a main theme of several theophanies. In Gen 9:1–17, Noah is ordered to be fruitful and multiply, a message emphasizing abundant life that comes on the heels of the destruction of almost all living creatures. In Gen 21:15–19, Hagar has resigned herself to her child's death when, in a theophany, God reveals that her son will not only live but will become a great nation, a message that enlivens Hagar. In 1 Kgs 19:11–18, Elijah is exhausted to the point of wishing his life to end before supernatural intervention nourishes him both with food and with encouraging words, the effect of which enliven him to perform the important task of anointing a new king. The multiple theophanies that Abraham receives in Genesis are all concerned with the promise of the birth of an heir who would grow into a prosperous nation—a promise of life that looks increasingly bleak the closer Abraham and Sarah come to their deaths (Gen 12:6–8; 15:1–17; 17:1–27; 18:7–14).[31] Even the theophanies that do not overtly

---

30. Ibid., 34.

31. Similarly, in a theophany God informs Minoah's wife that she will no longer be barren, but will bear a son (Judg 13:2–3).

foreground the overcoming of death with life do emphasize death and life *symbolism*. In Moses' theophany at the burning bush (Exod 3:10–17), for example, God tells Moses that he will lead Israel out from bondage and suffering in Egypt to a land flowing with milk and honey. The images of Israel's life in Egypt all stress confinement, bondage, control at the hand of others—what Lifton calls the death equivalent of "stasis"—while the images of Israel's future life stress deliverance, goodness, excess, abundance—life equivalents. Moses' theophany concerns the symbolic movement from death to life under his leadership.[32] Poetic descriptions of theophanies also frequently emphasize the life-giving quality of the divine appearance. The song Moses sings following the exodus from Egypt celebrates Yahweh's appearance as a warrior who delivers Israel in battle and brings them to a new life of goodness (Exod 15:1–18). Similarly, Deborah's song celebrates Yahweh's appearance as a warrior who aides Israel's deliverance from oppression by its enemies (Judg 5:1–31). The Psalmist overtly casts his experience of divine presence as one of deliverance from the grip of death to the realm of life (Ps 18:5–20),[33] as does Jonah (Jonah 2:3–10).[34] Lastly, in the phenomenology of some theophanies people sometimes fall into the danger of death (Isa 6:4–5) or a death-like trance (Ezek 3:15; Dan 8:18; 10:2–3) before being "revived" by divine agency.

In sum, the biblical theophany, although a stylized literary form, functions to represent a type of religious experience comparable to Lifton's category of experiential transcendence. Both involve the experience of the immediacy of the divine, or of a transcendental unity and wholeness; both take place outside of "normal" time; both function to alter the individual's life course; and both foreground issues and/or imagery of death and life.

6.2. *Theophany in* Job: *The Symbolic World of the Divine Speeches*

The important points of concern regarding the theophany in Job 38–41 are twofold. First is whether this particular theophany, like the mode of experiential transcendence, enables the movement from the experience of desymbolization to the reintegration and resymbolization of symbolic forms; and second, whether it provides new direction and purpose to life. If it accomplishes both, then the divine voice will bring ultimate closure to the book, giving a divine "last word" to the issues and theological problems that are raised in the book. If the Divine

---

32. Similar is Gideon's theophany where he is commissioned to deliver Israel from oppression at the hand of the Midianites (Judg 6:11–24).

33. See also Pss 46:1–6; 68:8–9; 83:2–19; 94:1–7.

34. A little more difficult to analyze along these lines is the theophany at Sinai (Exod 19–24). Although death is a major topic within these chapters, the main theme is to avoid death by not approaching the sacred mountain (Exod 19:12–13, 21–22, 24). The recounting of the Sinai theophany in Exodus does not seem to display the same type of overcoming of death with life as the other theophanies do. In Deuteronomy, however, the importance of the giving of the Law is revealed in its capacity to bring life to the one who obeys it, while disobedience brings death (see, e.g., Deut 4:1, 10, 26; 5:33; 8:1, etc.). The purpose of the theophany, therefore, is to ensure life.

Speeches fail to provide a picture of symbolic order and direction for future action, then one must probe further regarding what work the Divine Speeches accomplish and how they relate to Lifton's writings about experiential transcendence.

6.2.1. *Symbolic Order or Symbolic Disorder*

The first issue—whether or not the Divine Speeches present a picture of symbolic order—is not so easy to solve. Some scholars argue that the Divine Speeches do offer a symbolically whole picture, that of God's ultimate control of the universe, represented as the divine ordering of the most intractable forces of chaos. Habel, for example, argues that the key term in the Divine Speeches is עצה (38:2), God's design of the cosmos. First, God points to the "primordial structures of the universe"[35] (38:4–7), demonstrating how he constructed the universe like a master architect, giving concern to "stability and precision, not anarchy and disorder."[36] Likewise, God keeps in check the Sea, a symbol of chaos in the ANE, and governs it by his law, as he does both Behemoth and Leviathan, "the classic representatives of primordial chaos."[37] God also regulates the meteorological phenomena—snow, hail, and thunderstorms—and imbues the wild creatures with a patterned wisdom, protecting and preserving them as "their unseen midwife."[38] Significantly, these creatures participate in the natural cycle of birth, nourishment, and death—"the delicate ecology of life that God sustains in the wild…"[39] Indeed, "Every corner of the cosmos is embraced in this providential design."[40] Even the descriptions of Behemoth and Leviathan, creatures that represent the chaotic, are for the purpose of demonstrating that God controls them.[41] As Habel argues, the Divine Speeches reveal God "as the sage who designed a world of rhythms and paradoxes, of balanced opposites and controlled extremes, of mysterious order and ever-changing patterns, of freedom and limits, of life and death."[42]

The interpretation of the Divine Speeches that Habel offers suggests that the theophany does, indeed, provide a glimpse of acute wholeness and unity, and of the interconnection and abundance of life. This interpretation understands the theophany to operate like Lifton's experiential transcendence: the images and forms of the divine symbolic universe function not only to alter Job's existing forms, but to provide him with a new sense of symbolic unity.

---

35. Norman C. Habel, "In Defense of God the Sage," in Perdue and Gilpin, eds., *The Voice from the Whirlwind*, 21–38 (34).

36. Ibid.

37. Ibid., 35.

38. Ibid., 36.

39. Ibid., 36–37.

40. Ibid., 36.

41. Habel, *Job*, 559–66. See also Mettinger, "God of Job," 48–49; Perdue, *Wisdom in Revolt*, 221–32. However, many of the verses that deal with Behemoth and Leviathan are extremely textually difficult.

42. Habel, "God the Sage," 38. See also Habel, *Job*, 534–37; Karen Pidcock-Lester, "'Earth has No Sorrow the Earth Cannot Heal': Job 38–41," in *God Who Creates: Essays in Honor of W. Sibley Towner* (ed. William P. Brown and S. Dean McBride; Grand Rapids: Eerdmans, 2000), 125–32.

Other scholars, however, are not as convinced of the order and wholeness that Habel discerns. Newsom, for example, argues that key to interpreting the Divine Speeches is not the fundamental order of the cosmos (Habel's עצה), but "the nature of the relationship established in [the] images between God and the symbols of the chaotic."[43] Rhetorically, the Divine Speeches move from displaying the order of the cosmos (38:4–38) to emphasizing the providential care given to creatures that belong to the realm of the threatening and chaotic (38:39–39:30) to focusing on two mythic creatures who represent chaos and the threat to order. According to Newsom,

> [T]he divine speeches move Job, imaginatively, from places of secure boundaries to places where boundaries are threatened. In narrative sequence, they run counter to the mythic schema in which the creator god's defeat of the chaos monster precedes the creation of the structures of the cosmos.... An element of 'uncreation' takes place in the experience provided by means of the divine speeches, as Job is led to a sustained and intimate encounter with the symbol of the chaotic.[44]

Similarly, Patton argues that the focus on Behemoth and Leviathan, rather than emphasizing God's control over these chaos monsters, implies "(1) that chaos is created by God, (2) that chaos is created for God's enjoyment, and (3) that chaos is beautiful."[45] Patton argues that the Divine Speeches affirm that chaos exists in the universe, in God, and in humans.

Contrary to Habel, for whom the Divine Speeches imply a symbolic world of wholeness, unity, and order, Newsom and Patton suggest that the divine symbolic order consists of the disorderly and chaotic as much as the orderly and balanced. If this is so, then the theophany in *Job* would seem to run counter to the type of symbolic unity that Lifton describes in regard to experiential transcendence. Furthermore, the theophany would seem to fail to register the symbolic overcoming of death by life and fail to organize its forms and images into a new symbolization. If the Divine Speeches present to Job a symbolization of the chaotic and disorderly, and if the divine voice is supposed to be the authoritative voice that puts an end to all conversation and debate, then Job would be left seemingly in a state of desymbolization, without direction for symbolic unity and wholeness.

In order to determine whether or not this is the case, I would like to examine two particular aspects of the Divine Speeches. First is the general symbolic world of the Divine Speeches, namely, how their symbolic patterns compare to those of Job's resymbolization in chs. 29–31. Second, I will examine the symbolic place that life and death have in the Divine Speeches. One would

---

43. Newsom, *Contest of Moral Imaginations*, 243.

44. Newsom, "Job," 597. See also idem, *Contest of Moral Imaginations*, 243–52.

45. Corrine L. Patton, "The Beauty of the Beast: Leviathan and Behemoth in Light of Catholic Theology," in *The Whirlwind: Essays on Job, Hermeneutics and Theology in Memory of Jane Morse* (ed. Stephen L. Cook, Corrine L. Patton, and James W. Watts; JSOTSup 336; London: Sheffield Academic Press, 2001), 142–67 (156). Patton's understanding of the rhetorical movement of the Divine Speeches is similar to Newsom's. Patton argues that the first Divine Speech (chs. 38–39) emphasizes God's mastery over creation while the second Divine Speech (chs. 40–41) addresses the relationship between creation and chaos (pp. 155–56).

expect, if the Divine Speeches were to present a picture of symbolic unity and wholeness, that the images of life and death would occupy discrete symbolic "zones" that form a coherent and identifiable symbolization. I will argue that the Divine Speeches present neither a picture of symbolic unity and wholeness, but neither do they simply present a picture of symbolic chaos and desymbolization. In fact, the issue in the Divine Speeches is not so much "order" vs. "chaos" (though these terms are crucial), but complete and closed symbolic systems vs. ongoing and open symbolic systems. For if Lifton envisions a return to the symbolic unity and wholeness as the goal of the survivor after the experience of desymbolization, and if the book of Job seems to depict this same movement to symbolic unity and wholeness in Job's last speech, the Divine Speeches present a new possibility: resymbolization without closure, symbolic systems without finality.

6.2.1.1. *The Symbolic Patterns of the Divine Speeches.* The symbolic world of the Divine Speeches differs markedly from the one Job articulated in chs. 29–31. A glance at the initial images of each signals their radically different symbolic conceptions. For Job, the imagery of the village patriarchy establishes the symbolic parameters of his conception, as examined above. In the Divine Speeches, however, the imagery connects hardly at all with the village patriarchy and does not draw on imagery of the civilized human world, but rather, pushes back to the mythic past, drawing on imagery of creation to establish its symbolic connections. Whereas Job's imagery is of the household, the city square, and the margins of society populated by "children," "youth," "elders," "nobles," "princes," "orphans," and "widows," God's imagery is of the "foundations of the earth," the earth's "bases" and "cornerstone," the gushing sea, the "recesses of the deep," and the "expanses of the earth." Job's symbolization evokes the familiar zones of human occupation, while the divine symbolization evokes the mythic zones outside of the realm of human knowledge.

Similarly, on a more personal level, the rhetorical questions God poses Job ("Where were you?"; "Who determined?"; "On what were?"; "Have you entered?"; and so on) serve to highlight Job's distance from what God evokes. That is, in Job's speech in chs. 29–31, as patriarch among his village, he occupies the center of the symbolic universe he conceives, whereas in the Divine Speeches Job and Job's realm are entirely absent.[46] Even in the one symbolic space where Job's speech and the Divine Speeches seem to overlap—the reference to the wasteland—there actually is a deep rift. For Job the wasteland is a barren place outside the realm of the civilized, the undesirable zone that the outcasts and dishonorable inhabit, where structure and order do not prevail. For

---

46. Veronika Kubina, *Die Gottesreden im Buche Hiob: ein Beitrag zur Discussion um die Einheit von Hiob 38,1–42,6* (Freiburger theologische Studien; Freiburg: Herder, 1979), 131–43, examines the Divine Speeches in light of the similar dispute questions in Deutero-Isaiah (41:1–5, 21–29; 43:8–15; 44:6–8; 45:20–25). She argues that the challenge questions do not solicit information, but function to emphasize Yahweh as the only one capable of accomplishing the described action.

the deity, however, the wasteland is a positive place, the place for which he has specific concern, appointing the rain to disperse in order that vegetation may grow.[47] Significantly, this beautiful place is a place devoid of humans (לֹא אִישׁ; 38:26), a place Job does not know.

From the mythical structures of creation the divine symbolic universe moves to the creatures that inhabit therein. Again, Job and his realm of civilized humans does not register. Instead, the creatures God emphasizes are primarily animals of threat who were traditionally associated with the wasteland and the realm of the chaotic—creatures, that is, who represent the opposite of Job's ordered, civilized universe.[48] Even the warhorse (39:19–25), which is the only *domesticated* animal mentioned, and therefore seemingly associated with order and civility, is celebrated for its unbridled ferocity and its uncontrollable lust for battle—a zealous passion beyond the realm of human comprehension or domestication.

From the mythic structures of the universe to the wild and untamed creatures that inhabit it, the Divine Speeches close with an extended look at two creatures who embody the qualities of both of the previous: Behemoth and Leviathan represent both the mythic and the wild and chaotic (40:15–41:26).[49] And in each case, the creatures are described in terms that emphasize their distance from human control and domination.

Nowhere do the Divine Speeches explicitly engage Job's conception of the symbolic universe. Instead they present to him that which is completely beyond the realm of his experience and a far distance from the structures of knowledge that he can possibly attain. God speaks from a different symbolic universe, and its effect on Job is disorienting. So foreign is this new symbolic universe that Job is almost unable to speak in these terms (40:4–5), and when he does, his message itself is rife with ambiguities (42:6).[50] Once again, Job seems to be facing the disorientation of the desymbolization of his symbolic forms.

47. For more on this contrast, see Newsom, *Contest of Moral Imaginations*, 240.

48. Othmar Keel, *Jahwes Entgegnung an Ijob: eine Deutung von Ijob 38–41 vor dem Hintergrund der zeitgenössischen Bildkunst* (FRLANT 121; Göttingen: Vandenhoeck & Ruprecht, 1978), 63–81.

49. Of course, there is considerable debate concerning exactly what these creatures represent. Some, citing Egyptian literature argue that Behemoth is the hippopotamus and represents the wicked, while Leviathan represents the crocodile (see, e.g., ibid., 127–56). Some, connecting Behomoth with the hippopotamus as the symbol for the enemy of the king/gods in Egypt, and Leviathan as the mythic symbol for the enemy of the gods in Northwest Semitic literature, suggest that these creatures symbolize the historical forces that Yahweh controls (Eberhard Ruprecht, "Das Nilpferd im Hiobbuch," *VT* 21 [1971]: 209–31). Others argue that Behemoth and Leviathan are simply mortal creatures like Job and are didactic symbols to teach Job God's ways (see, e.g., John G. Gammie, "Behemoth and Leviathan: On the Siginificance of Job 40:14–41:26," in *Israelite Wisdom: Theological and Literary Essays in Honor of Samuel Terrien* [ed. John G. Gammie et al.; Missoula, Mont.: Scholars Press, 1978], 217–31). Others argue that Behemoth and Leviathan are mythic symbols of the chaos forces overcome by the deity in the ANE (see, e.g., Pope, *Job*, 268–70, 276–78; Kubina, *Gottesreden*, 68–75). For more on these discussions, see Habel, *Job*, 557–58.

50. I will examine his reaction in more detail below.

6.2.1.2. Life and Death in the Divine Speeches. The Divine Speeches are disorienting not only because they deal with symbols of the unknown and the chaotic, but also because when they deal with matters of death and life—matters of fundamental importance in a coherent symbolic system—they reverse and distort their symbolic resonance, providing a bewildering conflagration of images that are normally distinct.

At first glance, however, this may seem not to be the case, for the only explicit mention of death in God's recounting of cosmic design in 38:2–38 (v. 17) seems to emphasize a traditional understanding of death's place in the cosmos. God asks Job about the location of the limits of death—"Have the gates of death been revealed to you? Have you seen the gates of the darkness of death (צלמות)" (38:17)—questions that fit with his emphasis on the extremities of the cosmos, of which Job could have no possible knowledge. The question also recalls a traditional Mesopotamian conception of death, namely, the myth of the descent of Inanna/Ishtar to the netherworld, where she descends through seven gates as she gradually loses her life qualities.[51] The "gate" imagery is also fairly common in the HB where the gates of death represent the threshold that separates life from death. When one's life was near the end, one was considered to be near the gates of death. When one was dead, one had passed through the gates.[52]

God's question to Job about the threshold of life and death, however, is preceded immediately by a prior question about the threshold of the sea, a traditional symbol of chaos: "Have you penetrated the sources of the sea? Have you walked through the recesses of the deep?" (38:16). The images of the sea and the deep recall the creation story in Gen 1 where the act of creation is described as God's ordering of the primordial waters from their previous undifferentiated, chaotic state (Gen 1:6). In the deluge, the earth is destroyed by the release of these same waters, causing the earth to return again to this chaotic, uncreated state (Gen 7:11), while the end of the deluge is marked by the containment of these chaotic waters again (Gen 8:2). As in the deluge story, where the release of the waters means the death of all the living creatures, so here in Divine Speeches, where the threshold of the primordial waters is paralleled to the threshold of death.[53]

The imagery here suggests an ordered cosmos rather than one marked by the unleashing of disorder and death as in the deluge. As with the previous imagery of the earth's foundations, bases, and cornerstone, the images of the thresholds of the chaotic primordial waters and death convey the impression of stability and wholeness, that the cosmos is neatly structured.

Life imagery in this section (38:2–38), however, is a little less straightforward and appears in less expected places. The first such image occurs in 38:8–11, a unit that also refers to a tradition of the sea and creation, although a

51. "Inanna's Descent to the Nether World," translated by S. N. Kramer (*ANET*, 52–57); "Descent of Ishtar to the Nether World," translated by E. A. Speiser (*ANET*, 106–9).

52. See, e.g., Pss 9:14; 107:18. See, also Wis. 16:13; *3 Macc* 5:51; 6:31.

53. For more on the divine containment of the primordial waters, see Ps 33:7. For the parallel between the primordial waters and death, see Ps 71:20; Ezek 26:19; Jonah 2:5.

different one than the separation of the primordial waters in Genesis. This time the poet refers to the traditional ANE theme of the Sea as a force hostile to the gods, whom the chief god ultimately subdues in creation.[54] Typically the taming of the Sea is described in a battle scene that employs a variety of death imagery of destruction: God "shatters" (פרר; Ps 74:13), "breaks the head" (שבר; Ps 74:13), "crushes the head" (רצץ; Ps 74:14), "crushes like a corpse" (דכאת כחלל; Ps 89:11), "scatters" (פזר; Ps 89:11); "hacks into pieces" (חצב; Isa 51:9); "pierces" (חלל; Isa 51:9). As casualties in battle, the metaphorical carcasses of the Sea and its chaos creatures are given as food to the wild animals (Ps 74:14). While the Divine Speeches allude to this tradition, representing the Sea in aggressive terms ("bursting forth" [גיח; 38:8], requiring "bar and doors" to restrain it) the poet removes the battle/death imagery and replaces it, surprisingly, with birth imagery. The Sea is now depicted as a newborn, wrapped in swaddling bands[55] of cloud and darkness by the divine midwife (38:9). Although the image still suggests the containment of the Sea by the deity, the Sea is no longer a hostile force, but a helpless infant who is dependent upon the deity for life. Even the restraints the deity places upon it are for nurture rather than confinement.[56]

The implications of this life imagery are startling. Whereas in 38:16–17 the Sea, as a symbol of chaos, is associated with death, both of which have demarcated domains in the cosmos from which they are barred from transgressing, here, the Sea/chaos loses its association with battle/death imagery, instead now representing birth and new life. The image of the Sea, therefore, suggests that chaos, first of all, is not just a symbol of death, but also of life; and second, that even while the deity restrains the Sea, he also lovingly nurtures and protects chaos.

The second Divine Speech (40:7–41:26) alludes to a similar ANE tradition of the subduing of the sea, this time the tradition of the creator god slaying the sea monster, Leviathan (40:25–41:26).[57] However, like the startling image of the Sea nurtured by the divine midwife, the extended passage about Leviathan is not for the purposes of describing the divine conquest of the chaos monster as in ANE literature and in other places in the HB.[58] Rather, the deity seems to be in

---

54. See Pss 74:13–14; 89:9–11; Isa 51:9–10; *Enuma Elish* IV (*ANET*, 66–67).

55. Cf. Ezek 16:4; 30:21 for this translation.

56. For more on this point, see Newsom, "Job," 602; idem, *Contest of Moral Imaginations*, 244.

57. On the ANE background to Leviathan, see John Day, *God's Conflict with the Dragon and the Sea: Echoes of a Canaanite Myth in the Old Testament* (University of Cambridge Oriental Publications 35; Cambridge: Cambridge University Press, 1985), 1–18; Mary K. Wakeman, *God's Battle with the Monster: A Study in Biblical Imagery* (Leiden: Brill, 1973), 62–68. There are several good studies of ANE parallels to Job. See, in particular, Day, *God's Conflict*, 38–49, 62–87; Perdue, *Wisdom in Revolt*, 32–72; Pope, *Job*, 276–78, 281–87.

58. In the Baal epic, Baal is credited with slaying Lotan (Gibson, *Canaanite Myths*, 68). As in other ANE literature, the HB associates several creatures with the Sea: Rahab, the sea dragon (Job 9:13; 26:12; Ps 89:11; Isa 51:9); Leviathan (Job 3:8; Pss 74:14; 104:26; Isa 27:1); and *tannin* (Gen 1:21; Job 7:12; Pss 74:13; 148:7; Isa 27:1; Ezek 29:3; 32:2).

Some scholars argue that the Leviathan passage in the Divine Speeches does portray God's conquest over the chaos creature. The translation of the extremely obscure 41:4 is key. Because of

awe of the creature's beauty, describing in exquisite detail its protective skin (41:5), face (41:6),[59] teeth (41:6–9),[60] eyes (41:10), mouth (41:11, 13), nostrils (41:12), neck (41:14), and flesh (41:15). Patton writes,

> The description itself (41:4–16) travels down and up the monster's body, starting in his mouth as if the poet were somehow clenched in its teeth. The reader can picture its scaly body, can almost smell the sulfur from the fire in its mouth and nose.... [T]he closing of the poem pictures the sea monster slithering off into the sea, a slivery wake marking its path, a beautiful if frightening image.[61]

In fact, like the Sea imagery in 38:8–11 where the traditional subduing of the Sea is replaced by the birthing and coddling of the Sea, here not only is the traditional slaying of Leviathan imagery replaced by a lavish description of Leviathan's awesome beauty, but emphasis also falls on the fact that Leviathan absolutely *cannot* be slain.[62] This sea creature cannot be captured by traditional fishing methods (hook, cord, rope, barb [40:24–26], harpoon,[63] fish-spear [40:31][64]) with its carcass then being divided up and sold at market (41:30). Nor do the traditional war weapons work, not the sword, spear, dart, or javelin[65]

---

the ambiguity of almost every word/phrase in the verse (חין ערכו; דבר גבתרות; בדיו), it can be taken as a statement of God's conquest over Leviathan ("Did I not silence his boastings, his mighty word, and his persuasive case?"; Habel, *Job*, 551) or it can be taken as a statement about Leviathan's mystery ("I will not keep silence concerning his limbs or his mighty strength, or the grace of his form"; Gordis, *Job*, 470; see also, Hartley, *Job*, 527). Though both translations are equally possible, I follow the latter given that much of the Leviathan passage deals precisely with Leviathan's exquisite form, and as Gibson argues, there is no evidence of a tradition wherein God silences Leviathan's boasting (J. C. L. Gibson, "A New Look at Job 41.1–4 [English 41.9–12]," in *Text as Pretext: Essays in Honour of Robert Davidson* [ed. Robert P. Carroll; JSOTSup 138; Sheffield: JSOT Press, 1992], 129–39 [134]). See also Newsom, "Job," 622–23; idem, *Contest of Moral Imaginations*, 251–52, for a closer examination of the ambiguities of this passage.

59. Some, based on the Syriac and LXX, emend פניו ("face") to פיו ("mouth"; e.g., Dhorme, *Job*, 633–34).

60. Many argue that 41:8–9 is a reference to the scales on Leviathan's back, although the word for scales is missing. This is based on a revocalization of גאוה in 41:7 so that "pride" translates, rather, as "back" ("Its back is as rows of shields"; Hartley, *Job*, 527). Verses 8–9, therefore, would describe how the scales interlock with each other on the beast's back (for this common argument, see, e.g., Gordis, *Job*, 470, 484–85; Habel, *Job*, 551–52, 555; Hartley, *Job*, 527–28). Newsom, however, argues that one ought to read the MT "pride" (his rows of shields are his pride"), keeping the emphasis on Leviathan's teeth, which then continues in vv. 8–9 (Newsom, "Job," 624).

61. Patton, "Beauty of the Beast," 159. For more on the descriptive beauty, see Robert Alter, "The Voice from the Whirlwind," *Commentary* 77 (1984): 33–41 (40–41).

62. Habel's translation of 40:24 reads "El takes him by the mouth with rings; He pierces his nose with hooks." This verse, however, does not mention El. Habel can only maintain his translation by transposing אל פיהו from v. 23b and then understanding עיניו ("his eyes") as "rings" or "cords" in parallel to מוקש ("hooks") in the following line (Habel, *Job*, 553–54).

63. The word שעבות is a *hapax*. Likely it is related to שכים, meaning "thorn" (also the Arabic *sakka*, "pierce"). Gordis (*Job*, 482), therefore, translates the word "harpoon," whereas Dhorme (*Job*, 628) translates it as "darts."

64. Most take צלצל to mean "whirl" or "buzz" based on Isa 18:1. It would then be a reference to a spear.

65. The MT שריה is a *hapax* likely related to the Arabic *sirwat* ("short arrow") and *siryat* ("arrowhead"; see Gordis, *Job*, 488).

(41:18); nor the arrow, sling-stone, club[66] or javelin (41:20–21). In an image that completely overturns the traditional Leviathan myth, even the gods[67] are depicted as "shuddering"[68] and "withdrawing"[69] from Leviathan's presence (41:17). This creature who represents chaos and whose death traditionally represents order and life is depicted as gloriously alive and not threatened by death either from humans or from the gods. Again, traditional categories of life, death, chaos, and order have been mixed.

This blurring of the categories of life and death occurs also in the list of meteorological phenomena in 38:22–30. Many of the items listed are invoked precisely for their properties as destructive, death-dealing elements: hail (38:22) is a traditional weapon of God, bringing death to the objects of his wrath,[70] as are lightening (38:24)[71] and the "east-wind" (38:24).[72] Likewise, snow is identified as an element reserved for divine usage in war (38:22). In v. 25, however a subtle shift occurs. While the image of the "torrents" shares in the symbolism of divine destruction and devastation, and likewise, the "thunderstorm" might give the impression of a wild and ferocious meteorological display,[73] here these images of destruction and death are celebrated precisely for their *life-giving properties* as precipitation. The life they bring is life in the *desert waste* (מִדְבָּר; 38:27), the uninhabited nether-region associated with the chaotic.[74] Again, the categories of life, death, and the chaotic are blurred.

---

66. The *hapax* חותה likely means "shaft" or "club" based on an Akkadian cognate of the same root (Dhorme, *Job*, 641–42).

67. The term אלים normally means "gods" or "God," but it may also mean "chiefs" (cf. Ezek 31:11; 32:21).

68. Pope argues that the participle משברים ("breaking") refers to shuddering in fear, being a short form for the idiom "breaking of the loins," a euphemism for the loss of courage and trembling in fear (Pope, *Job*, 286). Habel offers another plausible solution: he takes the term to mean "crashings" (thus, "at [his] crashings"; cf. Zeph 1:10; Habel, *Job*, 556). Others revocalize the word, suggest the meaning "breakers" (of the sea; see, e.g., Dhorme, *Job*, 639).

69. The root usually has the sense "to miss the mark" or "purify oneself." Most suggest the derived sense of "fail" or "draw back" (e.g. Dhorme, *Job*, 640), with Ethiopic and Arabic cognates (Pope, *Job*, 287).

70. Exod 9:18–33; Josh 10:11; Pss 78:47, 48; 105:32; Isa 28:2, 17; 30:30; Hos 2:17.

71. אור has caused some commentators problems because it does not form a neat parallelism with קדים ("east-wind"). Many therefore suggest an alternative to אור: Gordis argues that the word actually means "air, cloud, mist" (Gordis, *Job*, 448–49); Tur-Sinai cites an Akkadian cognate, *amurru* ("land of the west-wind"), and so argues the word means "west-wind" (Tur-Sinai, *Job*, 529; see also Hartley, *Job*, 498); Driver cites an Arabic parallel and vocalizes it as אֹר ("heat"; Driver, "Problems in the Hebrew Text," 91); some argue, following the LXX, that the word ought to read אר ("mist" or "cosmic reservoir"; Dhorme, *Job*, 586; Pope, *Job*, 252–53; and many others); others emend אור to רוח in order to make a more exact parallel with קדים (Driver and Gray, *Job*, 1:332, 2:304; Fohrer, *Hiob*, 492). I choose to leave the MT as it stands, translating אור as "lightening," as is fairly frequent in *Job* (36:32; 37:3, 11, 15; cf., Habel, *Job*, 522). See also 2 Sam 22:15; Ps 144:6; Ezek 21:15, 20, 28, although the word translated "lightning" in these examples is ברק not אור.

72. See Gen 41:6, 23, 27; Exod 10:13; Job 27:21; Ps 48:8; Isa 27:8; Jer 18:17; Ezek 17:10; 19:12; 27:26; Hos 13:15; Jonah 4:8.

73. Cf. Habel, *Job*, 542.

74. See Keel, *Jahwes Entgegnung*, 57–58.

Even more striking is the birth imagery in vv. 28–29. The deity asks Job a rhetorical question similar in tone to the previous ones. However, instead of questioning if Job understands the sources and pathways of the meteorological phenomena that God has delineated, God asks Job if he understands who is the parent of these, and who gave birth to them: "Does the rain have a father? Who has begotten the dew drops? From whose belly did the ice come forth? Who bore the frost of heaven?" While the items listed (rain, dew, ice, and frost) do not have the same association with elements of destruction as do the previous, like their counterparts they do represent mysterious phenomena beyond Job's comprehension. And yet the imagery is of God giving birth to the mysteries, bringing new life into the cosmos. The imagery is similar to that in vv. 8–9 in reference to the Sea. As previously, the deity brings life, but life is shrouded in mystery, and associated with potential destruction, devastation, and chaos.

The animal imagery of 38:39–39:30 makes even more explicit this blending of the categories of life, death, and chaos. As Keel first noted, nearly all of the animals mentioned are wild animals belonging to realm of the wilderness, that hostile realm against which human culture was defined. In the ANE, these animals, like the Sea, represented the chaotic forces that were kept under control by the deity. ANE art often depicts kings hunting wild animals, which suggests the protection the king provides against hostile and threatening forces. Another common scene in Mesopotamian art is that of a divine figure surrounded by wild animals, which he holds in each hand as evidence of divine control over chaos and hostility.[75] In the HB, divine punishment is frequently depicted as the transformation of human society into a wilderness inhabited by the wild animals,[76] representing the conversion of civilization into chaos. Often these wild animals include the lion, the raven, the wild ass, and the ostrich—all creatures that appear in the Divine Speeches.[77] Furthermore, in the HB these creatures are also associated with death. This is obviously the case in these divine punishment texts where the wild creatures occupy a city or land only after its inhabitants have been killed. But it is also true in other texts where these creatures are depicted, themselves, as killers. Lions (לביא, כפיר; 38:39), for example, are known as killers, who rampage, ambush, tear their prey to pieces, and devour them.[78] To the Psalmist the lion deals death like the weapons of war: "I lie in the midst of lions that devour humans; their teeth are spears and arrows, their tongues are sharp swords" (Ps 57:5). Likewise, the wild ass (פרא; 39:5) was renown as a contentious creature, seeking its prey in the wilderness.[79] The wild ox (ראם; 39:9)[80] devours its enemies and crushes their bones (Num 24:8), and

---

75. Ibid., 86–125; *ANEP*, 110, pl. 464.

76. See, e.g., Ps 107:33–38; Isa 34:8–15; Hos 2:5, 14.

77. See, e.g., Isa 13:19–22; 34:8–15; Jer 2:15; 25:38; 50:39–40; Zeph 2:13–15.

78. See Num 23:24; Deut 33:20; 1 Kgs 20:36; Pss 10:9; 17:12; 35:17; 57:5; Isa 5:29; 15:9; 31:4; Jer 2:15, 30; 4:7; 5:6; 25:38; Lam 3:10; Ezek 19:3, 6; Hos 13:8; Joel 1:6; Amos 3:4; Mic 5:7; Nah 2:12, 13.

79. Gen 16:12; Job 24:5.

80. The LXX identifies this creature are a unicorn, while the Vulgate identifies it as a rhinoceros. More recently, however, scholars have identified it as a bison, buffalo, or aurochs. See Allen H.

the Psalmist pleas for deliverance from its ferocity (Ps 22:22). The ostrich (רננים[81]) is a cruel animal that refuses to nurture life. And the vulture (נץ[82]) lies in wait and pursues its victims, devouring its prey.[83]

Traditionally, therefore, these creatures represent the forces of chaos subduing culture, and the forces of death subduing life.[84] In the Divine Speeches, however, while the reference to these wild creatures cannot help but suggest the chaotic, the link to death is entirely absent. The contrary, in fact, is true: the imagery associated with these creatures is, on the whole, life imagery. This is most obviously the case for the descriptions of the animals in ch. 39.

The deity celebrates the mountain goat and hind precisely for their capacity as reproductive creatures. In fact, so focused is the imagery on their life-giving qualities that the poet strings together a series of parallel images of reproduction: they "give birth" (ילד; 39:1a), "calve" (חלל; 39:1b), "complete months" (ירחים תמלאנה; 39:2a), "give birth" (ילד; 39:2b), "crouch and bring forth offspring" (תכרענה ילדיהן תפלחנה; 39:3a),[85] "send forth their fetuses" (חבליהם תשלחנה; 39:3b).[86] They are creatures who produce offspring who are healthy, who roam unfettered in the open field—life imagery of movement (39:4).

The imagery that describes the wild ass and onager likewise is life imagery, though not cast as birth imagery, but rather as the life imagery of movement in the face of the death equivalent of stasis. Emphasis, therefore, is both on freedom and movement, but also on the stasis of captivity and confinement that such movement overcomes. The wild ass is "set free" (שלח חפשי) while the onager has its "bonds loosened" (מוסר פתח). Both sets of images draw on traditional slave imagery, the former on legal stipulations regarding the conditions in which a slave may be set free;[87] the latter on traditional expressions for emancipation following foreign occupation.[88] Just as the freed slave no longer is subject to the control and confinement of the master, so also these creatures are not subject to

Godbey, "The Unicorn in the Old Testament," *AJSL* 56 (1939): 256–96; John W. Klotz, "Notes on the Unicorn," *CTM* 32 (1961): 286–87. Cf. Pss 22:22; 92:11; Num 23:22.

81. This term is not the normal word for ostrich (יען). The term in 39:13 means "screechers" or "screeching birds," an epithet of the ostrich. This description of the bird in vv. 14–18 fits with that of the ostrich in other places in the HB. See Dhorme, *Job*, 603–4; Driver and Gray, *Job*, 1:342–45, for extended discussions of these issues.

82. נץ is also a term that applies to the eagle, and the imagery associated with the eagle is strikingly positive, compared to the vulture: Exod 19:4; Deut 32:11; Ps 103:5; Isa 40:31.

83. Job 9:26; Prov 30:17; Lam 4:19; Hos 8:1; Hab 1:8.

84. One exception to this argument is the hind (אילה; 39:5). In the HB this animal is associated with all manner of positive imagery, from divine favor, to security, to love (see Gen 49:21; 2 Sam 22:34; Ps 18:34; Prov 5:19; Sol 2:7; 3:5; Hab 3:19).

85. For the term "crouch in childbirth," see 1 Sam 4:19.

86. One might expect the feminine suffix on חבל, not the masculine. Hartley suggests that there is either an error here or when this was composed the distinction between the feminine and masculine suffixes had been lost (Hartley, *Job*, 505–6). Frequently this word suggests the pain of labor. Guillaume, however, argues that since there is no emphasis here on pain, it means "fetus," the cause of the pain (Guillaume, *Studies in the Book of Job*, 132; see also Rowley, *Job*, 248).

87. See Exod 21:2, 5, 26, 27; Deut 15:12, 13, 18; Jer 34:9, 10, 11, 14, 16. See, also, 1 Sam 17:25; Job 3:19; Isa 58:6.

88. See Ps 107:14; Jer 2:20; 5:5; 30:8; Nah 1:13.

the control and confinement of the "driver" (נגש; 39:7). Rather, they "explore" (תור; 39:8) the mountains—a life-image of movement. Interestingly, the words that describe the freedom and movement of these creatures are precisely those that Job used to describe the paradoxical life-giving qualities of Sheol in 3:18–19: in death the prisoner does not hear the voice of the "taskmaster" (נגש), and the slave is "free" (חפשי) from his master. As in Job's description of life-in-death, so also in the description of these creatures: symbols of chaos and death do not register on traditional grids, but merge with life imagery, creating a fluidity between supposed symbolic opposites.

The admixture of chaos, death, and life becomes more complex in the next set of images in 39:9–12 pertaining to the wild ox. Although the deity, on the whole, does not seem to respond directly either to Job's challenges or to his resymbolized universe divided between the civilized/coherent and the uncivilized/chaotic, here Job's world of the symbolically cultivated confronts the chaotic head on. The deity alludes to Job's world by referring to the normal activities of an agrarian village: the keeping of livestock (the "crib"; 39:9); plowing (39:10); and harvesting and storing grain (39:12). Such activities are the basic chores of survival in village life, and in Job's well-structured symbolic world they would be associated with life, vitality, order, and wholeness. However, in the Divine Speeches, emphasis falls not on the bearing of such activities on *Job's* experience of life, but on the *animals'* experience of life. Such activities do not bring life and vitality, but cause confinement, stasis, and servitude. The animals' experience is of slavery and hard service: they "serve" Job (עבד; 39:9); Job "relies" on them (בטח; 39:11); Job leaves his work for them to do (39:11); like faithful servants, Job "trusts" (אמן) them to accomplish his vital tasks (39:12). Imagery of confinement, subjugation, and stasis are most obvious in v. 10: "Can you bind the wild ass in the furrow with ropes?[89] Would he plow the valleys behind you?" With the description of the animal bound with ropes and being forced to do manual labor, emphasis falls inevitably on images of servitude and constraint, rather than on the life-sustaining qualities that this type of labor produces for humans. More jarring, however, is the following line, where the animal plows the valley "after you" (עמקים אחריך). This image even more clearly suggests utter servitude: "the poet is playing with the idea of total subservience. The incongruity of a wild ox following after a man in docile obedience would not be lost on the Israelite farmer."[90]

And yet the thrust of this section is that the wild ox is not subservient or confined, is not identified with these images of stasis. The wild ox is wild and free. While in Job's resymbolized symbolic universe of chs. 29–31 the work of cultivating land for planting would be typical of a civilized society and would lead literally to the sustenance of life, and while for Job wild animals represent

---

89. The MT's בתלם עבתו seems to make little sense. Various emendations have been suggested (see the list in Gordis, *Job*, 457). The translation suggested here follows Gordis, who translates the MT, arguing that עבתו is an abbreviation for עבתות, a type of abbreviation common in Rabbinic Hebrew. עבתו "is an accusative of specification to express means" ("by means of"). See Gordis, *Job*, 457.

90. Habel, *Job*, 524.

the forces of chaos and death that belong to the realm outside of the civilized, in the Divine Speeches, land cultivation represents the death equivalent of stasis and confinement, and the wild animal represents freedom and life. Again, the categories of life, death and chaos mix.

The mixture continues with the depiction of the next two animals, the ostrich and the war horse. The ostrich, like the mountain goat and hind (39:1–4), also is described as a creature who gives birth, although unlike for the mountain goat and hind, this focus on the processes of life gives way quickly to a meditation on potential death (39:14–16). This strange creature normally associated with the chaotic and death "lays (עזב) her eggs on the ground" (39:14), an image of life and vitality, but then abandons (עזב) the eggs, allowing them to be destroyed. Thus the ostrich is noted both for its association with life (the egg) and for its association with death (the potential destruction of the egg).

The war horse, for its part, is the only domesticated animal to appear in this list (39:19–25). Yet the imagery surrounding this creature exhibits a similar confusion regarding the categories of life and death. Initially the horse represents a vibrant, powerful life force described in terms normally reserved for a warrior god—might, thunder, majesty, and terror.[91] The horse is a model of fierce and awesome movement: it "leaps" like a locust (39:20), "snorts" (39:20), "paws," (39:21), and "charges" (יצא; 39:21). And yet what brings the horse to this state of exaggerated life-force is the anticipation of warfare: it charges into battle in order "to meet weapons" (לקראת נשק; 39:21). Far from paralyzing in deathly fear before the "sword" (39:22), the "spear" (39:23), or the "lance" (39:23), the horse "quivers and trembles" in excitement (39:24). When death presents itself, the horse then comes alive. Again, in the divine imagery there is a mixture of the categories of life and death.

The sense of a mixture of the categories climaxes with the last image of the first speech: "[The vulture's] young gulp[92] blood; where the slain are, there it is" (39:30). The word for "young," אפרח, suggests that these are new hatchlings,[93] which, as previously, emphasizes this strange creature's capacities as a life-giver. Yet life is sustained only insofar as the creatures feed off of death—the blood of the corpses slain in battle. Death, for some creatures, represents life.

6.2.2. *The Divine Speeches and Direction for Future Action*
Above, I argued that the biblical theophany functions in a manner similar to Lifton's category of experiential transcendence: both involve the experience of

---

91. See 9:34; 13:21; 37:22; 40:9 for these terms used of the warrior deity. See ibid., 547, for more.

92. The verb יעלעו is a *hapax*. Many suggest it is from the root לוע, which, in Syriac, means "lick up," or the root לעע, which, in the Arabic, has a similar meaning. Either the MT is a Pilpel form with a lost initial ל (ילעלעו) or it is a Qal form (ילעו) with the MT's initial ע being a *matres lectionis* (so Dhorme, *Job*, 612). Gesenius argues that the root is עלע (Wilhelm Gesenius and Emil Roediger, *Thesaurus Philologicus Criticus Linguae Hebraeae et Chaldaeae Veteris Testamenti* [2d ed.; 3 vols.; Lipsiae: Vogelii, 1829], 2:1038), a suggestion followed in contemporary times by Fohrer, *Hiob*, 494, among others.

93. See Deut 22:6; Ps 84:4.

the immediacy of the divine, or of a transcendental unity and wholeness; both take place outside of "normal" time; both function to alter the individual's life course; and both pertain to matters of death and life. Moreover, the theophany, like the mode of experiential transcendence, is supposed to move one from the experience of desymbolization to the reintegration and resymbolization of symbolic forms, providing new direction and purpose to life.

I have attempted to demonstrate that the Divine Speeches lack this sense of wholeness and unity crucial to the mode of experiential transcendence. The Divine Speeches, instead, seem to offer a picture of symbolic disorder. Traditional mythological structures are invoked only to be subverted: chaos blends with order; life with death. In contrast to Job's resymbolization in chs. 29–31 where the discourse of honor and shame served to orient life and death onto a symbolically navigable grid, in the divine symbolization with its fluid imagery, life and death blend in unexpected ways. The Divine Speeches fail to resymbolize death and life into a new unity and to reintegrate and resymbolize symbolic forms. The theophany is disorienting and enigmatic.

Further, in contrast to the typical HB theophany, the Divine Speeches also fail to provide Job direction for future action. Unlike the experiences of Moses (Exod 3; 19–24), Gideon (Judg 6:11–24), Isaiah (Isa 6) or Ezekiel (Ezek 1), where the encounter with the deity provides clear instructions for future actions, altering the course of the individuals' lives, God offers Job no direction about how he ought to act in light of what God has revealed.

The contrast between Job's own resymbolization in chs. 29–31 and the symbolic universe of the Divine Speeches is most telling. In Job's speech what enables his sense of certainty for future action is his ability to conceive of an operative symbolic universe that renders actions meaningful again. Only by framing his existence along the symbolics of honor and shame is Job able to understand his experiences and his treatment at God's hand, and, most importantly, to make his appeal for his own vindication. In contrast, the Divine Speeches do not offer a coherent symbolic system which then becomes the backdrop against which Job's experiences are interpreted; rather, the Divine Speeches seem to present three overlapping but discrete symbolic pictures, and Job is offered no indication of how he ought to understand himself and his experiences in relation to any of them. First, God describes the symbolics of the orderly world, created new everyday, though still with the chaotic within it (29:4–38); second, God describes the symbolic world of the wild and threatening animals—creatures part of Job's world, but who represent the mysterious, the unknown, and the terrifying (38:39–39:30); and third, God presents the symbolics of the limits, of the encounter with the abyss of Leviathan (40:15–41:26). At no point in the Divine Speeches is Job instructed about who he should be and how he should act in light of the symbolic universes set out before him. On the contrary, instead of outlining Job's proper response to these and giving him direction for future action, God demands that Job perform the work of deciphering his relation to the symbolic universes that God describes (38:3). Just as Job had previously declared his way of being in the world organized by the symbolics of honor and shame (chs. 29–31), so now God asks Job to consider his precise place in the created world ("Where were you?"; "Do you know?"; "Have you commanded?"; "Have you penetrated?"; and so on), his relation to the wild and dangerous animals who roam the wilderness ("Can you hunt prey?"; "Do you know the season?"; "Who sets free?"; "Do you give?"; and so on), and how he interacts with the great and terrifying sea monster, Leviathan ("Can you draw out?"; "Can you press down?"; "Can you fill his skin?"; and so on). The questions serve to demonstrate to Job that though he may be confident of who he is and how he should act in light of the symbolics of honor and shame, the symbolics of the created universe, of the wild and untamed animals, and of the terrifying Leviathan require a different sort of knowing and acting subject. In the pages that follow I will suggest possibilities about what sort of self Job must be in relation to these and how this differs from what he previously articulated in chs. 29–31.

6.2.2.1. *Job and the Created Order.* The opening section of the Divine Speeches introduces Job to a new field of vision and asks him to locate his place and his experiences in light of it. Specifically, the deity appeals to the symbolics of the primordial structures of the universe and demands that Job identify his own relation to these. Most importantly, God makes clear that it is he who provides the order and structure to the universe, acting as the grand architect by measuring and fixing the dimensions of the earth's foundations (38:4–5), setting its cornerstone (42:6), and establishing limits for the chaotic sea (38:10–11). Each part of creation has an appointed place, known only by God: dawn (38:12); the deep (38:16); death (38:17); light and darkness (38:19–20); snow and hail (38:22); wind (38:24); torrents and thunderstorms (38:25); and the constellations (38:31–33). Further, God is the agent responsible for the proper and regular functioning of the universe, appointing the dawn to break each day (38:12), reserving snow and hail for their proper times (38:23), causing rain to saturate the land and vegetation to spring (38:26–27), and dispatching lightning (38:35). Habel argues that "Here is not a God who intervenes or reacts, but one who modulates and constrains... Yahweh's appearance to Job is not to disrupt the grand design of things but to point Job precisely to that design."[94]

The appeal to the orderliness of the creation serves to shift Job's field of vision from the reality of his own social setting as the patriarch of a well-ordered village (chs. 29–31) to reality of the orderliness of the universe under God's direction. This frame of reference moves Job from the known world that he inhabits and that he is responsible for upholding to a universe in whose operation he has no hand. This has several implications for Job's own conception of himself and his experiences. First of all, Job must concede that all that occurs in the universe does so as part of God's design. Though the forces of chaos are not abolished, God does hold them at bay, providing barriers beyond which they may not cross (38:8–11). Importantly, however, Job is not privy to the operations of the divine order. He does not know where light and darkness

---

94. Habel, "In Defense," 35.

dwell (38:19), has not seen the vaults of hail (38:22), has not dispatched lightning (38:35), and likewise would not know the how or the why of the chaos of
his suffering. The Job of the symbolic world of ch. 38 is one tiny piece of a very
large cosmos whose operation depends on the carefully orchestrated direction
of God. The type of "self" that Job must be in this type of universe is one who
trusts unfailingly in God's direction of the universe—one who, though not
understanding the world's operations, nevertheless knows that a master design
ultimately undergirds all that surrounds him. In this symbolic system Job would
not question God's actions in the world and would not dispute the justice of the
difficult experiences he has endured.

Further, against the backdrop of ch. 38, God would not be held accountable to
a set of ethical norms, such as the code of honor to which Job appealed earlier.
Such accountability assumes both that Job can know these ethical norms and
that they apply equally to Job as they would to God. However, in the symbolics
of this portion of the Divine Speeches Job must let go of the possibility of the
confident knowledge of the operation of the universe and of the wisdom that
inheres therein (38:36). And God cannot possibly be held accountable to the
standards operative in the universe, for God is the only solely responsible for
endowing the universe with wisdom to begin with (38:36)—a wisdom that only
God comprehends

6.2.2.2. *Job and the Wilderness Animals.* From the symbolics of the orderly
creation, the Divine Speeches move to the symbolics of the animals that dwell
therein. As I discussed above, the particular animals of this section had specific
symbolic potency in the ANE, representing the wasteland and the realm of the
chaotic—the very opposite of Job's picture of society ordered by the symbolics
of honor and shame. Emphasis in this section, as in ch. 38, falls on *God's role* in
ensuring the processes of life among these creatures: providing food for the lion
(38:39–41); marking the season of the calving of the mountain goat (39:1–4);
ensuring the freedom of the wild ass (39:5–8); giving strength to the war horse
(39:19–25); enabling the vulture to soar (39:27–28). Even God's active role in
depriving the ostrich of wisdom ensures its peculiar behavior patterns (39:13–18).

However, the emphasis on God's role in ensuring orderliness among the wild
animals has a different resonance than does the earlier emphasis on God's role
in ensuring the orderliness of creation and the functioning of the cosmos. The
latter was a traditional conception in ancient Israel, finding expression in the
very first words of the HB, where God's act of creation is depicted as the process of structuring and ordering chaotic matter. By referring to this traditional
conception of God's relation to creation, the Divine Speeches invite Job to think
differently from how he had in chs. 29–31 about his relation to God and his
understanding of his experiences. That is, the symbolic universe shifted from the
realm of Job's familiar experience (society of honor) to the realm of the theologically familiar (ordered creation). In contrast, with the depiction of wild
animals, Job is invited to move from the realm of the familiar to the realm of the
foreign, mysterious, and threatening.

A comparison with Ps 104 will help illustrate the distinction. Psalm 104, like the Divine Speeches, celebrates God's ordering of creation. The Psalm also shares the same basic pattern, moving from God's act of ordering the foundations of the universe (vv. 1–9) to his ordering of the forces of nature (vv. 10–18), the luminaries (vv. 19–23), and the sea and its creatures (vv. 24–30). Included in the description of nature is God's provision for the creatures of the earth, both wild and domestic, including humans (vv. 14b–15). All the creatures of the earth receive their provisions from God, who structures the earth to meet their needs. The purpose of the Psalm is to describe the harmony of all of the created order, which elicits a response of praise. While the opening section of the Divine Speeches speak to the same harmonious creation, the animal imagery signifies differently. As Newsom argues, "Here the suppression of descriptions of human activity, the explicit opposition between the animals and human purposes, and repeated references to God's provisions for these creatures…destabilizes the customary binary oppositions of order and the chaotic, culture and nature, blessed and godforsaken."[95] Moreover, in contrast to the imagery surrounding the wild creatures of Ps 104, where all creatures hold a place in the harmonious, symbolically coherent creation, in the Divine Speeches the imagery of life, death, chaos, and order associated with the wild animals is in disarray, as argued earlier. Though God oversees and maintains the cycles and seasons of these animals, the animals represent the symbolically ambiguous threat of the wilderness.

This second portion of the Divine Speeches challenges Job to locate himself and his experiences in light of the symbolic disorientation of a God who actively upholds and maintains the affairs of the wild and chaotic. Though ch. 38 hinted at this depiction of God with the image of the deity wrapping the Sea in swaddling bands (v. 9), here there is no indication of the deity's restraint of chaos. Instead, the deity ensures its very vitality and vibrancy. This symbolic picture also represents a challenge to Job's earlier conception in chs. 29–31 of the neat division between the civilized society of honor and the uncivilized, shameful wilderness. For here the wilderness is not depicted as a place reserved for outcasts who know not how to live honorably; rather, the wilderness and its symbolic disorder is a place as blessed with the presence of the deity as is the ordered society that Job envisioned. Where Job might have earlier associated his experiences of suffering and death as "wilderness" experiences that God ought to remove and rectify (chs. 29–31), now Job is invited to understand God's operations in and through the wilderness. Where earlier Job interpreted disorder and chaos as a disruption of the well-ordered world, Job is invited to experience God's presence in the chaos of disruption. God is not only the foundation of order, harmony, and stability in the universe (ch. 38), but he is the foundation of disorder, ambiguity, and a threatening type of harmony in the wilderness.

6.2.2.3. *Job and Leviathan*. As abruptly as the Divine Speeches moved from the
, symbolics of the orderly cosmos to the symbolics of the wild animals of the earth, the speeches move to the symbolics of "the beyond"—of the realm of

---

95. Newsom, *Contest of Moral Imaginations*, 245.

Behemoth and Leviathan. As discussed earlier, in the ANE these creatures represented the mythical forces of chaos that threatened to undo the created order, and whose taming and defeat by the deity represented the primordial act of creation upon which all life was predicated. Yet, in contrast to the depiction of the deity in ch. 38 (vv. 8–11), here God not only is *not* depicted as the deity who orders creation by defeating and taming chaos, but much of the speech is devoted to celebrating the fact that no one, human or god, can slay the creature (40:24–26; 41:17–26).[96] In fact, to the divine eye, Leviathan is a creature of immense beauty who inspires reverential awe (41:4–16).

The presentation of this extended contemplation of Leviathan challenges Job once again to reconsider himself and his experiences in light of the symbolics of awesome and beautiful chaos. Where previously, in chs. 29–31, Job resymbolized the chaos of suffering as the problematic and undeserved punishment of a man of honor, here chaos is far from problematic, but is depicted in the form of Leviathan as having a natural place in creation, existing alongside the fishermen who would attempt to subdue it. In fact, the image of the fisherman, with their ineffectual attempts to conquer the chaos monster with spears and javelins, comes to represent Job himself as one who attempts to subdue the chaos of suffering by resymbolizing it as a problem that the deity ought to rectify. But this portion of the Divine Speeches indicates that chaos is not a problem that needs a solution, but is an independent force to be revered and celebrated. The symbolics of the beauty of Leviathan invite Job to embrace the apparent chaos of his experiences rather than to resist it. Moreover, Job is invited to reconsider God's involvement in the chaos of his experience. No longer is God depicted as the one who orders creation and who ensures the harmony of its operation, and no longer is God depicted as supporting and maintaining the wild creatures who represent threat. In both of these cases, God relates to Job as one who has ultimate control, both of the functioning of the universe, and of the terrifying and chaotic within creation. Here, however, the chaotic is depicted as a force separate from the deity, which God observes from a distance. This picture suggests that Job ought not to appeal to God to rectify the supposed wrong of chaotic experience, for God does not control chaos.

Taken together, these symbolic pictures of the Divine Speeches do not present to Job clear direction for his way of being in the world. Instead, they present to him various possibilities. Each possibility—ordered creation, the wild and untamed creatures, and the abyss of Leviathan—has its own accompanying implications about how Job is to understand himself and his experiences. But none lays out for Job exactly how he should proceed. Further, each possibility suggests a distinct mode of God's relation to the world, which, in turn, has implications for how Job ought to understand his experiences and move forward. In the first case, God is the divine architect who supplies an order to the world that Job, ultimately, is not able to discern; in the second case, God lovingly maintains the threatening creatures of creation, suggesting to Job that God's zone of operation is precisely in the chaos of experience; in the final case,

---

96. See above, section 6.2.1.2 for a discussion of these passages.

God operates at a distance from the forces of chaos, whose beauty Job is invited to revere along with the deity.

Instead of clear direction for future action, the Divine Speeches present open possibility. Though challenging Job's resymbolization in chs. 29–31 and inviting Job to conceptualize alternative ways-of-being in the universe, the Divine Speeches do not lay out for Job how his perspective ought to change or how he should alter his understanding of his situation.

Job's response in 42:1–6 reflects the open-endedness of the Divine Speeches. Responding to the disorienting imagery and open possibility of the Divine Speeches, Job, similarly, voices his mystification with words that are "elusive and enigmatic."[97] After acknowledging God's power (42:2), quoting God's words (42:3a, 4a), admitting his lack of knowledge (42:3b, c), and confessing that the theophany has altered his perspective dramatically (42:5), Job's only indication of exactly how his perspective has changed (42:6) is itself terse, enigmatic, and full of ambiguity.[98] As Newsom outlines, this verse can be translated in a number of legitimate ways:

(1)   "Therefore I despise myself and repent upon dust and ashes" (i.e. in humiliation; cf. NRSV; NIV);

(2)   "Therefore I retract my words and repent of dust and ashes" (i.e. the symbols of mourning);[99]

(3)   "Therefore I reject and forswear dust and ashes" (i.e. the symbols of mourning);[100]

(4)   "Therefore I retract my words and have changed my mind concerning dust and ashes" (i.e. the human condition);[101]

(5)   "Therefore I retract my words, and I am comforted concerning dust and ashes" (i.e. the human condition).[102]

Job's final words in the book of Job offer a fitting response to the Divine Speeches. Mirroring the sense of open possibility that the alternative symbolic

97. Newsom, "Job," 627.

98. See William S. Morrow, "Consolation, Rejection, and Repentance in Job 42:6," *JBL* 105 (1986): 211–25, for a discussion of the philological and grammatical problems as well as various scholars' solutions.

99. See Habel, *Job*, 583.

100. See Dale Patrick, "Translation of Job 42:6," *VT* 26 (1976): 369–71.

101. See Janzen, *Job*, 254–59.

102. See Perdue, *Wisdom in Revolt*, 232, 236–37 (though Perdue's translation of the sentence is "Therefore I reject but am comforted over dust and ashes"). Newsom, "Job," 627–29, outlines the following main points of disagreement among scholars (see also Morrow, "Consolation," 211–25; Newsom, "Considering Job," 111–12). First, is the object of the verb מאס ("I reject") to be supplied ("myself," "my words"; see Fohrer, *Hiob*, 535–36; Habel, *Job*, 582–83; Lester J. Kuyper, "Repentance of Job," *VT* 9 [1959]: 91–94), or is it the "dust and ashes" of the parallel line (see, e.g., Patrick, "Translation of Job 42:6," 369–71)? Alternatively, is the verb מאס, a variant of מסס ("to melt"), which would then be translated as "I submit" (Dhorme, *Job*, 646–47)? Second, the phrase ונחמתי על can be translated "I repent on account of," "I am consoled concerning," or "I forswear" (see Morrow, "Consolation," 215–16). Lastly, "dust and ashes" might refer to human mortality, humiliation (Morrow, "Consolation," 216–17), or the ash heap upon which Job sits (Dhorme, *Job*, 646–47; Pope, *Job*, 290).

universes of the Divine Speeches suggested, the ambiguity of Job's articulation of how his perspective has altered reflects this same sense of open possibility.

6.3. *The Divine Speeches and the Protean Self*

This sense of "possibility of being" of the Divine Speeches (and Job's response) is somewhat troubling from a Liftonian perspective, for, as I have been arguing throughout, Lifton envisions a return to symbolization as the goal of the human psyche after the unsettling experience of desymbolization. In terms of death imagery, when death becomes desymbolized, it ought then to be resymbolized in order to ensure a healthy psyche. The Divine Speeches, however, fail to resymbolize imagery of life and death and fail to provide a coherent and unified symbolic system.

Furthermore, for Lifton the mode of experiential transcendence is a special mode distinct from the other four (biological, theological, creative, and natural), for it depends entirely on a psychic *state*. The experience of transcendence is a particular quality of experience that "must connect with significant *content* (grounded relationship to any of the other four modes)" in order to vitalize the sense of life and connection to "the larger human process."[103] Lifton illustrates this point by referring to, among other things, the "Profound awareness of loving connection to the continuing human nexus through one's children...[that] can evoke moments of felt transcendence."[104] The experience of transcendence may be no more than a particular momentary feeling of pleasure and wholeness or a sense of near-perfect centering. "With inner forms in harmony, psychic action is intense and focused, and there is a free flow of psychic and bodily energy."[105]

In the Divine Speeches, however, the moment of transcendence—the divine communication—intentionally obfuscates a "grounded relationship" to traditional symbolizations and modes of symbolic immortality. In fact, the Divine Speeches play off of traditional imagery, creating a fluidity and mixture of symbolic forms. Moreover, by presenting the possibility of being in distinct symbolic universes (created order, wild animals, Leviathan), the Divine Speeches complicate the notion of "centeredness," implying the possibility of multiple symbolic centers, and the potential vacillation between them. This multiplicity and potential vacillation is *not* something that must be overcome by integration into a newer symbolic unity (as Lifton would seem to suggest), but is the divine final statement of the symbolic structure of the universe.

The Divine Speeches, therefore, fail to offer the type of resymbolization typical of the mode of experiential transcendence, but neither do they present a picture of desymbolization such as Job voiced earlier in the dialogues. Instead, they depict something different—not quite desymbolization, but not quite symbolic wholeness either. This sense of something new that is glimpsed in the Divine

---

103. Lifton, *Broken Connection*, 34.
104. Ibid.
105. Ibid.

Speeches also is glimpsed in Lifton's later writings concerning the particular style of self-formation common in the historically unique contemporary moment at the turn of the twenty-first century. Instead of describing the movement of the self in contemporary times with the familiar terms of desymbolization–resymbolization, Lifton refers to the mythology of Proteus, the shapeshifting Greek god, and argues that the contemporary historical situation—rapid historical change, mass media revolution, and the continual threat of extinction—has led ineluctably to a more flexible and shifting self-formation than in ages past. "The protean self emerges from confusion, from the widespread feeling that we are losing our psychological moorings. We feel ourselves buffeted about by unmanageable historical forces and social uncertainties."[106] But the self is resilient in the face of all this—it has become malleable.

Central to protean self are certain predominant features: first there is "a capacity for bringing together disparate and seemingly incompatible elements of identity and involvement in...'odd combinations,' and for continuous transformation of these elements";[107] second, there are feelings of "fatherlessness" and "homelessness" due to shifting conceptions of authority and mentorship; third, the psychology of survivorship is a common experience, as many undergo symbolic forms of dying and rebirth; fourth, mockery, irony, and absurdity are employed as ways to express lack of fit between how the world presents itself and how one actually experiences it; fifth, there is a considerable degree of uneasiness regarding commitment to idea systems, which, when held, can easily be tweaked and/or abandoned.[108]

Lifton argues that proteanism is, at the same time, sequential, simultaneous, and social. It is sequential in that there is "a changing series of involvements with people, ideas, and activities";[109] it is simultaneous "in the multiplicity of varied, even antithetical images and ideas held at any one time by the self, each of which it may be more or less ready to act upon";[110] and it is social "so that in any given environment—office, school, or neighborhood—one may encounter highly varied forms of self-presentation."[111]

At first glance, the protean style bespeaks not so much the familiar linear process of symbolization–desymbolization–resymbolization, but rather "an ongoing process of symbolization"[112] or "a wariness toward committing oneself to any particular form, [and] an anxiety around premature closure."[113] In the face

106. Lifton, *Protean Self*, 1.
107. Ibid., 5.
108. Ibid., 5–6.
109. Ibid., 8.
110. Ibid.
111. Ibid. For more on Lifton's conception of the protean self, see Anthon Molino and Christine Ware, "Protean Impulses: A Conversation with Robert Jay Lifton," in *Where Id Was: Challenging Normalization in Psychoanalysis* (ed. Anthony Molino and Christine Ware; Middletown: Wesleyan University Press, 2001), 138–46; Charles B. Strozier, "Proteanism and the Species Self: Interview with Robert Jay Lifton," *The Psychohistory Review* 20 (1992): 107–30.
112. Lifton, *Life of the Self*, 31.
113. Lifton, *Broken Connection*, 85.

of tenuous images and shifting institutions, contemporary humans struggle continually to attain "believable symbolizations of meaning and continuity."[114] This is the constant quest for continuity and meaning through the constant combination and recombination of forms and images. For, "The very tenuousness of the images around which that larger struggle takes place is also a source of possibility."[115]

In much of Lifton's discussions of the protean self one can sense the fluidity and open possibility of the Divine Speeches. Just as the Divine Speeches intermix traditionally opposite images of life and death, suggesting a symbolic overflow and inter-animation, so also the protean self combines paradoxical combinations of forms and images into loosely cohering and constantly shifting symbolizations. Just as the diverse and elusive imagery of the Divine Speeches radiates a surplus of meaning that resists the interpretive attempt at "containment" or "finalization," as is exhibited in the diverse history of interpretation, so also the protean self, in its unique combination of a diverse array of complementary and competing images and forms, resists the containment of resymbolization, of the move back to a unified symbolic system. And most importantly, just as the Divine Speeches present the possibility of multiple symbolic "centers" in whose light Job ought to locate himself, so also the protean self suggests the vacillation between different modes of being or symbolizations of the self in the world.

But Lifton does not allow the fluidity, open possibility, and potential incoherence of the protean self to stand. Instead he backs off from this radical formulation and asserts the self's fundamental orientation toward coherence: "The protean self seeks to be both fluid and grounded, however tenuous that combination... Proteanism, then, is a balancing act between responsive shapeshifting, on the one hand, and efforts to consolidate and cohere on the other."[116] Regardless of the odd combinations of form and their shifts and transformations, there is always a "certain continuity" about them,[117] for the protean self "requires a modicum of inner continuity, and of coherence as well."[118] And again, "however odd or bizarre [are the protean self's] components, something on the order of a coherent self comes on strong."[119]

With his conception of the protean self, Lifton opened the possibility of discussing the formation and maintenance of the "self" in a potentially radical manner. Yet, with his reluctance to surrender the metaphor of center/unity/wholeness Lifton never quite allows this insight to blossom. Instead, like the commentators who seize upon one particular aspect or implication of the imagery in the Divine Speeches and then resolve the ambiguity and fluidity of the Divine Speeches by foregrounding this one aspect at the expense of the

114. Ibid., 393.
115. Ibid.
116. Lifton, *Protean Self*, 9.
117. Ibid., 30.
118. Ibid., 88.
119. Ibid.

others, Lifton never quite relinquishes his dependence on the "center" metaphor and resolves the ambiguity, fluidity, and paradox of the formation of the protean self by asserting the ultimate recentering of the self.

In Job 38–41, however, the sense of fluidity, ambiguity, and open possibility that accompanies both the divine imagery and Lifton's discussion of the protean self is allowed to shine through without hindrance. In fact, these emerge as the last word in the book of Job—both chronologically in that this is the last substantive speech in the book, and theologically in that this word is presented as a theophany, the very word of God.

The Divine Speeches, therefore, form a critique of Lifton's conception of the protean self. Is it possible for the self to have this sort of fluidity, ambiguity, multiple commitments, and shifting imagery without, on the one hand, the self becoming diffuse "to the point of [becoming] incoherent and immobile: a 'chaos of possibilities'";[120] and, on the other hand, without a need for there also to be an inner core of stable and coherent imagery that grounds this fluctuation and vacillation? Is it possible that the self is always fluid, in process, and, to a degree, incoherent, and that any attempts to arrive at substantive form amid this flux are merely attempts to impose structure where structure does not exist? Could the very effort to attain structural coherence and inner form be the first step toward mental illness and/or the breakdown of the symbolic function of the psyche in that form is being imposed where form does not entirely belong? The implication of the Divine Speeches on Lifton's conception of the protean self is that instead of an inner sense of cohesion and form, one's self is forever in process, never centered, never unified, and never completely resymbolized, but always identifying itself against a backdrop of potential symbolizations.

Lifton argues that a recognition of proteanism helps diverse humans to realize a common humanity amid so many ostensible differences. "We can experience, amidst our cultural diversity, that common humanity. The diversity is integral to the process, as: 'We are multiple from the start.'"[121] The Divine Speeches push Lifton to expand this vision of multiplicity. The divine word is that the self, along with the world, is multiple, fluid, ambiguous, and forever in process.

---

120. Ibid., 190.
121. Ibid., 213.

Chapter 7

CONCLUSION: DEATH AT THE END
AND THE QUESTIONS OF SYMBOLIC
WHOLENESS AND MEANING

The book of Job does not end with the unsettling implications of the Divine Speeches. From images of symbolic flux, including the mingling of categories of life and death, order and chaos, the narrative returns, in 42:7–17, to the perfect order and wholeness of the symbolization of abundant life from the introduction to the prologue (1:1–5). God restores Job to his previous state of life, liveliness, and fecundity. From the alienation from his community and the experience of the death equivalent of separation, Job experiences the intimacy of human connection (42:11–12). From the sense of life as the death equivalent of stasis and confinement, Job experiences the excitement of celebration (42:11). Life to Job now is the abundance of material goods (42:11) and the multiplication of livestock that is even more virile now than before (42:12). And again, seven sons and three daughters are born to Job: symbolic numbers that suggest wholeness and completion. Life, for Job, once again is bursting at the seams. Alongside this restoration of abundant life is the restoration to relationship with the deity. As before, God uses the term of intimacy, "my servant," to refer to Job, and grants to Job special requests (42:8).

The climax to the story of Job's restoration to abundant life is the description of Job's abundant death. Surrounded by sons and beautiful daughters, Job dies a rich man who has lived a full, long life. Just as Abraham died "in peace" (בשלם; Gen 15:15), "in a good old age" (בשיבה טובה; Gen 15:15; 25:8), "old and sated" (זקן ושבע; Gen 25:8), so also Job died "old and full of years" (זקן ושבע ימים; 42:7). The type of death Job dies is the death of the pious, reserved for those in right relationship with the deity, whose lives were marked by abundance and happiness.

The lasting image of the book of Job, therefore, is of the traditional death of a pious man, which, in the symbolization of abundant life, is a satisfying and pleasant death. However, given Job's earlier articulation of the experience of desymbolization and his attempts to resymbolize, and given the implications of the Divine Speeches, the question must be asked: Is a return to the symbolization of abundant life with its image of an abundant death believable and/or satisfying? Some scholars seem to think it is. Crouch, for one, argues that given the prose tale's narrative strategies, the scene of Job's death does bring a high degree of closure to the book and that "The totalizing of the narrative effectively overcomes the disruptions of the poetic dialogues and has a sense of an 'and he lived happily ever after' ending."[1] According to Crouch, though the poetic dialogues raise a bevy of theological and moral issues, in the end, the perspective of the prose tale trumps that of the poetic sections. Instead of leaving the reader with the sense of protest and disquiet of the poetic dialogues, the book leaves the reader with the theologically satisfying position of "retributive justice."[2]

Burkes agrees that the type of death depicted at the end of the book of Job cancels out the rather heterodox musings about death in the poetic dialogues. "Job confronts the sort of circumstances which could lead to a new treatment of mortality, but the problem is never really raised since he is restored... The righteous man dies 'full of days,' and the problem is averted."[3]

Zuckerman, however, argues the opposite regarding death in the prose and poetic sections. According to Zuckerman, the original prose tale included the resurrection of Job's children from the dead as part of Job's "restoration." The message of the original legend of Job was that "God's merciful power knows no boundaries, not even the boundaries of death."[4] To the author of the poetic dialogues, however, the belief in resurrection was false hope. He, therefore, countered the message of the legend with his own message of the finality of death in the dialogues. Though Zuckerman does not overtly argue this, it seems that the perspective of the poetic dialogues trumps that of the prose narrative, given that Job's children's supposed resurrection from the dead no longer even appears in the prose tale. Only the perspective of the poetic dialogues remains.

All of these scholars understand that certain tensions exist between the prose tale and the poetic sections of the book, but they argue that ultimately the perspective of the one triumphs over that of the other. I, however, am not convinced that the relationship of the one to the other is that of an either/or: either this one dominates or that one does. Throughout the previous pages I have been interpreting the book of Job as a whole, interpreting the various sections (prose tale, dialogues, Divine Speeches) in the order they appear in the book. I believe that just as the first half of the prose tale functions as a prologue to the entire book (chs. 1–2), introducing the main problems that the dialogues and then the Divine Speeches will address (including the problems surrounding death), so also the second half of the prose tale now functions as an epilogue to the entire book (42:7–12), offering one final perspective on the fundamental issues of the book, including, importantly, death.

The prose epilogue, that is, operates in concert with, not opposition to, the poetic sections, though as Crouch, Burkes, and Zuckerman note, certain tensions exist between the two. First, God's approval of Job, that he has spoken of God "what is right" (נכונה; 42:8) directly contradicts God's earlier rebuke of Job, that he spoke "words without knowledge" (38:2). Second, though God condemns

---

1. Crouch, *Death and Closure*, 157.
2. See ibid., 135–68.
3. Burkes, *God, Self, and Death*, 250.
4. Zuckerman, *Job the Silent*, 128.

Eliphaz and the friends for the untruths they spoke about God, God actually confirms their arguments by restoring Job's wealth and granting him abundant offspring because of his piety. God "blessed Job's latter days more than the earlier ones" (42:7), just as Bildad had previously predicted would happen (8:7). So, on the one hand, God's approval goes to the one who questioned him, challenged him, and charged him with injustice and murder, but, on the other hand, his rebuke goes to those who resolutely supported the same theological system that God ultimately upholds, and whose predictions about God's actions God ultimately proves to be true. This most readily applies to the last and most lasting image of the book of Job, that of Job's own death. Far from the death of an embittered man, alienated from both humans and God, Job dies the perfect death of one who lived an abundant life. Just as Eliphaz predicted that Job's offspring would be many ("like the grass of the earth"; 5:25) and that he would come to the grave "at a ripe old age"[5] (5:26), so Job died "old and full of years" (42:17), surrounded by generations of offspring. And yet God charged Eliphaz, not Job, with speaking untruths.

Only on the surface does the prose epilogue present a neat and tidy, fairytale conclusion to the book of Job. Upon closer examination the simplicity and earnestness of the epilogue belies a host of perplexing issues. Which perspective on suffering and the divine–human relationship is ultimately correct? Perhaps the one Job voiced in the dialogues, which God seems to validate in his affirmation of Job in the epilogue. But God also condemned this perspective earlier, in the Divine Speeches, and his actions in the epilogue suggest that Job was wrong. Perhaps the perspective of the friends is correct since what they predicted ultimately came to pass in the epilogue. However, in the epilogue the deity also condemned their words as untrue. Perhaps God's perspective from the Divine Speeches is the correct one. However, in the epilogue the deity acts and speaks in a manner that scarcely can be reconciled with the deity's perspective in the Divine Speeches. Rather than closing down the narrative and bringing to a halt the dialogic nature of the poetic sections, the epilogue actually ensures that dialogue and inquiry into these matters continues among readers and interpreters long after the story has ended.

The same type of questions apply to the lasting image of the book: the depiction of Job's abundant death. For though the book ends with this traditionally satisfying death, the book of Job, as a whole, presents numerous perspectives on death's meaning. Job has understood death several ways: as the prospect of a hopeful future; as the subjective experience of life as stasis, separation, and disintegration; as the unjust attack of a murderous deity; as an indication of the destruction of all hope and optimism; and, ultimately, as the realm of dishonor and shame. The friends understood death to function two ways: abundant and full death as the climax to an abundant life lived piously in relation to the deity; untimely and impoverished death as the result of a life of impiety lived in alienation from the deity. God, however, blurred the distinctions between life

---

5. See, above, section 3.5.2 for this translation.

and death, suggesting that the symbolic realms of the ordered and the chaotic commingle with both life and death. And now the book ends with a depiction of a death that is, on the surface, the satisfying death of a man who lived an abundant life.

But just as the epilogue, in general, rather than shutting down and concluding the book of Job, ensures that questions and dialogue persist, so also this final depiction of seemingly satisfying death also belies a deeper and more complex conversation about death. For whatever the outcome of Job's attempted resymbolization in chs. 29–31, and whatever the implications of the divine symbolization in chs. 38–41, one thing for certain is that Job cannot return to the same symbolic world he once inhabited in the introduction to the prologue. The narrative of the book of Job depicts Job as, in Liftonian terms, a survivor: one for whom symbols of long-standing authority have collapsed in the wake of disaster, who has encountered death in a bodily or psychic fashion and has remained alive, who has struggled toward inner form and formulation, who has engaged the quest to find significance in his death encounter and remaining life experiences. Job has moved from symbolic wholeness to desymbolization and he has groped toward resymbolization. Though the depiction of Job's death in 42:17 resonates with the picture of symbolic wholeness in the introduction to the prologue in 1:1–5, this symbolic world has collapsed for Job and this type of death no longer applies, as the dialogues display. And yet if this type of death no longer applies, just what does Job's own death mean? How do we interpret it? On what basis do we evaluate it? If the symbolic system that would render it meaningful has collapsed, then in what symbolic system ought the meaning of death to be judged? Even as a host of questions hover above the epilogue's apparent simplicity, so also a host of questions hover above this final, apparently satisfying, death.

The depiction of Job's death in the epilogue raises one more important question, this one in reference to Lifton's observations about the return to symbolic wholeness after desymbolization. Earlier I argued that in Lifton's writings about the experience of disaster and desymbolization he envisions a return to symbolic wholeness as the goal of the survivor. He indicates this in his usage of "the center" metaphor to describes the movement of healthy psychic functioning as centering to decentering to recentering. As argued in the previous chapter, however, the Divine Speeches offer a critique of this emphasis on symbolic wholeness. Instead they suggest that Lifton's insights regarding the protean style be pressed and be allowed to reach their full conclusion: symbolic wholeness is never quite achieved, but humans are always operating amid the flux of symbolic possibility, always negotiating the challenges of new experiences, always working with systems that are forever in motion.

The narrative progression of Job's attempted return to symbolic wholeness in chs. 29–31, to the Divine Speeches that affirm symbolic "messiness" and possibility, to the epilogue's return to a type of symbolic wholeness that certainly no longer applies, raises the question not just of the appropriateness of the symbolization of abundant life, but of the type of symbolic wholeness that the symbolization of abundant life represents. For after the Divine Speeches, where the divine voice declares the fundamental symbolic openness of reality in a theophany, any return to symbolic wholeness—whether in the form of the symbolization of abundant life or in some other form—is bound to appear inappropriate. By ending the book of Job with a return to a form of symbolic wholeness whose desymbolization was the premise of the entire book, the epilogue foregrounds the issue of the impossibility of *this* form of symbolic wholeness, which also raises the issue of the potential impossibility of *any* form of symbolic wholeness. Stated differently, given the desymbolization of Job's symbolic world in the prologue, certainly *this* picture of symbolic wholeness in the epilogue no longer applies. But given the divine sanction of symbolic incoherence and messiness can *any* picture of symbolic wholeness apply?

I began this project with a brief discussion of the particular resonance that the book of Job has in the contemporary age. "Modern Job" is the apt epithet that Friedman gives to those contemporary humans who, living in a "post-traumatic" age, articulate meaning and purpose only by grappling head-on with the horrifying events and experiences that plague this era. For similar reasons, Elie Wiesel calls Job "our contemporary," despite the millennia that separate Wiesel from the composition of the biblical book, a contemporaneity that springs from Job's honest expression of suffering.

For Job, this expression of suffering is the articulation of the experience of survival—in Lifton's terms, the movement from desymbolization and back to resymbolization. However, in *Job*, resymbolization as a complete return to wholeness, centeredness, and symbolic unity is problematized in the Divine Speeches. Here resymbolization is not straightforward or well-delineated. It is even fraught with danger. Though the book seemingly ends with ultimate closure in the epilogue, this closure fittingly opens up new discussions, new interpretations, new possibilities for ways forward. *Job*'s resistance to resymbolization enacts what Caruth describes as the "impossible history"[6] that trauma victims carry: an event that exists outside all schemes of meaning that would tame it by rendering it comprehensible and bring it inside the realm of the familiar. Perhaps this is another way that the book of Job becomes "contemporary": it bears witness to the rupture of disaster and the shattering of patterns of interpretation and knowledge that disaster brings.

---

6. Cathy Caruth, "Introduction," in *Trauma: Explorations in Memory* (ed. Cathy Caruth; Baltimore: The Johns Hopkins University Press, 1995), 5.

BIBLIOGRAPHY

Abercrombie, John R. "Palestinian Burial Practices from 1200 to 600 B.C.E." Ph.D. diss., University of Pennsylvania, 1979.

Albright, William Foxwell. "The High Place in Ancient Palestine." Pages 242–58 in *Volume du Congrès, Strasbourg, 1956*. Edited by G. W. Anderson. Supplements to Vetus Testamentum 4. Leiden: Brill, 1957.

Allan, Keith, and Kate Burridge. *Euphemism and Dysphemism: Language Used as Shield and Weapon*. New York: Oxford University Press, 1991.

Alter, Robert. "From Line to Story in Biblical Verse." *Poetics Today* 4 (1983): 615–37.

—"The Voice from the Whirlwind." *Commentary* 77 (1984): 33–41.

Andersen, Francis I. *Job: An Introduction and Commentary*. Tyndale Old Testament Commentaries. Downers Grove, Ill.: Inter-Varsity, 1976.

Anderson, Gary A. *A Time to Mourn, a Time to Dance: The Expression of Grief and Joy in Israelite Religion*. University Park: Pennsylvania State University Press, 1991.

Anderson, Hugh. "The Book of Job." Pages 1–41 in *Wisdom Literature and Poetry: A Commentary on Job, Psalms, Proverbs, Ecclesiastes, The Song of Solomon*. Edited by Charles M. Laymon. Interpreter's Concise Commentary 3. Nashville: Abingdon, 1983.

Aquinas, Thomas. *The Literal Exposition on Job: A Scriptural Commentary Concerning Providence*. Translated by Anthony Damico. Classics in Religious Studies 7. Atlanta: Scholars Press, 1989.

Ariès, Philippe. *The Hour of Our Death*. Translated by Helen Weaver. New York: Oxford University Press, 1991.

—*Images of Man and Death*. Translated by Janet Lloyd. Cambridge, Mass.: Harvard University Press, 1985.

—*Western Attitudes toward Death: From the Middle Ages to the Present*. Translated by Patricia M. Ranum. Johns Hopkins Symposia in Comparative History. Baltimore: The Johns Hopkins University Press, 1974.

Aristotle, *Poetics*. Edited and translated by Stephen Halliwell. Loeb Classical Library. Cambridge, Mass.: Harvard University Press, 1995.

Avery-Peck, Alan J., and Jacob Neusner, eds. *Judaism in Late Antiquity*. Vol. 4, *Death, Life-after-Death, Resurrection and the World-to-Come in the Judaisms of Antiquity*. Leiden: Brill, 2000.

Bailey, Lloyd R. *Biblical Perspectives on Death*. Overtures to Biblical Theology. Philadelphia: Fortress, 1979.

—"Death as a Theological Problem in the Old Testament." *Pastoral Psychology* 22 (1971): 20–32.

Barr, James. "Theophany and Anthropomorphism." Pages 31–38 in *Congress Volume: Oxford, 1959*. Edited by G. W. Anderson et al. Supplements to Vetus Testamentum 7. Leiden: Brill, 1960.

Barr, James, and Jeremy Hughes. "Hebrew *'ad*, Especially at Job 1:18 and Neh 7:3." *JSS* 27 (1982): 177–92.

Barrick, W. Boyd. "The Funerary Character of 'High Places' in Ancient Palestine: A Reassessment." *Vetus Testamentum* 25 (1975): 564–95.

Barth, Christoph. *Die Errettung vom Tode in den individuellen Klage- und Dankliedern des Alten Testamentes.* Zollikon: Evangelischer Verlag, 1947.

Barton, George A. "The Composition of Job 24–30." *Journal of Biblical Literature* 30 (1911): 66–77.

Becker, Ernest. *The Denial of Death.* New York: Free Press, 1973.

Bentzen, Aage. *Introduction to the Old Testament.* 6th ed. 2 vols. Copenhagen: G. E. C. Gad, 1961.

Berger, Peter L. *The Sacred Canopy: Elements of a Sociological Theory of Religion.* Garden City, N.Y.: Doubleday, 1967.

Blenkinsopp, Joseph. "Deuteronomy and the Politics of Post-Mortem Existence." *Vetus Testamentum* 45 (1995): 1–16.

Bloch, Maurice, and Jonathan P. Parry. "Introduction: Death and the Regeneration of Life." Pages 1–44 in *Death and the Regeneration of Life.* Edited by Maurice Bloch and Jonathan P. Parry. New York: Cambridge University Press, 1982.

Bloch-Smith, Elizabeth. "The Cult of the Dead in Judah: Interpreting the Material Remains." *Journal of Biblical Literature* 111 (1992): 213–24.

—*Judahite Burial Practices and Beliefs about the Dead.* Journal for the Study of the Old Testament: Supplement Series 123. Sheffield: JSOT Press, 1992.

Blommerde, Anton C. M. *Northwest Semitic Grammar and Job.* Biblica et orientalia 22. Rome: Pontifical Biblical Institute, 1969.

Blumenthal, Elke. "Hiob und die Harfnerlieder." *Theologische Literaturzeitung* 115 (1990): 721–30.

Bowker, John Westerdale. *The Meanings of Death.* Cambridge: Cambridge University Press, 1991.

Box, George Herbert. *Judaism in the Greek Period, from the Rise of Alexander the Great to the Intervention of Rome (333–63 B.C.).* Clarendon Bible Old Testament 5. Oxford: Clarendon, 1932.

Bradbury, Mary. *Representations of Death: A Social Psychological Perspective.* London: Routledge, 1999.

Brenner, Athalya. "God's Answer to Job." *Vetus Testamentum* 31 (1981): 129–37.

Brichto, H. C. "Kin, Cult, Land and Afterlife: A Biblical Complex." *Hebrew Union College Annual* 44 (1973): 1–54.

Bronfen, Elisabeth. "Death: The Navel of the Image." Pages 79–90 in *The Point of Theory: Practices of Cultural Analysis.* Edited by Mieke Bal and Inge E. Boer. New York: Continuum, 1994.

Bronfen, Elisabeth, and Sarah Webster Goodwin. "Introduction." Pages 3–25 in *Death and Representation.* Edited by Elisabeth Bronfen and Sarah Webster Goodwin. Baltimore: The Johns Hopkins University Press, 1993.

Brooks, Peter. *Reading for the Plot: Design and Intention in Narrative.* New York: Knopf, 1984.

Brueggemann, Walter. "Death, Theology of." Pages 219–22 in *Interpreter's Dictionary of the Bible: Supplementary Volume.* Edited by Keith R. Crim. Nashville: Abingdon, 1976.

Buber, Martin. *The Prophetic Faith.* Translated by Carlyle Witton-Davies. New York: Macmillan, 1949. Repr., New York: Harper & Row, 1960.

Burke, Kenneth. "Thanatopsis for Critics: A Brief Thesaurus of Deaths and Dying." *Essays in Criticism* 2 (1952): 369–75.

Burkes, Shannon. *God, Self, and Death: The Shape of Religious Transformation in the Second Temple Period.* Supplements to the Journal for the Study of Judaism 79. Boston: Brill, 2003.

Burns, John Barclay. "Cursing the Day of Birth." *Proceedings* 13 (1993): 11–22.

—"The Identity of Death's First-Born (Job 18:13)." *Vetus Testamentum* 37 (1987): 362–64.

Buss, Martin. "Role and Selfhood in Hebrew Prophecy." Pages 277–94 in *Psychology and the Bible: A New Way to Read the Scriptures*. Vol. 2, *From Genesis to Apocalyptic Vision*. Edited by J. Harold Ellens and Wayne G. Rollins. Westport, Conn.: Prager, 2004.

Caruth, Cathy. "Introduction." Pages 3–12 in *Trauma: Explorations in Memory*. Edited by Cathy Caruth. Baltimore: The Johns Hopkins University Press, 1995.

Charles, Robert Henry. *Eschatology, the Doctrine of a Future Life in Israel, Judaism, and Christianity: A Critical History*. Schocken Paperbacks 49. New York: Schocken Books, 1963.

Clines, David J. A. "The Etymology of Hebrew *Ṣelem*." *Journal of Northwest Semitic Languages* 3 (1974): 19–25.

—"False Naivety in the Prologue to Job." *Hebrew Annual Review* 9 (1985): 127–36.

—*Job 1–20*. Word Biblical Commentary 17. Dallas: Word, 1989.

—"Verb Modality and the Interpretation of Job 4:20–21." *Vetus Testamentum* 30 (1980): 354–57.

Cooley, Robert E. "The Contribution of Literary Sources to the Study of the Canaanite Burial Pattern." Ph.D. diss., New York University, 1968.

Cooper, Alan. "Reading and Misreading the Prologue to Job." *Journal for the Study of the Old Testament* 46 (1990): 67–79.

Cooper, Brian. "Euphemism and Taboo of Language (with Particular Reference to Russian)." *Australian Slavonic and East European Studies* 7 (1993): 61–84.

Cooper, Jerrold S. *The Curse of Agade*. Johns Hopkins Near Eastern Studies. Baltimore: The Johns Hopkins University Press, 1983.

Cox, Dermot. "'As Water Spilt on the Ground' (Death in the Old Testament)." *Studia Missionalia* 31 (1982): 1–17.

Crenshaw, James L. "Flirting with the Language of Prayer." Pages 110–23 in *Worship and the Hebrew Bible: Essays in Honour of John T. Willis*. Edited by M. Patrick Graham, Rick R. Marrs, and Steven L. McKenzie. Journal for the Study of the Old Testament: Supplement Series 284. Sheffield: Sheffield Academic Press, 1999.

Critchley, Simon. *Very Little—Almost Nothing: Death, Philosophy, Literature*. Warwick Studies in European Philosophy. London: Routledge, 1997.

Crook, Margaret Brackenbury. *The Cruel God: Job's Search for the Meaning of Suffering*. Boston: Beacon, 1959.

Cross, Frank Moore. *Canaanite Myth and Hebrew Epic: Essays in the History of the Religion of Israel*. Cambridge, Mass.: Harvard University Press, 1973.

Crouch, Walter B. *Death and Closure in Biblical Narrative*. Studies in Biblical Literature 7. New York: Peter Lang, 2000.

Curtis, John B. "On Job's Witness in Heaven." *Journal of Biblical Literature* 102 (1983): 549–62.

Dahood, Mitchell J. "Hebrew–Ugaritic Lexicography IV." *Biblica* 47 (1966): 403–19.

—"Immortality in Proverbs 12,28." *Biblica* 41 (1960): 176–81.

—"Northwest Semitic Philology and Job." Pages 55–74 in *The Bible in Current Catholic Thought*. Edited by John L. McKenzie. Saint Mary's Theology Studies 1. New York: Herder & Herder, 1962.

—*Psalms III*. Anchor Bible 17a. Garden City, N.Y.: Doubleday, 1970.

Davidson, A. B., and H. C. O. Lanchester. *The Book of Job with Notes, Introduction and Appendix*. New ed. Cambridge: Cambridge University Press, 1895.

Day, John. *God's Conflict with the Dragon and the Sea: Echoes of a Canaanite Myth in the Old Testament*. University of Cambridge Oriental Publications 35. Cambridge: Cambridge University Press, 1985.

Dell, Katharine J. *The Book of Job as Sceptical Literature.* Beihefte zur Zeitschrift für die alttestamentliche Wissenschaft 197. Berlin: de Gruyter, 1991.

Derrida, Jacques. *Aporias: Dying—Awaiting (One Another at) the "Limits of Truth."* Translated by Thomas Dutoit. Meridian: Crossing Aesthetics. Stanford: Stanford University Press, 1993.

—*Of Grammatology.* Translated by Gayatri Chakravorty Spivak. Corrected ed. Baltimore: The Johns Hopkins University Press, 1998.

Dhorme, Edouard. *A Commentary on the Book of Job.* Translated by Harold Knight. Nashville: Nelson, 1984. Repr., London: Thomas Nelson, 1967.

Dhorme, P. "Les chapitres XXV–XXVIII du livre de Job." *Revue Biblique* 33 (1924): 343–56.

Dick, Michael B. "Legal Metaphor in Job 31." *Catholic Biblical Quarterly* 41 (1979): 37–50.

Driver, Godfrey Rolles. "Problems in the Hebrew Text of Job." Pages 72–93 in Noth and Winton Thomas, eds., *Wisdom in Israel.*

Driver, Samuel Rolles. *An Introduction to the Literature of the Old Testament.* Meridian Library 3. New York: Meridian Books, 1963.

Driver, Samuel Rolles, and George Buchanan Gray. *A Critical and Exegetical Commentary on the Book of Job: Together with a New Translation.* 2 vols. International Critical Commentary 14. Edinburgh: T. & T. Clark, 1921.

Eichhorn, Johann Gottfried. *Einleitung in das Alte Testament.* 3d ed. 3 vols. Leipzig: Weidmann, 1803.

Eichrodt, Walther. *Theology of the Old Testament.* Translated by J. A. Baker. 2 vols. Old Testament Library. Philadelphia: Westminster, 1961.

Eissfeldt, Otto. *The Old Testament: An Introduction, Including the Apocrypha and Pseudepigrapha, and also the Works of Similar Type from Qumran: The History of the Formation of the Old Testament.* Translated by Peter R. Ackroyd. New York: Harper & Row, 1965.

Eslinger, Lyle, and Glen Taylor, eds. *Ascribe to the Lord: Biblical and Other Essays in Memory of Peter C. Craigie.* JSOTSup 67. Sheffield: JSOT Press, 1988.

Fackenheim, Emil L. *The Jewish Bible after the Holocaust: A Re-reading.* Bloomington: Indiana University Press, 1990.

Feinberg, Charles L. "Job and the Nation of Israel." *Bibliotheca Sacra* 96 (1939): 405–11.

Fohrer, Georg. *Das Buch Hiob.* Kommentar zum Alten Testament 16. Gütersloh: Gütersloher Verlagshaus G. Mohn, 1963.

—"Form und Funktion in der Hiobdichtung." Pages 60–77 in *Studien zum Buche Hiob (1956–1979).* Edited by Georg Fohrer. Beiheft zur Zeitschrift für die alttestamentliche Wissenschaft 159. Berlin: de Gruyter, 1983.

Forrest, Robert W. E. "The Two Faces of Job: Imagery and Integrity in the Prologue." Pages 385–98 in Eslinger and Taylor, eds., *Ascribe to the Lord.*

Fowler, Mervyn D. "The Israelite *bāmâ.*" *Zeitschrift für die alttestamentlische Wissenschaft* 94 (1982): 203–13.

Fox, Michael V. *Proverbs 1–9: A New Translation with Introduction and Commentary.* Anchor Bible 18a. New York: Doubleday, 2000.

—*Qohelet and His Contradictions.* Bible and Literature Series 18. Sheffield: Almond, 1989.

Freedman, David Noel. "Elihu Speeches in the Book of Job." *Harvard Theological Review* 61 (1968): 51–59.

Freud, Sigmund. *The Ego and the Id.* Translated by Joan Riviere. The International Psycho-Analytical Library 12. London: Hogarth, 1950.

Frey, Johannes. *Tod, Seelenglaube und Seelenkult im alten Israel: eine religionsgeschichtliche Untersuchung.* Leipzig: Deichert, 1898.

Friedman, Alan Warren. *Fictional Death and the Modernist Enterprise.* Cambridge: Cambridge University Press, 1995.

Friedman, Maurice. *Problematic Rebel: Melville, Dostoievsky, Kafka, Camus.* Rev. ed. Chicago: University of Chicago Press, 1970.

—*To Deny Our Nothingness: Contemporary Images of Man.* Chicago: University of Chicago Press, 1978. Repr., Chicago: Midway, 1984.

Friedman, Richard Elliott, and Shawna Dolansky Overton. "Death and Afterlife: The Biblical Silence." Pages 35–59 in Avery-Peck and Neusner, eds., *Judaism in Late Antiquity.* Vol. 4, *Death, Life-after-Death, Resurrection and the World-to-Come in the Judaisms of Antiquity.*

Frye, J. B. "The Legal Language of the Book of Job." Ph.D. diss., University of London, 1973.

Gadd, C. J. "Harran Inscription of Nabonidus." *Anatolian Studies* 8 (1958): 35–92.

Gammie, John G. "Behemoth and Leviathan: On the Siginificance of Job 40:14–41:26." Pages 217–31 in *Israelite Wisdom: Theological and Literary Essays in Honor of Samuel Terrien.* Edited by John G. Gammie et al. Missoula, Mont.: Scholars Press, 1978.

Geller, Stephen A. "'Where is Wisdom?': A Literary Study of Job 28 in its Settings." Pages 155–88 in *Judaic Perspectives on Ancient Israel.* Edited by Jacob Neusner, Baruch A. Levine, and Ernest S. Frerichs. Philadelphia: Fortress, 1987.

Gemser, Berend. "The *rib-* or Controversy-Pattern in Hebrew Mentality." Pages 120–37 in Noth and Winton Thomas, eds., *Wisdom in Israel.*

Gese, Hartmut. *Lehre und Wirklichkeit in der alten Weisheit: Studien zu den Sprüchen Salomos und zu dem Buche Hiob.* Tübingen: Mohr, 1958.

Gesenius, Wilhelm. *Gesenius' Hebrew Grammar.* Edited by E. Kautzsch. Translated by A. E. Cowley. 2d English ed. Oxford: Clarendon, 1910.

Gesenius, Wilhelm, and Emil Roediger. *Thesaurus Philologicus Criticus Linguae Hebraeae et Chaldaeae Veteris Testamenti.* 2d ed. 3 vols. Lipsiae: Vogelii, 1829.

Gibson, J. C. L. *Canaanite Myths and Legends.* Edinburgh: T. & T. Clark, 1978.

—"Eliphaz the Temanite." *Scottish Journal of Theology* 28 (1975): 259–72.

—*Job.* The Daily Study Bible Series. Philadelphia: Westminster, 1985.

—"A New Look at Job 41.1–4 (English 41.9–12)." Pages 129–39 in *Text as Pretext: Essays in Honour of Robert Davidson.* Edited by Robert P. Carroll. Journal for the Study of the Old Testament: Supplement Series 138. Sheffield: JSOT Press, 1992.

—"On Evil in the Book of Job." Pages 399–419 in Eslinger and Taylor, eds., *Ascribe to the Lord.*

Ginsberg, H. L. "Job the Patient and Job the Impatient." *Scottish Journal of Theology* 17 (1968): 98–107.

Godbey, Allen H. "The Unicorn in the Old Testament." *American Journal of Semitic Languages and Literature* 56 (1939): 256–96.

Goldingay, John. "Death and Afterlife in the Psalms." Pages 61–85 in Avery-Peck and Neusner, eds., *Judaism in Late Antiquity.* Vol. 4, *Death, Life-after-Death, Resurrection and the World-to-Come in the Judaisms of Antiquity.*

Gonen, Rivka. *Burial Patterns and Cultural Diversity in Late Bronze Age Canaan.* American Schools of Oriental Research Dissertation Series 7. Winona Lake, Ind.: Eisenbrauns, 1979.

Good, Edwin M. *In Turns of Tempest: A Reading of Job, with a Translation.* Stanford: Stanford University Press, 1990.

Gordis, Robert. *The Book of God and Man: A Study of Job.* Chicago: University of Chicago Press, 1965.

—*The Book of Job: Commentary, New Translation, and Special Studies.* Moreshet Series 2. New York: Jewish Theological Seminary of America, 1978.

Grabbe, Lester L. "Comparative Philology and the Text of Job: A Study in Methodology." Ph.D. diss., Claremont Graduate School, 1975.

Gross, John. "Intimations of Mortality." Pages 203–19 in *Fair of Speech: The Uses of Euphemism*. Edited by D. J. Enright. Oxford: Oxford University Press, 1985.

Grüneisen, Carl. *Der Ahnenkultus und die Urreligion Israels*. Halle: Max Niemeyer, 1900.

Gualtieri, Antonio R. *The Vulture and the Bull: Religious Responses to Death*. Lanham: University Press of America, 1984.

Guillaume, Alfred. "The Arabic Background of the Book of Job." Pages 106–27 in *Promise and Fulfilment: Essays Presented to Professor S. H. Hooke in Celebration of His Ninetieth Birthday*. Edited by F. F. Bruce. Edinburgh: T. & T. Clark, 1963.

—*Studies in the Book of Job*. Edited by John Macdonald. Annual of Leeds University Oriental Society Supplement 2. Leiden: Brill, 1968.

—"The Use of חלש in Exod. XVII. 13; Isa. XIV. 12, and Job XIV. 10." *JTS* 14 (1963): 91–92.

Guillaume, Philippe. "Caution: Rhetorical Questions!" *Biblische Notizen* 103 (2000): 11–16.

Gunkel, Hermann, and Joachim Begrich. *Introduction to Psalms: The Genres of the Religious Lyric of Israel*. Translated by James D. Nogalski. Mercer Library of Biblical Studies. Macon, Ga.: Mercer University Press, 1998.

Gunn, David M., and Danna Nolan Fewell. *Narrative in the Hebrew Bible*. Oxford Bible Series. New York: Oxford University Press, 1993.

Habel, Norman C. *The Book of Job*. Cambridge Bible Commentary: New English Bible. London: Cambridge University Press, 1975.

—*The Book of Job: A Commentary*. Old Testament Library. Philadelphia: Westminster, 1985.

—"In Defense of God the Sage." Pages 21–38 in Perdue and Gilpin, eds., *Voice from the Whirlwind*.

—"Symbolism of Wisdom in Proverbs 1–9." *Interpretation* 26 (1972): 131–57.

Hallote, Rachel S. *Death, Burial, and Afterlife in the Biblical World: How the Israelites and their Neighbors Treated the Dead*. Chicago: Dee, 2001.

Halpern, Baruch. "Yhwh's Summary Justice in Job XIV 20." *Vetus Testamentum* 28 (1978): 472–74.

Hartley, John E. *The Book of Job*. The New International Commentary on the Old Testament. Grand Rapids: Eerdmans, 1988.

Healey, John F. "Das Land ohne Wiederkehr: Die Unterwelt im antiken Ugarit und im Alten Testament." *Theologische Quartalschrift* 177 (1997): 94–104.

—"Death, Underworld and Afterlife in the Ugaritic Texts." Ph.D. diss., University of London, 1977.

—"The Immortality of the King: Ugarit and the Psalms." *Orientalia* 53 (1984): 245–54.

Heider, George C. *The Cult of Molek: A Reassessment*. Journal for the Study of the Old Testament: Supplement Series 43. Sheffield: JSOT Press, 1985.

Hesse, Franz. *Hiob*. 2d ed. Zürcher Bibelkommentare 14. Zürich: Theologischer Verlag, 1992.

Hiebert, Theodore. "Theophany in the OT." Pages 505–11 in vol. 6 of *The Anchor Bible Dictionary*. Edited by David Noel Freedman. 6 vols. New York: Doubleday, 1992.

Higonnet, Margaret. "Speaking Silences: Women's Suicide." Pages 68–83 in *The Female Body in Western Culture: Contemporary Perspectives*. Edited by Susan Rubin Suleiman. Cambridge, Mass.: Harvard University Press, 1986.

Holbert, John C. "The Rehabilitation of the Sinner: The Function of Job 29–31." *Zeitschrift für die alttestamentliche Wissenschaft* 95 (1983): 229–37.

Horst, Friedrich. *Hiob*. 2d ed. Biblischer Kommentar, Altes Testament 16. Neukirchen–Vluyn: Neukirchener Verlag, 1969.

Huntington, Richard, and Peter Metcalf. *Celebrations of Death: The Anthropology of Mortuary Ritual*. Cambridge: Cambridge University Press, 1979.

Hurvitz, Avi. "Date of the Prose-Tale of Job Linguistically Reconsidered." *Harvard Theological Review* 67 (1974): 17–34.

Jackson, Donald. "LSD and the New Beginning." *Journal of Nervous and Mental Disease* 135 (1962): 435–39.

Jacobsen, Thorkild, and Kirsten Nielsen. "Cursing the Day." *Scandinavian Journal of the Old Testament* 6 (1992): 187–204.

Janzen, J. Gerald. *Job*. Interpretation. Atlanta: John Knox, 1985.

Jastrow, Morris. "Dust, Earth, and Ashes as Symbols of Mourning among the Ancient Hebrews." *Journal of the American Oriental Society* 20 (1904): 133–50.

Jeremias, Jörg. *Theophanie: die Geschichte einer alttestamentlichen Gattung*. Wissenschaftliche Monographien zum Alten und Neuen Testament 10. Neukirchen–Vluyn: Neukirchener Verlag, 1965.

Johnson, Aubrey R. *The Vitality of the Individual in the Thought of Ancient Israel*. Cardiff: University of Wales Press, 1949.

Johnston, Philip S. *Shades of Sheol: Death and Afterlife in the Old Testament*. Downers Grove, Ill.: Apollos, 2002.

—"The Underworld and the Dead in the Old Testament." Ph.D. diss., Cambridge University, 1993.

Keel, Othmar. *Jahwes Entgegnung an Ijob: eine Deutung von Ijob 38–41 vor dem Hintergrund der zeitgenössischen Bildkunst*. Forschungen zur Religion und Literatur des Alten und Neuen Testaments 121. Göttingen: Vandenhoeck & Ruprecht, 1978.

Kepnes, Steven. "Job and Post-Holocaust Theodicy." Pages 252–66 in Linafelt, ed., *Strange Fire*.

Kermode, Frank. "The Uses of Error." *Theology* 89 (1986): 425–31.

Kirkpatrick, Kathryn. "The Figurative Language of Death." *The Secol Review* 7 (1983): 27–35.

Kittel, Gisela. *Befreit aus dem Rachen des Todes: Tod und Todesüberwindung im Alten und Neuen Testament*. Biblisch-theologische Schwerpunkte 17. Göttingen: Vandenhoeck & Ruprecht, 1999.

Klotz, John W. "Notes on the Unicorn." *Concordia Theological Monthly* 32 (1961): 286–87.

König, Franz. *Zarathustras Jenseitsvorstellungen und das Alte Testament*. Wien: Herder, 1964.

Kopf, Lothar. "Arabische Etymologien und Parallelen zum Bibelwörterbuch." *Vetus Testamentum* 8 (1958): 161–215.

Kubina, Veronika. *Die Gottesreden im Buch Hiob: ein Beitrag zur Diskussion um die Einheit von Hiob 38,1–42,6*. Freiburger theologische Studien. Freiburg: Herder, 1979.

Kuntz, John Kenneth. *The Self-Revelation of God*. Philadelphia: Westminster, 1967.

Kutsche, E. " 'Trauerbräuche' und 'Selbstminderungsriten' im AT." *Theologische Studiën* 78 (1965): 25–42.

Kuyper, Lester J. "Repentance of Job." *VT* 9 (1959): 91–94.

Lapsley, Jacqueline E. "Feeling Our Way: Love for God in Deuteronomy." *Catholic Biblical Quarterly* 65 (2003): 350–69.

Laski, Marghanita. *Ecstasy: A Study of Some Secular and Religious Experiences*. Bloomington: Indiana University Press, 1962.

Lévêque, Jean. *Job et son Dieu: essai d'exégèse et de théologie biblique*. 2 vols. Etudes bibliques. Paris: Gabalda, 1970.

Lewis, Theodore J. *Cults of the Dead in Ancient Israel and Ugarit*. Harvard Semitic Monographs 39. Atlanta: Scholars Press, 1989.

Lifton, Robert Jay. *America and the Asian Revolutions*. Chicago: Aldine, 1970.

—*Boundaries: Psychological Man in Revolution*. New York: Random House, 1970.

—*The Broken Connection: On Death and the Continuity of Life.* New York: Simon & Schuster, 1979.

—*Death in Life: Survivors of Hiroshima.* New York: Random House, 1968.

—*The Future of Immortality and Other Essays for a Nuclear Age.* New York: Basic Books, 1987.

—*History and Human Survival: Essays on the Young and Old, Survivors and the Dead, Peace and War, and on Contemporary Psychohistory.* New York: Random House, 1970.

—*Home from the War: Learning from Vietnam Veterans.* Boston: Beacon, 1992.

—*The Life of the Self: Toward a New Psychology.* New York: Simon & Schuster, 1976.

—*The Protean Self: Human Resilience in an Age of Fragmentation.* New York: Basic Books, 1993.

—*Revolutionary Immortality: Mao Tse-tung and the Chinese Cultural Revolution.* New York: Random House, 1968.

—*Thought Reform and the Psychology of Totalism: A Study of "Brainwashing" in China.* Chapel Hill: University of North Carolina Press, 1989.

Lifton, Robert Jay, and Nicholas Humphrey, eds. *In a Dark Time.* Cambridge, Mass.: Harvard University Press, 1984.

Lifton, Robert Jay, and Eric Markusen. *The Genocidal Mentality: Nazi Holocaust and Nuclear Threat.* New York: Basic Books, 1990.

Lifton, Robert Jay, and Greg Mitchell. *Hiroshima in America: Fifty Years of Denial.* New York: Putnam's Sons, 1995.

—*Who Owns Death? Capital Punishment, the American Conscience, and the End of Executions.* New York: Morrow, 2000.

Lifton, Robert Jay, and Eric Olson, eds. *Explorations in Psychohistory: The Wellfleet Papers.* New York: Simon and Schuster, 1974.

Linafelt, Tod. "The Undecidability of BRK in the Prologue to Job and Beyond." *Biblical Interpretation* 4 (1996): 154–72.

—ed. *Strange Fire: Reading the Bible after the Holocaust.* New York: New York University Press, 2000.

Lindblom, Johannes. "Theophanies in Holy Places in Hebrew Religion." *Hebrew Union College Annual* 32 (1961): 91–106.

Lipiński, Edward. *La liturgie pénitentielle dans la Bible.* Lectio Divina 52. Paris: Cerf, 1969.

Lippert, Julius. *Der Seelencult in seinen Beziehungen zur althebräischen Religion: eine ethnologische Studie.* Berlin: Hofmann, 1881.

Lods, Adolphe. *La croyance à la vie future et le culte des morts dans l'antiquité israélite.* 2 vols. Paris: Fischbacher, 1906.

Lohfink, Norbert. "Enthielten die im Alten Testament bezeugten Klageriten eine Phase des Schweigens." *Vetus Testamentum* 12 (1962): 260–77.

Lugt, Pieter van der. *Rhetorical Criticism and the Poetry of the Book of Job.* Oudtestamentische Studiën 32. Leiden: Brill, 1995.

Mann, Thomas W. *Divine Presence and Guidance in Israelite Traditions: The Typology of Exaltation.* Johns Hopkins Near Eastern Studies. Baltimore: The Johns Hopkins University Press, 1977.

Markusen, Eric. "Comprehending the Cambodian Genocide: An Application of Robert Jay Lifton's Model of Genocidal Killing." *The Psychohistory Review* 20 (1992): 145–69.

Martin-Achard, Robert. *From Death to Life: A Study of the Development of the Doctrine of the Resurrection in the Old Testament.* Translated by John Penney Smith. Edinburgh: Oliver & Boyd, 1960.

—"'Il engloutit la mort à jamais'. Remarques sur Esaïe 25,8aα." Pages 283–96 in *Mélanges bibliques et orientaux en l'honneur de M. Mathias Delcor.* Edited by André Caquot, S.

Légasse, and Michel Tardieu. Alter Orient und Altes Testament 215. Kevelaer: Butzon & Berker, 1985.

Meier, Sam. "Job 1–2: A Reflection of Genesis 1–3." *Vetus Testamentum* 39 (1989): 183–93.

Mettinger, Tryggve N. D. "The God of Job: Avenger, Tyrant, or Victor?" Pages 39–49 in Perdue and Gilpin, eds., *Voice from the Whirlwind.*

——"Intertextuality: Allusion and Vertical Context Systems in Some Job Passages." Pages 257–80 in Perdue and Gilpin, eds., *Voice from the Whirlwind.*

Meyers, Eric M. "Secondary Burials in Palestine." *Biblical Archaeologist* 33 (1970): 2–29.

Michel, Walter L. *Job in the Light of Northwest Semitic.* Vol. 1, *Prologue and First Cycle of Speeches, Job 1:1–14:22.* Biblica et Orientalia 42. Rome: Biblical Institute Press, 1987.

——"ṢLMWT, 'Deep Darkness' or 'Shadow of Death.'" *Biblical Research* 29 (1984): 5–20.

——"The Ugaritic Texts and the Mythological Expressions." Ph.D. diss., University of Wisconsin, 1970.

Miller, David Leonard. "The Development of the Concept of Immortality in the Old Testament." Ph.D. diss., New York University, 1977.

Molino, Anthon, and Christine Ware. "Protean Impulses: A Conversation with Robert Jay Lifton." Pages 138–46 in *Where Id Was: Challenging Normalization in Psychoanalysis.* Edited by Anthony Molino and Christine Ware. Middletown: Wesleyan University Press, 2001.

Moore, Michael S. "Resurrection and Immortality: Two Motifs Navigating Confluent Theological Streams in the Old Testament (Dan 12,1–4)." *Theologische Zeitschrift* 39 (1983): 17–34.

Morgenstern, Julian. *The Rites of Birth, Marriage, Death, and Kindred Occasions among the Semites.* Cincinnati: Hebrew Union College Press, 1966.

Morrow, William S. "Consolation, Rejection, and Repentance in Job 42:6." *Journal of Biblical Literature* 105 (1986): 211–25.

Mowinckel, Sigmund. "Hiobs *go'el* und Zeuge im Himmel." Pages 207–12 in *Vom Alten Testament.* Edited by Karl Budde. Beihefte zur Zeitschrift für die Alttestamentliche Wissenschaft 41. Giessen: Töpelmann, 1925.

Muilenburg, James. "Speech of Theophany." *Harvard Divinity Bulletin* 28 (1964): 35–47.

Murphy, Roland Edmund. *The Book of Job: A Short Reading.* New York: Paulist, 1999.

——"Death and Afterlife in the Wisdom Literature." Pages 101–16 in Avery-Peck and Neusner, eds., *Judaism in Late Antiquity.* Vol. 4, *Death, Life-after-Death, Resurrection and the World-to-Come in the Judaisms of Antiquity.*

——*The Wisdom Literature: Job, Proverbs, Ruth, Canticles, Ecclesiastes, and Esther.* Forms of the Old Testament Literature 13. Grand Rapids: Eerdmans, 1981.

Neher, André. *The Exile of the Word: From the Silence of the Bible to the Silence of Auschwitz.* Translated by David Maisel. Philadelphia: Jewish Publication Society of America, 1981.

Nemo, Philippe. *Job and the Excess of Evil.* Translated by Michael Kigel. Pittsburgh: Duquesne University Press, 1998.

Neusner, Jacob. *Bavli Tractate Baba Batra. A. Chapters I through VI.* Vol. 22 of *The Talmud of Babylonia: An Academic Commentary.* South Florida Academic Commentary Series. Atlanta: Scholars Press, 1996.

Newsom, Carol A. *Book of Job: A Contest of Moral Imaginations.* New York: Oxford University Press, 2003.

——"Considering Job." *Currents in Research: Biblical Studies* 1 (1993): 87–118.

——"Job." Pages 319–637 in vol. 4 of *The New Interpreter's Bible.* Nashville: Abingdon, 1994.

Niditch, Susan. *Ancient Israelite Religion.* New York: Oxford University Press, 1997.

Niehaus, Jeffrey Jay. *God at Sinai: Covenant and Theophany in the Bible and Ancient Near East.* Studies in Old Testament Biblical Theology. Grand Rapids: Zondervan, 1995.

Niehr, Herbert. "Aspekte des Totengedenkens im Juda der Königszeit." *Theologische Quartalschrift* 178 (1998): 1–13.

Noth, Martin, and David Winton Thomas, eds. *Wisdom in Israel and in the Ancient Near East.* Vetus Testamentum Supplements 3. Leiden: Brill, 1969.

Oorschot, Jürgen van. *Gott als Grenze: Eine literar- und redaktionsgeschichtliche Studie zu den Gottesreden des Hiobbuches.* Beihefte zur Zeitschrift für die alttestamentliche Wissenschaft 170. Berlin: de Gruyter, 1987.

Ovid. *Metamorphoses.* Translated by Neil Hopkinson. Cambridge Greek and Latin Classics. Cambridge: Cambridge University Press, 2000.

Patrick, Dale. "Translation of Job 42:6." *Vetus Testamentum* 26 (1976): 369–71.

Patton, Corrine L. "The Beauty of the Beast: Leviathan and Behemoth in Light of Catholic Theology." Pages 142–67 in *The Whirlwind: Essays on Job, Hermeneutics and Theology in Memory of Jane Morse.* Edited by Stephen L. Cook, Corrine L. Patton, and James W. Watts. Journal for the Study of the Old Testament: Supplement Series 336. London: Sheffield Academic Press, 2001.

Pedersen, Johannes. *Israel: Its Life and Culture.* Translated by A. Møller and A. I. Fausbell. 2 vols. London: Oxford University Press, 1926.

Perdue, Leo G. *Wisdom in Revolt: Metaphorical Theology in the Book of Job.* Journal for the Study of the Old Testament: Supplement Series 112. Bible and Literature Series 29. Sheffield: Almond, 1991.

Perdue, Leo G., and W. Clark Gilpin, eds. *Voice from the Whirlwind: Interpreting the Book of Job.* Nashville: Abingdon, 1992.

Pfeiffer, Robert Henry. "The Dual Origin of Hebrew Monotheism." *Journal of Biblical Literature* 46 (1927): 193–206.

—*Introduction to the Old Testament.* New York: Harper, 1948.

Pham, Xuan Huong Thi. *Mourning in the Ancient Near East and the Hebrew Bible.* Journal for the Study of the Old Testament: Supplement Series 302. Sheffield: Sheffield Academic Press, 1999.

Piaget, Jean, and Bärbel Inhelder. *The Psychology of the Child.* Translated by Helen Weaver. New York: Basic Books, 1969.

Pidcock-Lester, Karen. "'Earth has No Sorrow the Earth Cannot Heal': Job 38–41." Pages 125–32 in *God Who Creates: Essays in Honor of W. Sibley Towner.* Edited by William P. Brown and S. Dean McBride. Grand Rapids: Eerdmans, 2000.

Pietikainen, Petteri, and Juhani Ihanus. "On the Origins of Psychoanalytic Psychohistory." *History of Psychology* 6 (2003): 171–94.

Podella, Thomas. "Nekromantie." *Theologische Quartalschrift* 177 (1997): 121–33.

Pope, Marvin H. "Euphemism and Dysphemism in the Bible." Pages 279–91 in *Probative Pontificating in Ugaritic and Biblical Literature: Collected Essays.* Edited by Mark S. Smith. Ugaritisch-biblische Literatur 10. Münster: Ugarit-Verlag, 1994.

—*Job.* 3d ed. Anchor Bible 15. Garden City, N.Y.: Doubleday, 1973.

Preuss, Horst Dietrich. *Old Testament Theology.* Translated by Leo G. Perdue. 2 vols. Old Testament Library. Louisville, Ky.: Westminster John Knox, 1991.

Rad, Gerhard von. *Old Testament Theology.* Translated by D. M. G. Stalker. 2 vols. OTL. Louisville, Ky.: Westminster John Knox, 2001.

Rahmani, L. Y. "Ancient Jerusalem's Funerary Customs and Tombs. Part Two." *Biblical Archaeologist* 44 (1981): 229–35.

Regnier, A. "La distribution des chapitres 25–28 du livre de Job." *Revue Biblique* 33 (1924): 186–200.

Reventlow, Henning Graf. "Tradition und Redaktion in Hiob 27 im Rahmen der Hiobreden des Abschnittes Hi 24–27." *Zeitschrift für die Alttestamentliche Wissenschaft* 94 (1982): 279–93.

Ribar, John Whalen. "Death Cult Practices in Ancient Palestine." Ph.D. diss., University of Michigan, 1973.

Richter, Heinz. *Studien zu Hiob: Der Aufbau des Hiobbuches, dargestellt an den Gattungen des Rechtslebens.* Theologische Arbeiten 11. Berlin: Evangelische Verlagsanstalt, 1959.

Ricoeur, Paul. "The Narrative Function." *Semeia* 13 (1978): 177–202.

Ringgren, Helmer. *Israelite Religion.* Translated by David E. Green. Philadelphia: Fortress, 1966.

Roberts, J. J. M. "Job and the Israelite Religious Tradition." *Zeitschrift für die Alttestamentliche Wissenschaft* 89 (1977): 107–14.

—"Job's Summons to Yahweh: The Exploitation of a Legal Metaphor." *Restoration Quarterly* 16 (1973): 159–65.

—"Young Lions of Psalm 34:11." *Bib* 54 (1973): 265–67.

Robertson, David A. *Linguistic Evidence in Dating Early Hebrew Poetry.* Society of Biblical Literature Dissertation Series 3. Missoula: Society of Biblical Literature, 1972.

Rowley, Harold Henry. *The Book of Job.* New Century Bible Commentary. Grand Rapids: Eerdmans, 1980.

—"The Future Life in the Thought of the Old Testament." *Congregational Quarterly* 33 (1955): 116–32.

—*From Moses to Qumran: Studies in the Old Testament.* New York: Association Press, 1963.

Rubenstein, Richard L. "Job and Auschwitz." Pages 233–51 in Linafelt, ed., *Strange Fire.*

Ruprecht, Eberhard. "Das Nilpferd im Hiobbuch." *Vetus Testamentum* 21 (1971): 209–31.

Saggs, H. W. F. *The Encounter with the Divine in Mesopotamia and Israel.* Jordan Lectures in Comparative Religion 12. London: Athlone, 1978.

Sarna, Nahum M. "Mythological Background of Job 18." *Journal of Biblical Literature* 82 (1963): 315–18.

Sasson, Victor. "The Literary and Theological Function of Job's Wife in the Book of Job." *Biblica* 79 (1998): 86–90.

Schmidt, Brian B. "Memory as Immortality: Countering the Dreaded 'Death after Death' in Ancient Israelite Society." Pages 87–100 in Avery-Peck and Neusner, eds., *Judaism in Late Antiquity.* Vol. 4, *Death, Life-after-Death, Resurrection and the World-to-Come in the Judaisms of Antiquity.*

—*Israel's Beneficent Dead: Ancestor Cult and Necromancy in Ancient Israelite Religion and Tradition.* Forschungen zum Alten Testament 11. Tübingen: Mohr, 1994.

Scholnick, Sylvia Huberman. "Lawsuit Drama in the Book of Job." Ph.D. diss., Brandeis University, 1975.

Schwally, Friedrich. *Das Leben nach dem Tode: nach den Vorstellungen des alten Israel und des Judentums einschliesslich des Volksglaubens im Zeitalter Christi, eine biblisch-theologische Untersuchung.* Giessen: Ricker, 1892.

Segal, Alan F. "Some Observations about Mysticism and the Spread of Notions of Life after Death in Hebrew Thought." Pages 385–99 in *SBL Seminar Papers, 1996.* Society of Biblical Literature Seminar Papers 35. Atlanta: Scholars Press, 1996.

Sellin, E. "Die alttestamentliche Hoffnung auf Auferstehung und ewiges Leben." *Neue kirchliche Zeitschrift* 30 (1919): 232–89.

Shirun-Grumach, Irene. *Untersuchungen zur Lebenslehre des Amenope.* Edited by Hans Wolfgang Müller. Münchner Ägyptologische Studien. Munich: Deutscher Kunstverlag, 1972.

Silberman, Lou H. "Death in the Hebrew Bible and Apocalyptic Literature." Pages 13–32 in *Perspectives on Death*. Edited by Liston O. Mills. Nashville: Abingdon, 1969.

Smith, Gary V. "Job IV 12–21: Is it Eliphaz's Vision?" *Vetus Testamentum* 40 (1990): 453–63.

Snaith, Norman Henry. *The Book of Job: Its Origin and Purpose*. Studies in Biblical Theology Second Series 11. London: SCM Press, 1968.

Spiess, Edmund. *Entwicklungsgeschichte der Vorstellungen vom Zustande nach dem Tode: auf Grund vergleichender Religionsforschung*. Jena: Hermann Costenoble, 1877.

Spronk, Klaas. *Beatific Afterlife in Ancient Israel and in the Ancient Near East*. Alter Orient und Altes Testament 219. Kevelaer: Butzon & Bercker, 1986.

Stewart, Garrett. *Death Sentences: Styles of Dying in British Fiction*. Cambridge, Mass.: Harvard University Press, 1984.

Strauss, Hans. "Tod (Todeswunsch; »Jenseits«?) im Buch Hiob." Pages 239–49 in *Gottes Recht als Lebensraum: Festschrift für Hans Jochen Boecker*. Edited by Werner H. Schmidt, Peter Mommer, and Hans Strauss. Neukirchen–Vluyn: Neukirchener Verlag, 1993.

Strozier, Charles B. "Introduction." *The Psychohistory Review* 20 (1992): 103–5.

—"Proteanism and the Species Self: Interview with Robert Jay Lifton." *The Psychohistory Review* 20 (1992): 107–30.

Strozier, Charles B., and Michael Flynn. "Lifton's Method." *The Psychohistory Review* 20 (1992): 131–44.

Strozier, Robert. "The Euphemism." *Language Learning* 16 (1966): 63–70.

Tambor-Krzyzanowska, Anna. "L'euphemisme: Comment parler de la mort en français et en polonais." *Verbum* 16 (1993): 125–30.

Terrien, Samuel L. "Job." Pages 875–1198 in vol. 3 of *The Interpreter's Bible*. New York: Abingdon-Cokesbury Press, 1951–57.

—*Job: Poet of Existence*. Indianapolis: Bobbs-Merrill, 1957.

Thomas, D. Winton. "צלמות in the Old Testament." *Journal of Semitic Studies* 7 (1962): 191–200.

—"Use of נצח as a Superlative in Hebrew." *Journal of Semitic Studies* 1 (1956): 106–9.

Toorn, Karel van der. "Ein verborgenes Erbe: Totenkult im frühen Israel." *Theologische Quartalschrift* 177 (1997): 105–20.

Torge, Paul. *Seelenglaube und Unsterblichkeitshoffnung im Alten Testament*. Leipzig: Hinrichs, 1909.

Tournay, Raymond. "L'ordre primitif des chapitres 24–28 du livre de Job." *Revue Biblique* 64 (1957): 321–34.

Tromp, Nicholas J. *Primitive Conceptions of Death and the Nether World in the Old Testament*. Biblica et orientalia 21. Rome: Pontifical Biblical Institute, 1969.

Tur-Sinai, Naphtali H. *The Book of Job: A New Commentary*. Translated by Sefer Iyov. Jerusalem: Kiryath Sepher, 1957.

Uchelen, Nico von. "Death and the Afterlife in the Hebrew Bible of Ancient Israel." Pages 77–90 in *Hidden Futures: Death and Immortality in Ancient Egypt, Anatolia, the Classical, Biblical and Arabic-Islamic World*. Edited by Jan Maarten Bremer, P. J. van den Hout, and Rudolph Peters. Amsterdam: Amsterdam University Press, 1994.

Vall, Gregory. "The Enigma of Job 1,21a." *Biblica* 76 (1995): 325–42.

Vaughan, Patrick H. *The Meaning of "bāmâ" in the Old Testament: A Study of Etymological, Textual and Archaeological Evidence*. Society for Old Testament Studies Monograph Series 3. London: Cambridge University Press, 1974.

Vaux, Roland de. *Ancient Israel*. 2 vols. New York: McGraw-Hill, 1965.

Vawter, Bruce. "Post-Exilic Prayer and Hope." *Catholic Biblical Quarterly* 37 (1975): 460–70.

Volgger, David. "Auch in Israel haben die Toten eine Botschaft." *Antonianum* 74 (1999): 227–52.

Wakeman, Mary K. *God's Battle with the Monster: A Study in Biblical Imagery.* Leiden: Brill, 1973.

Walters, Gregory J. "Religious Totalism in the Preconciliar and Postconciliar Church: An Application and Critique of Robert Jay Lifton's Psycohistorical Paradigm." *The Psychohistory Review* 20 (1992): 171–80.

Ward, Eileen F. de. "Mourning Customs in 1, 2 Samuel." *Journal of Jewish Studies* 23 (1972): 1–27.

Weiser, Artur. *Das Buch Hiob.* Das Alte Testament Deutsch 13. Göttingen: Vandenhoeck & Ruprecht, 1951.

—*The Old Testament: Its Formation and Development.* Translated by Dorothea M. Barton. New York: Association Press, 1961.

Weiss, Meir. *The Story of Job's Beginning: Job 1–2; A Literary Analysis.* Jerusalem: Magnes, 1983.

Wenning, Robert. "Bestattungen im königszeitlichen Juda." *Theologische Quartalschrift* 177 (1997): 82–93.

Wensinck, Arent Jan. *Some Semitic Rites of Mourning and Religion: Studies on their Origin and Mutual Relation.* Verhandelingen der Koninklijke akademie van wetenschappen te Amsterdam. Afdeeling Letterkunde. Nieuwe reeks 18. Amsterdam: Müller, 1917.

Westermann, Claus. *The Structure of the Book of Job: A Form-Critical Analysis.* Translated by Charles A. Muenchow. Philadelphia: Fortress, 1981.

Wette, Wilhelm Martin Leberecht de. *A Critical and Historical Introduction to the Canonical Scriptures of the Old Testament.* Translated by Theodore Parker. 3d ed. 2 vols. Boston: Rufus Leighton, 1859.

Whybray, Roger Norman. *Job.* Readings: A New Biblical Commentary. Sheffield: Sheffield Academic Press, 1998.

Widlak, S. "L'interdiction linguistique en français d'aujourd'hui." *Revue Belge de Philologie et d'Histoire* 43 (1965): 932–45.

Wied, Günther. "Der Auferstehungsglaube des späten Israel in seiner Bedeutung für das Verhältnis von Apokalyptik und Weisheit." Ph.D. diss., Universität Bonn, 1967.

Wiesel, Elie. *Messengers of God: Biblical Portraits and Legends.* Translated by Marion Wiesel. New York: Summit Books, 1976.

Wilde, A. de. *Das Buch Hiob.* Oudtestamentische studiën 22. Leiden: Brill, 1981.

Williamson, H. G. M. *Ezra, Nehemiah.* Word Biblical Commentary 16. Waco, Tex.: Word, 1985.

Witte, Markus. *Vom Leiden zur Lehre: der dritte Redegang (Hiob 21–27) und die Redaktionsgeschichte der Hiobbuches.* Beihefte zur Zeitschrift für die alttestamentliche Wissenschaft 230. Berlin: de Gruyter, 1994.

Wolde, Ellen van. "A Text-Semantic Study of the Hebrew Bible: Illustrated with Noah and Job." *Journal of Biblical Literature* 113 (1994): 19–35.

Wolfers, David. "The Speech-Cycles in the Book of Job." *Vetus Testamentum* 43 (1993): 385–403.

Wolff, Hans Walter. *Anthropology of the Old Testament.* Translated by Margaret Kohl. Philadelphia: Fortress, 1974.

Zuckerman, Bruce. *Job the Silent: A Study in Historical Counterpoint.* New York: Oxford University Press, 1991.

INDEXES

INDEX OF REFERENCES

INDEX OF AUTHORS